in works not readily accessible to the student or general reader.

Texts have been somewhat modernized in spelling and punctuation for clearer understanding, and each selection is preceded by an editorial note placing it in the context of the developing movement.

E. GRAHAM WARING is Beach-Garton Professor of Religion and Chairman of the Department of Religion, Lawrence University, Appleton, Wisconsin. He is represented in the Milestones of Thought series also as co-editor of Ludwig Feuerbach's *The Essence of Christianity*. Outside the series he is editor of the abridged version of Friedrich Schleiermacher's *On Religion* (Ungar).

DEISM AND NATURAL RELIGION

MILESTONES OF THOUGHT

DEISM AND
NATURAL RELIGION

A Source Book

BL 2710 .W3

Edited, with an introduction, by

E. GRAHAM WARING

Lawrence University

FREDERICK UNGAR PUBLISHING CO.

NEW YORK

MILESTONES
OF THOUGHT
in the History of Ideas

INTRODUCTION

The controversy over deism represents the principal development in religious thought during the Age of Enlightenment. Though the movement had profound repercussions and eminent representatives in France, Germany, and America, the main intellectual positions were worked out in Great Britain during the last decade of the seventeenth century and the first half of the eighteenth.

The Age of Enlightenment marks the early stages of a revolution in the total world-view of Western man. Only one who adequately apprehends the magnitude of the change can wrestle fruitfully with present issues in social, religious and philosophic thought. The shift in mood, assumptions, and general outlook from the Medieval-Reformation world to that of the Age of Enlightenment can be depicted in many ways. Negatively, there was an attempt to organize a civilization which would in all dimensions be emancipated from the Christian world-view. Positively, the age evolved a remarkable new faith which had revolutionary implication for all modes of thought, as well as for developments in political and economic institutions.

Many factors coalesced to bring about the drastic shift in outlook. The most evident is the rise of the mechanical model of nature associated with the name of Newton. Physical science provided not only specific conclusions but also an atmosphere of thought.

By means of a rational method it had achieved the picture of a universe whose parts were harmoniously interrelated, and whose laws were universal, objective, and simple. The "mystery" of nature was penetrated and dissolved. Alexander Pope gave voice to a common mood:

Nature and Nature's law lay hid in night.
God said: "Let Newton be," and all was light.

"Nature," in the medieval view, had involved a hierarchy of beings, graded in quality. All levels of reality, however, had relevance to man's existence and destiny. The universe was one of purposive law, filled with awesome and beautiful qualities. This nature lived in the shadow of supernature, which "lured" all beings to their destined ends, and which completed and brought to perfection the realm of nature.

The "nature" of the Newtonian world-machine was one in which the mystery and hazard—and the moral meaning—of the older "nature" were replaced by uniformity and purposelessness. It was a universe throughout which the same law reigned supreme, in the tiniest things on earth as well as on the farthest stars. The key to unlock nature's secrets had been found; it was that distinctive fusion of mathematical formulation and empirical experiment and observation with which Newton had brought grand, simple harmony to the work of his great predecessors. The simplicity and clarity of the new model of nature exhilarated the age. Newton had not only shown how to explain natural phenomena; he was understood to have shown in principle how all phenomena are to be explained. The man of the Enlightenment felt at home in Newtonian nature, or at least he thought he did. Its orderliness and rationality seemed wholly good, its interpreters wholly pious.

In the background of the religious thought of the period were other factors besides the scientific developments. One was the emotional reaction to the religious wars and persecutions which had marred the preceding era. Another was the confusion promoted by the growing multiplicity of religious groups, each claiming to be the vehicle of (conflicting) absolute truths. Devotion to classical thought, continued from the Renaissance, made men conscious of older cultural patterns. Perhaps the most significant non-scientific factor, however, was the impact of a growing awareness of non-European cultures and religions.

The era of geographical discoveries and colonial and commercial expansion opened new horizons to the minds of the men of the age. Their sources of information were seldom accurate; often they were fictional. But the net effect was to provide an alien norm against which the customs, beliefs, and institutions of Europe could be measured.

The impact had two forms. First, there were the tales of the simple and noble savage, unruined by the artificialities of civilization, living a happy and righteous life. Secondly, there were the accounts of other religions and civilizations. The life of Mohammed had a literary vogue. Highly colored reports from Jesuit missionaries in China, in which Chinese religion and morality seemed the purest forms of "natural religion," challenged the assumption of Christianity's monopoly of religious truth.

More significant and permanent, however, was the intellectual shock to Christendom of having to cope with the fact of the great non-Western religions. The "sacred history" which was the center of the Christian world-view had always seemed illuminative of the whole general history of mankind. But now, as that general history had to be expanded, the question of the universal significance of the sacred history could not long be evaded. What relevance did the divine revelation in the Exodus or in the crucifixion of Jesus Christ have for Asia? The religious isolation of Europe from the great cultures of India and China was coming to an end, and the intellectual problems posed by the new encounter were to increase steadily until our own time.

Part of the climate of opinion of the Enlightenment was represented in its rejection of authorities. Politically such rejection was the most marked feature of an age which reached its climax in the American and French revolutions. But parallel to such political upheaval was the intellectual one. Ideas and institutions which represented a traditional authority were increasingly called into question in the name of "reason." The hold of the institutional church and its theology on the lives and minds of men was steadily weakened. One after another, the major forms of thought declared their independence of a theological framework. Science's struggle for such freedom is symbolized by the episode of Galileo. The emancipation of political and economic theory, and of philosophy and psychology, was achieved more slowly and less dramatically, but just as surely. The acceptance of divine law as the normative principle behind positive state legislation gave way to views of natural law or the social contract. In the name of the autonomy of the political sphere attempts were made to disengage morality from its traditional foundation in religion. Every area of thought sought a divorce from theology in order to ground itself anew in "reason" and "nature."

The controversy over deism in Great Britain arose as a distinctive part of the social and intellectual atmosphere of the time. The Enlightenment's reaction to the older Christian world-view was articulated primarily through the contrast between "natural religion" and "revealed" (or "traditionary") religion. The older Christian world-view had, of course, used terms that seemed similar; it had made numerous attempts to relate and distinguish a "natural" knowledge of God and a "revealed" knowledge of God. Yet the Enlightenment's way of posing the issue was genuinely new; the concept of "revealed religion" was revolutionary. Indeed, the idea of "religions" can be seen as itself arising because of the period's increasing alienation from the older tradition.[1]

The concept of "natural religion" was used in the controversy in two ways, in the face of the new consciousness of religious diversity. (1) It served as a common denominator, representing that upon which all religions are believed to agree, that which is "reasonable" and "natural"; this common agreement, it must be noted, was usually assumed rather than demonstrated. (2) It served as a norm (on the assumption that the truly valid is necessarily universal) against which to measure the separate eccentricities of particular historical "religions," especially Christianity.

Three positions emerged in the discussion, though they were not always separated by the controversialists. (1) Natural religion leads to, and is completed and purified by, revealed religion. (2) The content of both modes of religion is the same, but they differ in the manner and clarity of our knowing.

---

[1] See the historical argument in Wilfred Cantwell Smith, *The Meaning and End of Religion* (New York: Macmillan, 1963), pp. 41ff.

(3) Natural religion contains all that is true in revealed religion; where the latter differs, the differences are either morally insignificant or superstitious.
This last position may most strictly be termed "deism,"
an appellation which was very loosely used in the
Enlightenment itself.

The heart of the deist position may be expressed
most simply in terms of five cardinal propositions:

(a) All men possess the faculty of reason adequate
to all the important needs of human life.

(b) Reason, the image of God in man, can know
God and God's will.

(c) Man's duty is to do God's will = man's duty is
to seek the happiness of all men.

(d) Man has always had this possibility of knowledge of the good, or natural religion.

(e) No religion can be higher than natural religion.

This "logic," of course, depends upon a whole series
of assumptions about reason, man's nature and existence, and God. Only through controversy did the
full deist position emerge; only through criticism did
the assumptions become evident.

While there are earlier figures who may properly
be called deists (in particular, Lord Herbert of Cherbury), the main British development began in the
last decade of the seventeenth century. In many ways
the literary source was the thought of John Locke.
The end-point of fruitful controversy may be found
in the thought of David Hume.

Though it is difficult to see any clear-cut progres-
sion in the discussion, certain key ideas develop.
Many central themes were adumbrated by Locke,
whose reputation guaranteed that his position on

religion would be influential. Locke had argued in his *Essay Concerning Human Understanding* (1690) that the existence of God is rationally demonstrable. Man, by his God-given reason (that which makes him man), can know the natural law of his duty. Of what significance, then, is the Christian revelation? Would it not be better to discard the idea, and to see in Jesus Christ simply a preacher of pure natural religion? In *The Reasonableness of Christianity* (1695) Locke rejected this possibility, and thereby sharply divided from the road the deists were to take, in spite of their frequent use of his ideas. He saw that exclusive emphasis on natural religion really assumes that man is not in need of redemption; such an assumption violated Locke's own considered judgment of human experience. As the debate proceeded, however, Locke's view of man's sinfulness was commonly diluted; fulfillment of the highest moral standards often was treated as a matter of relative simplicity.

Locke spoke of two sources of knowledge, reason and revelation. Revelation can be recognized only when reason finds it accompanied by unmistakable marks of divine authority; the "marks" of miracle and fulfillment of prophecy are evidence that a revelation comes from God. As the controversy continued, these two "marks" increasingly occupied a central place.

Locke also spoke of ideas which, though not contrary to reason, are "above reason." [2] This notion, so easily associated with the idea of "mystery," was soon attacked by Toland. The term "mystery" had too

---

[2] For a provocative analysis of this Lockian idea, see I. T. Ramsey's introduction to John Locke, *The Reasonableness of Christianity* (Stanford: Stanford U. P., 1958).

many associations with authority and obscurantism to be palatable to a consistent Enlightenment rationalist.

Locke also gave clear voice to the need for freedom of thought and expression (in his *Letters Concerning Toleration*). This theme was to be pursued by Collins and others, and in general one may say that the legal pressures brought against the deists provided them with a powerful argument for their position.

A strange feature of the controversy is the apparent acceptance by all parties of the conviction of the existence of God. Locke had said in the *Essay* that "we have a more certain knowledge of the existence of a God than of anything that our senses have not immediately discovered to us." (IV, x, 6) The reason for the common agreement is not hard to find; the Newtonian view seemed to demand a God. The world-machine is an intricate mechanism displaying order; such order implies an intelligent designer. Indeed, many of the scientists (and Newton in particular) regarded their ideas as essentially religious in nature; they were making clearer than ever before the basic lineaments of the divine purpose. The first impact of the "scientific theism" of the age was to broaden greatly the scope of the inherited idea of God. The immensity of the universe revealed by the new science made the God of the older world-view seem quite provincial.

But, increasingly, the God postulated as necessary to the ordering of the world-machine was removed from an active part in human affairs. Theologically, "God" became increasingly transcendent; psychologically, "God" became increasingly abstract. God was seen as the author of the natural law (in both the scientific and the moral senses of the term). But as the author of the law which describes the regular, orderly inter-relations of things, "God" receded behind the battery of secondary causes with which men have daily to do. And to speak of "God" as the author of the moral law of nature was often to do little more than bestow an honorific on man's ability to make autonomous rational calculations in matters of personal and social morality.

The abstractness of "God" is illustrated by a consideration of the idea of divine providence. Though many authors of the time bowed piously in the direction of "providence," any notion of a particular providence was gradually ruled out. As the idea of a particular revelation to a given people at a specific time and place in history seemed repugnant to the prevailing "cosmopolitanism" of the age, so the idea that the almighty sustainer of the world-machine should bother with the particularities of trivial finite beings seemed absurd and unworthy. The whole discussion about miracles is colored by this increasingly abstract notion of providence, in which the older sense of the divine concern for the creature and the divine purpose for history is gradually attenuated.

Thus the common acceptance of the idea of "God" resulted largely from the way in which the idea was emptied of most of its concrete religious connotations. "Knowledge of God" seldom carried with it in this period (Law and Wesley being the most conspicuous exceptions) the awesome sense of encounter with a mystery through which emerged a new, humbling, transforming awareness of self.

The problem of the relation between the Enlightenment's "faith," as represented most extremely in deism, and the faith embodied in the older Christian world-view, arises particularly in the area of the view of man, his nature, and his possibilities. If we may briefly indicate the Christian view by saying that it postulated a dialectical tension between man as made in the image of God and man as in existence always a sinner, then we may say that the consistent tendency of most thinkers in the Enlightenment was to break that tension through emphasizing the first term while denying the second. Here is the root of that "optimism" which all students of the period notice.

Positively, the age saw man's reason as the instrument for his individual and corporate betterment. Evils there are in human life, of course; indeed, one notes the philanthropic activities of the time as practical attacks on some of these evils. But this is precisely the point—it was believed that man can attack and overcome by educational and technical means, and good will, all the evils of life. Few believed seriously in that warping of reason and aspiration which the older doctrine of original sin had presupposed as a mysterious vitiation of human hopes. Man seemed no mystery to himself. Both ends of the spectrum of psychic experience—the darker end of the "demonic" as well as the lighter end of the ecstatic and the creative—tended to be sloughed off; the norms of rationality and universality clearly favored the middle of the spectrum. The pejorative sense the period gave to the term "enthusiasm" is a clear example.

The critics of deism were alert to the weaknesses of many of the standard assumptions of their time. On one side were the spokesmen for Christianity. William Law saw that the understanding of human nature was the central problem, and ridiculed the deists' idea of "reason" as unreal to experience, abstract and unhistorical. Bishop Joseph Butler, whose

The Analogy of Religion, Natural and Revealed, to the Constitution and Course of Nature (1736) was the weightiest exposition of "orthodoxy" against deism, showed that there were as many mysteries in natural religion as there were in revealed, and as many in our knowledge of nature as in our knowledge of morality. John Wesley pointed to dimensions of religious experience which the deists had largely ignored in their rationalistic approach.

But the critic who most thoroughly exposed the weaknesses of the deist position did so, not from the standpoint of Christianity, but from that of philosophical skepticism.

David Hume's *The Natural History of Religion* (written about 1751) was a presentation of the origin of religion conceived as a social phenomenon amenable to dispassionate, external observation. Hume saw man's earliest religion as polytheistic, from which slowly and tentatively there developed monotheism. The origin of religion was chiefly to be found in fear. The clear reasonableness of natural religion disappeared before a semi-historical look at what can be known about uncivilized man—"a barbarous, necessitous animal," as Hume termed him. Natural religion, if by that term one means the actual religious beliefs and practices of uncivilized peoples, was seen to be a fabric of superstitions. Primitive man was no unspoiled philosopher, clearly seeing the truth of one God. And the history of religion was not, as the deists has implied, retrograde; the widespread phenomenon of superstition was caused less by priestly malice than by man's unreason as he confronted his experience.

Hume's *Dialogues Concerning Natural Religion,* (originally written about the same time as *The Natural History* but not published until after Hume's death) exposed with dialectical rigor the weaknesses in the elaborate rational constructions of the best of the exponents of natural religion. Profoundly conscious of the limits of reason, Hume distrusted man's ability to deal adequately with any problem precisely to the extent that the problem goes beyond common experience. As religious speculation moves from the simple to the complex and then to that which transcends all possible experience, reason's limits are more clearly demonstrated; here, where "we are like foreigners in a strange country," the undisciplined imagination, not reason, reigns unchecked. By careful logical analysis, but even more by varying modes of irony, Hume showed the weakness of "the religious hypothesis" as an explanation of order. The existence of God, with the traditional predicates, so quickly assumed by Locke to be rationally demonstrable, is reduced to the level of low probability. More significantly, "the religious hypothesis" is shown to be fruitless; on the basis of it, one can make no significant predictions. Throughout both works, Hume very tentatively adumbrated his own alternative to "natural religion"; sketchy and incomplete as it was, it carried almost no marks acceptable either to a deist or to an advocate of natural religion. Indeed, it represented a radical departure from the Western religious tradition, not a "half-way house" of the deist type.

As a phenomenon of intellectual history, the deist controversy is over, and no reputable thinker today adopts the deist solution (although deist ideas often appear in popular journalism, often uttered with great aplomb as if they were the most advanced of new notions). The whole discussion is significant for one who is concerned about the intellectual transition from the older accepted Christian world-view to the more modern secular one. As one reads the old controversialists, he can see the change taking place before him, as "defenders" accept their opponents' formulations of problems, concepts, and methods. So eminent a representative of "orthodoxy" as Bishop Butler, for example, had already gone halfway to deism in his arguments against the deists.

But though the old debate is over, many of the problems it posed remain very much alive today. The whole issue of how the Christian faith is to be understood in relation to non-Christian faiths has become, with increasing knowledge of Eastern religions and cultures, a still more pressing concern. If the scientific developments of the nineteenth century served to reinforce the Humian (and later Kantian) criticisms of the "proofs" of God, some contemporary religious thinkers are still deeply concerned to seek to relate man's knowledge of the natural order and his faith in God. And with our increasing consciousness of the actual pluralism of moral systems in divergent cultures, the question of whether there can be any meaningful moral consensus (whether defined in terms of natural law or not) becomes a vital issue.

The present edition seeks to present in abridged form the major contributions to the controversy, except for works which are readily available in reprint form. (Thus Locke, Berkeley, Butler and Hume are excluded.) Since most of the ideas were articulated through debate, some tracts and letters answering other works are included, and placed in relation to the work attacked. Texts have been modernized in spelling, capitalization, and punctuation; very rarely a connective has been interpolated without indication to make grammatical sense.

E.G.W.

SELECTED BIBLIOGRAPHY

This list includes only works in English, and it excludes works dealing with single thinkers.

BAUMER, Franklin L. *Religion and the Rise of Scepticism.* New York: Harcourt, Brace, 1960.

CASSIRER, Ernst. *The Philosophy of the Enlightenment,* tr. Fritz C. A. Koelin and James P. Pettegrove. Boston: Beacon, 1951.

CRAGG, Gerald R. *Reason and Authority in the Eighteenth Century.* London: Cambridge University Press, 1964.

HAZARD, Paul. *European Thought in the Eighteenth Century,* tr. J. Lewis May. New Haven: Yale University Press, 1954.

LOVEJOY, Arthur O. *Essays in the History of Ideas.* Baltimore: John Hopkins, 1948.

NICHOLS, James H. *History of Christianity, 1650–1950.* New York: Ronald, 1956.

STEPHEN, Leslie. *History of English Thought in the Eighteenth Century.* New York: Harcourt, Brace, 1962; original edition, 1876.

STROMBERG, Ronald N. *Religious Liberalism in Eighteenth-Century England.* London: Oxford University Press, 1954.

SYKES, Norman. *From Sheldon to Secker:* Aspects of English Church History, 1660–1768. London: Cambridge University Press, 1959.

WILLEY, Basil. *The Eighteenth Century Background.* London: Chatto and Windus, 1940.

SOURCES OF TEXTS

1. TOLAND, JOHN. Christianity Not Mysterious; Or, A Treatise Showing that there is nothing in the Gospel contrary to reason nor above it; and that no Christian doctrine can be properly called a mystery. London, 1696.

2. BROWNE, PETER. A Letter in Answer to a Book Entitled "Christianity Not Mysterious," as also to All those who set up for reason and evidence in opposition to revelation and mysteries. London, third ed., 1703.

3. LESLIE, CHARLES. A Short and Easy Method with the Deists, wherein the certainty of the Christian Religion is demonstrated by infallible proof from four rules, which are incompatible to any imposture that ever yet has been, or that can possibly be. London, ninth ed., 1745.

4. CLARKE, SAMUEL. A Discourse Concerning the Being and Attributes of God, the unchangeable Obligations of Natural Religion, and the Truth and Certainty of the Christian Revelation (Boyle Lectures), in The Works of Samuel Clarke. London, 1742, Vol. II.

5. COLLINS, ANTHONY. A Discourse of Free-Thinking, occasioned by the Rise and Growth of a Sect called Free-Thinkers. London, 1713.

6. WOOLSTON, THOMAS. (Six) Discourses on the Miracles of our Savior, in view of the present controversy between infidels and apostates. London, varying editions, 1728–1729.

7. SHERLOCK, THOMAS. The Trial of the Witnesses of the Resurrection of Jesus, in The Works of Bishop Sherlock, ed. T. S. Hughes. London, 1830, Vol. V.

8. TINDAL, MATTHEW. Christianity as Old as the Creation, or The Gospel a Republication of the Religion of Nature. London, 1730.

9. LAW, WILLIAM. The Case of Reason, or Natural Religion, fairly and fully stated, in answer to a book entitled "Christianity as Old as the Creation," in The Works of the Reverend William Law. London, 1892 reprint, Vol. II.

10. DODWELL, HENRY. Christianity Not Founded on Argument; and the true principles of Gospel-Evidence assigned. London, third ed., 1743.

11. WESLEY, JOHN. An Earnest Appeal to Men of Reason and Religion, in The Works of the Reverend John Wesley. New York, 1850, Vol. V.

12. MIDDLETON, CONYERS. A Free Inquiry into the Miraculous Powers Which are Supposed to have subsisted in the Christian Church, from the Earliest Ages through several successive centuries, in The Miscellaneous Works of Conyers Middleton. London, second ed., 1755, Vol. I.

13. WESLEY, JOHN. To Dr. Conyers Middleton, in The Letters of the Reverend John Wesley, ed. John Telford. London, 1931, Vol. II.

CONTENTS

JOHN TOLAND

Toland (1670–1722), an Irishman reared in childhood as a Roman Catholic, became a Protestant dissenter during his adolescence. Studying for the ministry, he attended college at Glasgow; Edinburgh bestowed the M.A. upon him in 1690. During that decade he read, conversed, and wrote in Holland and at Oxford. He was acquainted with John Locke, and shared many of Locke's ideas. The publication of *Christianity Not Mysterious* in 1696 touched off widespread discussion; Locke made a point of disavowing any identity of opinion between him and Toland. The Irish House of Commons condemned the book to be burned by the hangman, and ordered its author arrested and prosecuted. A comment of Toland's on this action will be found at the end of the selection from Peter Browne. Toland lived the rest of his life in England and on the Continent, writing occasional pieces and living on the fringes of political and intellectual society.

Christianity Not Mysterious

PREFACE

I hope to make it appear that the use of reason is not so dangerous in religion as it is commonly represented. Religion is not to be modelled according to our fancies, nor to be judged of as it relates to our private designs, else there would be full as many creeds as persons. But how little soever our notions agree, religion is always the same, like God its author, with whom there is no variableness, nor shadow of turning.

I don't pretend that we are able to explain the

terms or doctrines of this or that age, council or nation, but the terms and doctrines of the Gospel. They are not the articles of the East or West, Orthodox or Arian, Protestant or Papist, considered as such, that I trouble myself about, but those of Jesus Christ and his apostles. Since religion is calculated for reasonable creatures, 'tis conviction and not authority that should bear weight with them.

And for my own part, as I would have none by false or unfair consequences make me say what I never thought of, so I would not be told I contradict anything but Scripture or reason, which, I'm sure, agree very well. I readily submit myself to them, and give all the world the same right over me. I am not therefore to be put out of countenance by venerable names and pompous citations that have no value but such as an ugly rust and color give ancient coins. God alone, and such as are inspired by him, can prescribe injunctions relating to the world to come, while human powers regulate the affairs of this.

I have endeavored to speak very intelligibly; I have in many places made explanatory repetitions of difficult words. This labor is of no benefit to philosophers, but it is of considerable advantage to the vulgar. For why may not the vulgar be judges of the true sense of things? Truth is always and everywhere the same. The poor, who are not supposed to understand philosophical systems, soon apprehend the difference between the plain convincing instructions of Christ and the intricate ineffectual declamations of the scribes.

INTRODUCTION: *The State of the Question*

There is nothing that men make a greater noise about than the "mysteries of the Christian religion."

The divines gravely tell us "we must adore what we cannot comprehend." Some of them say the "mysteries of the Gospel" are to be understood only in the sense of the "ancient fathers." But that is so multifarious and inconsistent with itself as to make it impossible for anybody to believe so many contradictions at once. They themselves did caution their readers from leaning upon their authority without the evidence of reason. They were as injudicious, violent, and factious as other men; they were for the greatest part very credulous and superstitious in religion; in a word, they were of the same nature and make with ourselves.

Some give a decisive voice in the unravelling of "mysteries," and the interpretation of Scripture, to a General Council, and others to one man whom they hold to be the head of the church universal upon earth, and the infallible judge of all controversies. But we do not think such Councils possible, nor (if they were) to be of more weight than the fathers, for they consist of such. As for the "one judge of all controversies," we suppose none but such as are strongly prepossessed by interest or education can in good earnest digest those chimerical supreme headships and monsters of infallibility. We read nowhere in the Bible of such delegate judges appointed by Christ to supply his office, and reason manifestly proclaims them frontless usurpers.

They come nearest the thing who affirm that we are to keep to what the Scriptures determine about these matters; there is nothing more true if rightly understood. But ordinarily 'tis an equivocal way of speaking. Some will have us always believe what the literal sense imports, with little or no consideration for reason, which they reject as not fit to be employed about the revealed part of religion. Others assert that we may use reason as the instrument but not the rule of our belief. The first contend some mysteries may be, or at least seem to be, contrary to reason, and yet be received by faith. The second, that no mystery is contrary to reason, but that all are "above" it.

On the contrary, we hold that reason is the only foundation of all certitude, and that nothing revealed, whether as to its manner or existence, is more exempted from its disquisitions than the ordinary phenomena of nature. Wherefore, we likewise maintain, according to the title of this discourse, that *there is nothing in the Gospel contrary to reason, nor above it; and that no Christian doctrine can be properly called a mystery.*

I: *Of Reason*

The order I design to observe is, first, to show what is meant by reason, and its properties; then to prove there's no doctrine of the Gospel contrary to reason; after that, to evince that neither is there any above reason; and by consequence, that none is a mystery.

Everyone experiences in himself a power or faculty of forming various ideas or perceptions of things; of affirming or denying, according as he sees them to agree or disagree; and so of loving and desiring what seems good unto him, and of hating and avoiding what he thinks evil. The right use of all these faculties is what we call common sense, or reason in general. Simple and distinct ideas, laid up in the great repository of the understanding, are the sole matter and foundation of all our reasoning. For the soul does upon occasion compare them together, compound them into complex ideas, enlarge, contract, or separate them. So that all our knowledge is, in effect, nothing else but the perception of the agreement or disagreement of our ideas in a greater or lesser number, whereinsoever this agreement or disagreement may consist. And because this perception is immediate or mediate, our knowledge is twofold.

First, when the mind, without the assistance of any other idea, immediately perceives the agreement or disagreement of two or more ideas, as that two and two is four, that red is not blue, it cannot be called reason, though it be the highest degree of evidence. But secondly, when the mind cannot immediately perceive the agreement or disagreement of any ideas, because they cannot be brought near enough together and so compared, it applies one or more intermediate ideas to discover it. As when by the successive applications of a line to two distant houses, I find how far they agree or disagree in length, which I could not effect with my eye. This method of knowledge is properly called reason or demonstration (as the former self-evidence or intuition); and it may be defined as that faculty of the soul which discovers the certainty of anything dubious or obscure by comparing it with something evidently known.

Though self-evidence excludes reason, yet all demonstration becomes at length self-evident. When we have no notions or ideas of a thing, we cannot reason about it at all; and where we have ideas, if intermediate ones, to show their constant and necessary agreement or disagreement, fail us, we can never go beyond probability.

But besides these properties of reason, we are yet most carefully to distinguish in it the means of information from the ground of persuasion. The means of information I call those ways whereby anything comes barely to our knowledge without necessarily commanding our assent. By the ground of persuasion I understand that rule by which we judge of all truth, and which irresistibly convinces the mind. The means of information are experience and authority. Experience is either external, which furnishes us with the ideas of sensible objects, or internal, which helps us to the ideas of the operations of our own minds. This is the common stock of all our knowledge; nor can we possibly have ideas any other way without new organs or faculties. Authority is either human or divine. Human authority is called also moral certitude. Thus all possible matters of fact, duly attested by coevous persons as known to them, and successively related by others of different times, nations or interests, who could neither be imposed upon themselves nor be justly suspected of combining together to deceive others, ought to be received by us for as certain and indubitable as if we had seen them through our own eyes or heard them with our own ears. By this means it is I believe there was such a city as Carthage, such a reformer as Luther, and that there is such a kingdom as Poland. The authority of God, or divine revelation, is the manifestation of truth by truth itself, to whom it is impossible to lie.

Nothing in nature can come to our knowledge but by some of these four means, viz.: the experience of the senses, the experience of the mind, human and divine revelation.

Now, as we are extremely subject to deception, we may, without some infallible rule, often take a questionable proposition for an axiom, old wives' fables for moral certitude, and human impostures for divine revelation. This infallible rule, or ground of all right persuasion, is evidence, and it consists in the exact conformity of our ideas or thoughts with their objects, or the things we think upon. It is impossible for us to err as long as we take evidence for our guide; and we never mistake, but when we wander from it by abusing our liberty, in denying that of any thing which belongs to it, or attributing to it what we do not see in its idea.

But God the wise creator of all, who has enabled us to perceive things and form judgments of them, has also endued us with the power of suspending our judgments about whatever is uncertain, and of never assenting but to clear perceptions. He is so far from putting us upon any necessity of erring that as he has thus privileged us on the one hand with a faculty of guarding ourselves against prepossession or precipitation, by placing our liberty only in what is indifferent or dubious and obscure, so he provides on the other hand that we should discern and embrace the truth, by taking it out of our power to dissent from an evident proposition. We must necessarily believe that it is impossible the same thing should be and not be at once; nor can all the world persuade us to doubt of it. But we need not admit that there's no void in nature, or that the earth absolves an annual course about the sun, till we get demonstrations to that effect.

Let us cheerfully thank our kind disposer, who has put us under a law of bowing before the light and majesty of evidence. And truly if we might doubt of anything that is clear, or be deceived by distinct conceptions, there could be nothing certain; neither conscience, nor God himself, should be regarded; no society or government could subsist.

II: *That the doctrines of the Gospel are not con-
     trary to reason*

I take it to be very intelligible from the precedent
section that what is evidently repugnant to clear and
distinct ideas, or to our common notions, is contrary
to reason. I go on therefore to prove that the doctrines of the Gospel, if it be the word of God, cannot
be so. No Christian I know of expressly says reason
and the Gospel are contrary to one another. But very
many affirm that, though the doctrines of the latter
cannot in themselves be contradictory to the principles of the former, as proceeding both from God, yet
that according to our conceptions of them they may
seem directly to clash. And that though we cannot
reconcile them by reason of our corrupt and limited
understandings, yet that from the authority of divine
revelation we are bound to believe and acquiesce in
them; or, as the fathers taught them to speak, to
"adore what we cannot comprehend."

This famous and admirable doctrine is the undoubted source of all the absurdities that ever were
seriously vented among Christians. Without the pretense of it, we should never hear of transubstantiation, and other ridiculous fables of the Church of
Rome. Nor should we be ever bantered with the
Lutheran impanation, or the ubiquity it has produced, as one monster ordinarily begets another. And
though the Socinians disown this practice, I am mistaken if either they or the Arians can make their
notions of a dignified and creature-God capable of
divine worship appear more reasonable than the ex-
travagancies of other sects touching the article of the
Trinity. In short, this doctrine is the known refuge

of some men when they are at a loss in explaining any passage of the word of God.

Let us enter upon the immediate examen of the opinion itself. The first thing I shall insist upon is that if any doctrine of the New Testament be contrary to reason, we have no manner of idea of it. To say, for instance, that a ball is white and black at once is to say just nothing, for these colors are so incompatible in the same subject as to exclude all possibility of a real positive idea or conception. So to say as the papists that children dying before baptism are damned without pain signifies nothing at all.

If any should think to evade the difficulty by saying that the ideas of certain doctrines may be contrary indeed to common notions, yet consistent with themselves and I know not what supra-intellectual truths, he's but just where he was. But supposing a little that the thing were so, it still follows that none can understand these doctrines except their perceptions be communicated to him in an extraordinary manner, as by new powers and organs. Four may be called five in Heaven, but so the name only is changed, the thing remains still the same. And since we cannot in this world know anything but by our common notions, how shall we be sure of this pretended consistency between our present seeming contradictions and the theology of the world to come? For as 'tis by reason we arrive at the certainty of God's own existence, so we cannot otherwise discern his revelations but by their conformity with our natural notices of him, which is in so many words to agree with our common notions.

The next thing I shall remark is that those who stick not to say they could believe a downright contradiction to reason, did they find it contained in the

Scripture, do justify all absurdities whatsoever, and by opposing one light to another undeniably make God the author of all incertitude. The very supposition that reason might authorize one thing and the Spirit of God another throws us into inevitable skepticism, for we shall be at a perpetual uncertainty which to obey. Nay, we can never be sure which is which. For the proof of the divinity of Scripture depending upon reason, if the clear light of the one might be any way contradicted how shall we be convinced of the infallibility of the other? Reason may err in this point as well as in anything else, and we have no particular promise it shall not, no more than the papists that their senses may not deceive them in everything as well as in transubstantiation. To say it bears witness to itself is equally to establish the Alcoran or the Poran. And 'twere a notable argument to tell a heathen that the church has declared it, when all societies will say as much for themselves, if we take their word for it. Besides, it may be he would ask whence the church had authority to decide this matter? And if it should be answered, from the Scripture, a thousand to one but he would divert himself with this circle.

But if we believe the Scripture to be divine, not upon its own bare assertion but from a real testimony consisting in the evidence of the things contained therein, from undoubted effects and not from words and letters, what is this but to prove it by reason? It has in itself, I grant, the brightest characters of divinity; but 'tis reason finds them out, examines them, and by its principles approves and pronounces them sufficient, which orderly begets in us an acquiescence of faith or persuasion. Now if particulars be thus severely sifted, if not only the doctrine of Christ and his apostles be considered, but also their lives, predictions, miracles, and deaths, surely all this labor would be in vain might we upon any account dispense with contradictions.

The natural result of what has been said is that to believe that divinity of Scripture, or the sense of any passage thereof, without rational proofs and an evident consistency, is a blameable credulity and a temerarious opinion, ordinarily grounded upon an ignorant and willful disposition, but more generally maintained out of a gainful prospect.

Against all that we have been establishing, the authority of revelation will be alleged with great show, as if without a right of silencing or extinguishing reason it were altogether useless and impertinent. But if the distinction I made be well considered, the weakness of the present objection will quickly appear, and this controversy be better understood hereafter. I said revelation was not a necessitating motive of assent, but a means of information. We should not confound the way whereby we come to the knowledge of a thing with the grounds we have to believe it. Now such is the nature of a matter of fact that, though it may be conceived possible enough, yet he only can with assurance assert its existence who is himself the author, or by some means of information comes first to the certain knowledge of it. That there was such an island as Jamaica no European could ever reasonably deny; and yet that it was precisely situated in such a latitude, was watered with those rivers, clothed with these woods, bore this grain, produced that plant, no Englishman before the discovery of America could positively affirm.

Thus God is pleased to reveal to us in Scripture several wonderful matters of fact, as the creation of

the world, the last judgment, and many other important truths which no man left to himself could ever
imagine, no more than any of my fellow-creatures can
be sure of my private thoughts. Yet we do not receive
them only because they are revealed. For besides the
infallible testimony of the revelation from all requisite circumstances, we must see in its subject the indisputable characters of divine wisdom and sound
reason, which are the only marks we have to distinguish the oracles and will of God from the impostures
and traditions of men.

Whoever reveals anything, that is whoever tells us
something we did not know before, his words must
be intelligible and the matter possible. This rule
holds good, let God or man be the revealer. If we
count that person a fool who requires our assent to
what is manifestly incredible, how dare we blasphe-
mously attribute to the most perfect being what is
an acknowledged defect of one of ourselves? Therefore all matters revealed by God or man must be
equally intelligible and possible; so far both revelations agree. But in this they differ, that though the
revelation of man should be thus qualified, yet he may
impose upon me as to the truth of the thing; whereas
what God is pleased to discover to me is not only
clear to my reason but likewise it is always true.

Thus all the doctrines and precepts of the New
Testament (if it be indeed divine) must agree with
natural reason and our own ordinary ideas. This
every considerate and well-disposed person will find
by the careful perusal of it. And whoever undertakes
this task will confess the Gospel "not to be hidden
from us, nor afar off, but very nigh us, in our mouths,
and in our hearts." (Deut. 30:11, 14) It affords the
most illustrious examples of close and perspicuous

ratiocination conceivable, which it is incumbent on
me in the explication of its "mysteries" to demonstrate.
And though the evidence of Christ's doctrine might
claim the approbation of the Gentiles; and its conformity with the types and prophecies of the Old
Testament, with all the marks of the Messiah con-
curring in his person, might justly challenge the
assent of his countrymen; yet to leave no room for
doubt he proves his authority and Gospel by such
works and miracles as the stiffnecked Jews themselves
could not deny to be divine.

Jesus himself appeals to his very enemies, ready to
stone him for pretended blasphemy, saying: "If I do
not the works of my Father, believe me not; but if
I do, believe not me, believe the works, that you may
know and believe that the Father is in me, and I in
him." (John 10:37, 38) That is, believe not rashly on
me, and so give a testimony to my works; but search
the Scriptures which testify of the Messiah; and consider the works I do, whether they be such as to
become God and are attributed to him. If they be,
then conclude and believe that I am he, etc. Peter
exhorts Christians "to be ready always to give an
answer to every one that asks them a reason of their
hope." (I Peter 3:15) Now to what purpose served
all these miracles, all these appeals, if no regard was
to be had of men's understandings? if the doctrines
of Christ were incomprehensible? or were we obliged
to believe revealed nonsense?

Nor is there any different rule to be followed in the
interpretation of Scripture from what is common to
all other books. Whatever unprejudiced person shall
use those means will find them notorious deceivers,
or much deceived themselves, who maintain the New
Testament is written without any order or certain

scope, but just as matters came into the apostles'
heads. They are strangers to true method who com-
plain of this confusion and disorder. The facility of
the Gospel is not confined only to method, for the
style is also most easy, most natural, and in the common dialect of those to whom it was immediately
consigned. "I came not to you," says Paul, "with
excellency of speech or wisdom, declaring unto you
the testimony of God. My speech and my preaching
was not with enticing words of human wisdom, but
in demonstration (or conviction) of the Spirit (or
mind), and in power (or efficacy)." (I Cor. 2:1, 4)
This he speaks in reference to the philosophers and
orators of those times, whose elocution was curious,
and periods elaborate, apt to excite the admiration
of the hearers but not to satisfy their reasons; charm-
ing indeed their senses while in the theatre or the
temple, but making them neither the better at home
nor the wiser abroad.

These men, as well as many of their modern successors, were fond enough of their own ridiculous
systems to "count the things of God foolishness," (I
Cor. 2:14) because they did not agree with their
precarious and sensual notions, because every sentence was not wrapped up in "mystery," and gar-
nished with a figure, not considering that only false
or trivial matters need the assistance of alluring
harangues to perplex or amuse. But they were enemies and strangers to the simplicity of truth. And as
he was esteemed the best orator that made the worst
cause appear the most equitable before the judges, so
he was the best philosopher that could get the wildest
paradox to pass for demonstration.

But the scope of the apostles was very different:
piety toward God and the peace of mankind was

their gain, and Christ and his Gospel their glory. They came not magnifying nor exalting themselves, not imposing but declaring their doctrine. They did not confound and mislead, but convince the mind. They were employed to dispel ignorance, to eradicate superstition, to propagate truth and reformation of manners; "to preach deliverance to captives," (Lk. 4:18), i.e., the enjoyment of Christian liberty to the slaves of the Levitical and pagan priesthoods, and to declare salvation to repenting sinners.

There remains one objection upon which some lay a mighty stress, though it's like to do them little service. Granting, say they, the Gospel to be as reasonable as you pretend, yet corrupt and depraved reason can neither discern nor receive divine verities. Aye, but that proves not divine verities to be contrary to sound reason. But they maintain that no man's reason is sound. Wherefore I hope so to state this question as to cut off all occasion of dispute from judicious and peaceable men. Reason, taken for the principle of discourse in us, or more particularly for that faculty everyone has of judging of his ideas according to their agreement or disagreement, and so of loving what seems good unto him, and hating what he thinks evil; reason, I say, in this sense, is whole and entire in every one whose organs are not accidentally indisposed. 'Tis from it that we are accounted men, and we could neither inform others nor receive improvement ourselves any more than brutes without it.

But if by reason be understood a constant right use of these faculties, viz., if a man never judges but according to clear perceptions, desires nothing but what is truly good for him, nor avoids but what is certainly evil, then, I confess, it is extremely corrupt.

We are too prone to frame wrong conceptions and erroneous judgments of things. We generally covet what flatters our senses, without distinguishing noxious from innocent pleasures; and our hatred is as partial. We gratify our bodies so much as to meditate little, and think very grossly of spiritual or abstract matters. We are apt to indulge our inclinations, which we term "to follow nature" (I Cor. 2:14); so that the natural man, that is he that gives the swing to his appetites, counts divine things mere folly. But these disorders are so far from being reason that nothing can be more directly contrary to it. We lie under no necessary fate of sinning. There is no defect in our understandings but those of our own creation, that is to say, vicious habits easily contracted but difficultly reformed.

Supposing a natural impotency to reason well, we could no more be liable to condemnation for not keeping the commands of God than those to whom the Gospel was never revealed for not believing on Christ. Were our reasoning faculties imperfect, or we not capable to employ them rightly, there could be no possibility of our understanding one another in millions of things, where the stock of our ideas should prove unavoidably unequal, or our capacities different. But 'tis the perfection of our reason and liberty that makes us deserve rewards and punishments. The deliberations we use about our designs, and the choice to which we determine ourselves at last, do prove us the free disposers of all our actions. Now what is sound reason except this be it? Doubtless it is. And no evangelical or other knowable truth can prove insuperable or monstrous to him that uses it after this manner. But when we abuse it against itself, and enslave it to our debauched imaginations, it is averse from all good. We are so habituated, I confess, to precarious and hasty conclusions, that without great constancy and exercise we cannot recover our innate freedom. Encouragements are proposed to such as do so. We can, upon serious reflection, see our faults, and find that what we held most unreasonable did only appear so from superficial disquisitions, or want of necessary helps, from deference to authority, and principles taken upon trust, from irregular inclinations and self-interest, or the hatred of a party.

But notwithstanding all this, some are at a world of pains to rob themselves (if they could) of their liberty or freewill, the noblest and most useful of all our faculties, the only thing we can properly call ours, and the only thing that neither power nor fortune can take from us. Not willing to own their ignorance and miscarriages (which proceed from passion, sloth or inconsideration), they would remove all the blame from their will and charge it upon a natural impotency not in their power to cure. Thus they ingeniously cheat themselves, and choose rather to be ranked in the same condition with brutes or machines than to be obliged to acknowledge their human frailties, and to mend.

Why should we entertain such mean and unbecoming thoughts, as if truth, like the Almighty, dwelt in light inaccessible, and not to be discovered by the sons of men? Things are always the same, how different soever the conceptions of men about them may be; and what another did not, I may happily find out. That nothing escaped the sight of former ages is a tale to be told where one person only speaks, and nobody present must contradict him. The slips and errors which are taken notice of in the

world everyday serve only to put us in mind that
many able men did not examine the truth with that
order and application they should or might have
done. There are a thousand things in our power to
know, of which, through prejudice or neglect, we
may be and frequently remain ignorant all our life.
And innumerable difficulties may be made by
imagining "mysteries" where there are none, or by
conceiving too discouraging and unjust an opinion
of our own abilities. Whereas, by a parity of reason,
we may hope to outdo all that outdid others before
us, as posterity may exceed both.

III. *That there is nothing mysterious or above reason
in the Gospel.*

We come at length to inquire whether any doctrine of the Gospel be above, though not contrary to,
reason. This expression is taken in a two-fold significance. First, it denotes a thing intelligible of itself, but so covered by figurative words, types and
ceremonies that reason cannot penetrate the veil,
nor see what is under it till it be removed. Secondly,
it is made to signify a thing of its own nature inconceivable, and not to be judged of by our ordinary
faculties and ideas, though it be never so clearly revealed. In both these senses "to be above reason" is
the same thing with "mystery," and, in effect, they are
convertible terms in divinity.

To understand aright what the word "mystery"
imports, we must trace the original of it as far back
as the theology of the ancient Gentiles. *Myein* in
their systems signified "to initiate"; *myesis*, "initia-
tion"; *mystes*, a name afterwards given the priests,

denoted the person to be initiated; and "mystery" the
doctrine in which he was initiated. There were different sorts of mysteries, the most famous the Samo-
thracian, the Eleusinian, the Egyptian, and those of
Bacchus.

From what has been said it is clear that they
understood by "mystery" in those days a thing intelligible of itself, but so veiled by others that it could
not be known without special revelation.

But many, not denying what is so plain, yet will
have some Christian doctrines to be still "mysterious"
in the second sense of the word, that is, inconceivable
in themselves however clearly revealed. If I can
demonstrate that in the New Testament "mystery"
is always used in the first sense of the word, viz.,
for things naturally very intelligible, but so covered
by figurative words or rites that reason could not
discover them without special revelation; and that
the veil is actually taken away; then it will manifestly
follow that the doctrines so revealed cannot now be
properly called mysteries.

First, I affirm that nothing can be said to be a
mystery because we have not an adequate idea of it,
or a distinct view of all its properties at once, for
then everything would be a mystery. The knowledge
of finite creatures is gradually progressive, as objects
are presented to the understanding. We are said to
know a thousand things, nor can we doubt of it; yet
we never have a full conception of whatever belongs
to them. I understand nothing better than this table
upon which I am now writing; I conceive it divisible
into parts beyond all imagination; but shall I say it
is above my reason because I cannot count these
parts, nor distinctly perceive their quantity and
figures?

Knowing nothing of bodies but their properties, God has wisely provided we should understand no more of these than are useful and necessary for us, which is all our present condition needs. Thus our eyes are not given us to see all quantities, nor perhaps anything as it is in itself, but as it bears some relation to us.

Rightly speaking, then, we are accounted to comprehend anything when its chief properties and their several uses are known to us. It is improper therefore to say a thing is above our reason because we know no more of it than concerns us, and ridiculous to supersede our disquisitions about it upon that score. The most compendious method therefore to acquire sure and useful knowledge is neither to trouble ourselves nor others with what is useless, were it known, or what is impossible to be known at all. Since I easily perceive the good or bad effects of rain upon the earth, what should I be the better did I comprehend its generation in the clouds?

The application of this discourse to my subject admits of no difficulty. It is, first, that no Christian doctrine, no more than any ordinary piece of nature, can be reputed a mystery because we have not an adequate or complete idea of whatever belongs to it. Secondly, that what is revealed in religion, as it is most useful and necessary, so it must and may be as easily comprehended, and found as consistent with our common notions, as what we know of wood or stone, of air, of water, or the like. And thirdly, that when we do as familiarly explain such doctrines as what is known of natural things, we may then be as properly said to comprehend the one as the other.

I conclude that neither God himself, nor any of his

attributes, are mysteries to us for want of an adequate idea; no, not eternity. Eternity is no more above reason, because it cannot be imagined, than a circle, because it may; for in both cases reason performs its part according to the different natures of the objects, whereof the one is essentially imaginable, the other not.

As we know not all the properties of things, so we can never conceive the essence of any substance in the world. To avoid ambiguity, I distinguish, after an excellent modern philosopher, the nominal from the real essence of a thing. The nominal essence is a collection of those properties or modes which we principally observe in anything. Thus the nominal essence of the sun is a bright, hot, and round body, at a certain distance from us, and that has a constant regular motion. Whoever hears the word "sun" pronounced, this is the idea he has of it. He may conceive more of its properties, or not all these, but it is still a collection of modes or properties that makes his idea. But the real essence is that intrinsic constitution of a thing which is the ground or support of all its properties, and from which they naturally flow or result. Now though we are persuaded that the modes of things must have such a subject to exist in, yet we are absolutely ignorant of what it is.

It follows very plainly that nothing can be said to be a mystery because we are ignorant of its real essence, since it is not more knowable in one thing than in another, and is never conceived or included in the ideas we have of things, or the names we give them. We certainly know as much of the soul as we do of anything else, if not more. We form the clearest conceptions of thinking, knowing, imagining, willing, hoping, loving, and the like operations of the mind. But we are strangers to the subject wherein these operations exist.

As for God, we comprehend nothing better than his attributes. We know not, it's true, the nature of that eternal subject or essence wherein infinite goodness, love, knowledge, power and wisdom coexist; but we are not better acquainted with the real essence of any of his creatures. I remarked in the beginning of this chapter that we knew nothing of things but such of their properties as were necessary and useful. We may say the same of God, for every act of our religion is directed by the consideration of some of his attributes, without ever thinking of his essence. Our love to him is kindled by his goodness, and our thankfulness by his mercy; our obedience is regulated by his justice; and our hopes are confirmed by his wisdom and power.

I think I may now warrantably conclude that nothing is a mystery because we know not its essence, since it appears that it is neither knowable in itself, nor ever thought of by us. So that the divine being himself cannot with more reason by accounted mysterious in this respect than the most contemptible of his creatures. Nor am I very much concerned that these essences escape my knowledge, for I am fixed in the opinion that what infinite goodness has not been pleased to reveal to us, we are either sufficiently capable to discover ourselves, or need not understand at all.

We come now to the main point upon which the whole controversy chiefly depends. The question being whether or no Christianity is mysterious, it ought to be naturally decided by the New Testament, wherein the Christian faith is originally contained.

Now by searching the Scriptures, I find some of the evangelical doctrines called "mysteries," in a more general or in a more particular sense. They are more generally so called with respect to all mankind, for being certain matters of fact only known to God and lodged in his decree, or such events as were quite lost and forgot in the world, it was impossible for any person, though never so wise or learned, to discover them. "The things of God knoweth none but the Spirit of God," (I Cor. 2:11) as none can find out the secret thoughts of man till he tells them himself. Such revelations then of God in the New Testament are called "mysteries," not from any present inconceivableness or obscurity, but with respect to what they were before this revelation. If any should question this, let him hear the apostle Paul. (Cf. I Cor. 2:7–10) The most perspicacious philosophers were not able to foretell the coming of Christ, to discover the resurrection of the body, nor any other matter of fact that is delivered in the Gospel. And if they happened now and then to say something like the truth, they did but divine at best, and could never be certain of their opinion.

But some doctrines of the Gospel are more particularly called mysteries because they were hid from God's peculiar people under the Mosaic economy. Not that they knew nothing concerning them, for "the law had a shadow of good things to come" (Heb. 10:1); but they were not clearly and fully revealed till the New Testament times, being veiled before by various typical representations, ceremonies, and figurative expressions. Christ tells his disciples, "Many prophets and kings have desired to see those things which you see, and have not seen them, and to hear things which you hear, and have not heard them." (Lk. 10:24). Paul says, "we use great plainness of speech, and not as Moses who put a veil over his face." And then expressly adds that "this veil is taken away in Christ," (II Cor. 3:12–14) which could not be truly affirmed were the things revealed still inconceivable. (Cf. Rom. 16:25f.).

These passages alone sufficiently prove the assertions, first, that the mysteries of the Gospel were certain things in their own nature intelligible enough, but called mysteries by reason of the veil under which they were formerly hid; secondly, that under the Gospel this veil is wholly removed; from which, thirdly, follows the promised conclusion, that such doctrines cannot now properly deserve the name of mystery.

The most material difficulty (made to me by a friend) is that my opinion destroys the nature of faith. Thus I shall with all the brevity I can deliver my sentiments concerning this subject. The word imports "belief" or "persuasion," as when we give credit to anything which is told us by God or man.

Now since by revelation men are not endued with any new faculties, it follows that God should lose his end in speaking to them if what he said did not agree with their common notions. Could that person justly value himself upon being wiser than his neighbors who, having infallible assurance that something called *Blictri* had a being in nature, in the meantime knew not what this *Blictri* was? Seeing the case stands really thus, all faith or persuasion must necessarily consist of two parts, knowledge and assent. 'Tis the last indeed that constitutes the formal act of faith, but not without the evidence of the first. And this is the true account we have of it all over the New Testament. The firm persuasion of a pious man that his requests will be granted is grounded upon his knowledge of the being, goodness and power of God. (Heb. 11:6) The author of the Epistle to the Hebrews does not define faith a prejudice, opinion or conjecture, but conviction of demonstration. (Heb. 11:1) Nor can any man show me in all the New Testament another signification of faith but a most firm persuasion built upon substantial reasons.

Faith is so far from being an implicit assent to anything above reason that this notion directly contradicts the ends of religion, the nature of man, and the goodness and wisdom of God. But at this rate, some will be apt to say, faith is no longer faith but knowledge. I answer that if knowledge be taken for a present and immediate view of things, I have nowhere affirmed anything like it, but the contrary in many places. But if by knowledge be meant understanding what is believed, then I stand by it that faith is knowledge; I have all along maintained it, and the very words are promiscuously used for one another in the Gospel. (John 4:42; Rom. 14:14; I Cor. 15:58)

Others will say that this notion of faith makes revelation useless. But, pray, how so? For the question is not whether we could discover all the objects of our faith by ratiocination; I have proved on the contrary that no matter of fact can be known without revelation. But I assert that what is once revealed we must as well understand as any other matter in the world, revelation being only of use to inform us, whilst the evidence of its subject persuades us. Then, reply they, reason is of more dignity than revelation. I answer, just as much as a Greek grammar is superior to the New Testament; for we make use of grammar to understand the language, and of reason to comprehend the sense of that book. But, in a word, I see no need of comparisons in this case, for reason is not less from God than revelation; 'tis the candle, the guide, the judge he has lodged within every man that cometh into this world.

Lastly, it may be objected that the poor and illiterate cannot have such a faith as I maintain. But the vulgar are more obliged to Christ, who had a better opinion of them than these men; for he preached his Gospel to them in a special manner, and they, on the other hand, "heard him gladly" (Mark 12:37); because, no doubt, they understood his instructions better than the mysterious lectures of their priests and scribes. The uncorrupted doctrines of Christianity are not above their reach or comprehension, but the gibberish of your divinity schools they understand not.

CONCLUSION

Thus I have endeavored to show others what I'm fully convinced of myself, that there is no mystery in Christianity, or the most perfect religion, and that by consequence nothing contradictory or inconceivable, however made an article of faith, can be contained in the Gospel, if it be really the Word of God. I acknowledge no orthodoxy but the truth; and I'm sure wherever the truth is there must be also the Church, of God I mean, and not any human faction or polity.

PETER BROWNE

Browne (c. 1661–1735) was an Irish academic and cleric. His letter attacking Toland was so widely read that Toland later boasted that he had been responsible for Browne's becoming a bishop (of Cork and Ross, 1710). Later works elaborated Browne's theory of man's knowledge of God as solely analogical; his view was attacked by Bishop Berkeley (in *Alciphron*) as one which really led to atheism.

A Letter

To any reasonable considering person it were a sufficient answer to this whole book to show in short how he mistakes the question, and proceeds in it all upon two false suppositions: one in logic, in the former part of his book, viz.,

that evidence is the only ground of persuasion;

the other in divinity, in the latter part of it,

that now under the Gospel the veil is perfectly removed.

What will this man deserve for that arrogant expression of his, "that the divine being himself cannot with more reason be accounted mysterious than the most contemptible of his creatures." His business was to let us have known what was the true notion of a mystery in Scripture. Now the clearest way I can think of for doing of this is to instance in some particular mystery of the Gospel. I shall take that of the resurrection of our bodies.

St. Paul says, "Behold, I show you a mystery. We shall all be changed in the twinkling of an eye." (I Cor. 15:51f.) Again St. John, speaking of the same matter, says, "It doth not yet appear what we shall be, but we know that when he shall appear, we shall be like him." (I John 3:2) From whence we see a Christian mystery is something which relates to another life, which it was impossible for us to know without divine revelation, and now that it is revealed we know it but in part, and cannot fully comprehend it. So that in a Christian mystery there is something we do understand, and something that we are wholly ignorant of.

Therefore now we see the question is not, "whether a man can believe what he knows nothing of," which no man in his wits ever yet affirmed, for there is a flat contradiction in the terms. But the question is, whether there be not some things in the Gospel concerning which we are bound to believe that there is much more in them than we are now able to comprehend.

I come now to consider his "clear and distinct ideas," which he lays down as the ground of evidence. He never considers the difference between these two propositions: "Clear and distinct ideas are the foundation of all our knowledge and assent" (which considered in a right sense is undoubtedly true; but for that other, which they make a consequence of it, it is absolutely false); "that we can believe nothing but what we have a clear and distinct idea of." It is upon the account of those things whereof we have clear and distinct ideas that we give a firm assent to the existence of things whereof we have no idea at all.

Because this is the fundamental error of all our quaint reasoners against revelation, and the fallacy whereby they impose upon others, I shall express myself as distinctly and plainly in this matter as I can.

What is meant by an "adequate idea" is a full and comprehensive knowledge of any thing, so as to know all that is knowable in it. But how far short what men call a clear and distinct idea comes of that adequate conception of a thing is impossible to determine, because our knowledge of things is varied almost in infinite degrees. He contends in his book "that we have as clear and distinct ideas of all things revealed to us in the Gospel as we have of the ordinary phenomena of nature; and that we are obliged to give our assent to them no further than we have clear and distinct ideas of them." In direct opposition to which, I shall lay down these two propositions: That we are so far from having clear and distinct ideas of those things of another world which are revealed to us, that we have no proper and immediate idea at all of them. And, that though we have no proper or immediate idea of those things, yet we are bound to believe them; and that our assent to them, according to his own principle, is founded upon clear and distinct ideas.

By a "proper and immediate idea," I mean a conception or notion of the thing as it is in itself. Now what I say is this: that we have no proper ideas of the things of another world, but frame to ourselves conceptions of them from those things in this world whereof we have clear and distinct ideas. There are but two ways of God's revealing anything to us: either by giving us new faculties, or by adapting his revelations to those we have, which are our senses and our reason. Now we can have no proper or im-

mediate idea from sense or reason of the real nature
of any thing relating to another life as it is in itself,
or indeed any other notion of them than that of being
in general. This will best appear by instancing in the
particulars. I shall begin with God himself and his
attributes.

Our imagination can frame no likeness or re-
semblance of God, as it can do of material and sensible objects. As we can form no similitude from the
senses, so neither hath the reason any the least
glimpse of his real nature as he is in himself, for the
only way we have of forming an idea of him is either
negatively (by removing from him all the imperfections of the creatures), or by enlarging those excel-
lencies we find in these and attributing them to God.
So that he is now incomprehensible to us. Therefore
when he made a particular revelation of himself, it
was only by the name "I am," (Ex. 3:14) which denoted nothing more of him than barely his existence,
and plainly intimated that it was impossible for them
to conceive any thing further of him. For this reason
'tis said that hereafter "we shall see him as he is,"
(I John 3:2) because we have no knowledge of him
now but by mediation of those ideas we have of the
things of this world.

To make this further appear, let us consider him
in those attributes of his whereof we are thought to
have the most clear and distinct ideas. 'Tis revealed
that "God is a spirit," (John 4:24) by which we
really understand nothing more than that he is a
being that is not matter. As for infinity, another attribute of God, the only way we are said to form a
notion of this is by continued accumulation, and
then a confused idea of what remains when we are
weary of this. How little this will help us to any

immediate positive idea of it is plain, because when we have imagined all the atoms that go to the composition of the universe, told as many times over as we can heap up numbers for it, we are as far from any true idea of infinity as when we began to reckon two. It is more conducive to true knowledge to own our ignorance, and say it is a perfection which we know nothing of. As to his omnipresence, we have no idea at all of it, for it is utterly impossible for us to conceive how the same thing should be here and there, and everywhere in the same instant; therefore we frame to ourselves a gross notion of it by that of continued extension, though at the same time we are sure this must be utterly inconsistent with the real nature of God. I might thus run through all the attributes of God, and show in every one of them how we make to ourselves some representations of them by compounding and enlarging those ideas we have either of sensible objects or of the operations of our minds. But as we can have no such proper and immediate idea of God himself, so neither have we such ideas of anything relating to another world.

Therefore it is that the Spirit of God in all his revelations hath made use, not only of the words and phrases commonly received and understood, but likewise of those common notions in the minds of men of things in this world, to represent truths which are in respect of us now unconceivable, and for which there are as yet no capacities in our nature. So that in truth all the ideas we at present have of the things of another world are no other than a sort of types and figures of things, the real nature of which is totally obscured from us. This is the literal meaning of those words of St. Paul, that "now we see through a glass darkly," (I Cor. 13:12), i.e., by analogy with the things of this world. But "then face to face," i.e., we shall have as immediate a view of those heavenly objects as we have now of these things which only represent them to us.

If I were to give an account of my belief of the divinity of the Son, it should be thus: I am convinced by the completion of prophecies, the miracles he wrought, and the agreeableness of his doctrine to the natural sentiments of our minds, that whatever Jesus Christ was, he came from God. I find him in many places assuming to himself the name, and titles, and worship of God. Therefore, if I act like a reasonable man, I am under a necessity either of giving my assent to this, or of utterly rejecting him as an impostor. Had he been an impostor, God, who showed himself always very jealous of his honor, would never have confirmed this doctrine of his with such repeated testimonies. Because I can't reject him as an impostor, therefore I believe this proposition, and confess the blessed Jesus the Son of God to be eternal God equal with the Father.

Now thus far I proceed in this mystery upon the strictest rules of reason and evidence, and my faith of this proposition is founded upon clear and distinct ideas. For I know clearly who I mean by Jesus Christ, that person who was born of the Virgin Mary and crucified under Pontius Pilate. I have a clear and distinct idea of what it is for one thing to be equal to another, and I apprehend very well what is signified by the name of "God" here. And I have a clear and distinct idea of what it is for one person to be the son of another. Thus I understand the meaning of the words; nor is there any thing in them contradictory to my reason. And lastly, I have clear and distinct ideas of those miraculous proofs to the senses of men. All which raise such an evidence or knowledge in my mind of the divinity of his mission that I must do violence to my reason if I do not give my assent to it. And thus far it is not so properly and strictly a mystery.

But when I think of this proposition again, "Jesus the Son of God is God equal with the Father," I must own at the same time I have no knowledge at all of that eternal generation which I form an improper idea of from the procreation of one man from another. Nor have I any notion of this wonderful union of the human nature with divinity. Nor can I in the least imagine wherein this equality consists. These and all other things relating to the manner of it are wholly out of reach of all my capacities, and totally obscured from me. These are the things which make it a mystery, and in respect of this part of it, the authority or veracity of God is the only ground of my persuasion.

Now by this time who so blind as not to see that the design of this book is to strike at the root and foundation of all revealed religion. And if we must give our assent to nothing but what we have clear and distinct ideas of, then farewell all religion both natural and revealed. For we know all religion, natural and revealed, is founded upon the belief of a deity, of the immortality of the soul, and of rewards and punishments in another world; but it is impossible for us now to have clear and distinct ideas of these, and therefore upon his principles we must utterly reject them all.

Even the most glorious of his creatures are finite and limited, whereas the nature of God is infinite; and therefore even when we come to heaven, he will be mysterious to us in a more proper sense than anything else, because we shall not even then have as full and comprehensive a knowledge of him as we shall have of the greatest of his creatures. But there is yet greater difference than this; for the things revealed in the Gospel are such as exceed our present capacities of knowledge, whereas all the things of nature fall within their sphere and are in themselves immediate and proper objects of our sense and reason. Though many of them are such that we neither do, nor ever can, actually know any thing of them. To lay this difference open to all, we must consider that this being "above reason" is an equivocal expression, and signifies two very different things.

1. It signifies a thing which does not exceed our powers of understanding, but is concealed from us and lies out of our reach by some accidental impediment or obstruction which it is impossible for us to remove. In this sense it is above our reason to know certainly whether there be any inhabitants in Saturn.

2. To be above our reason signifies a thing which in its own nature exceeds our present capacities, and is no proper object of those faculties of knowledge which we are now endued withal.

Let us suppose an illiterate person, who never heard of Christianity or the mathematics, is equally ignorant of these two propositions: the three angles of a triangle are equal to two right ones; and, "we shall be raised in the likeness of Christ." (Rom. 6:5) These two propositions this derider of all revealed truths will say are alike mysterious to this man. Whereas the contrary will evidently appear if we but take this man and teach him mathematics. Then he shall perfectly apprehend all that is to be known of that demonstration, and how it is impossible it should be otherwise. But teach him the Gospel, and make him as learned as he is capable in the Christian religion, he shall know nothing more of that proposition (though he shall be better convinced of the truth of it) than he did at the first hearing. And why? Because the one was a truth in nature within the sphere of his intellectual powers; the other is supernatural and he can never have any notion of the manner of it till he has new faculties or those he already hath are greatly enlarged.

If God had required us to give our assent to what we knew nothing at all of, he would have required impossibilities; if he had required us to give our assent to what we had no proof or evidence for, he would have required what was unreasonable; but when he adapts the revelation of things which we cannot apprehend to our capacities, under the notions of things which we do apprehend clearly and fully, it is the greatest argument of his wisdom. And when he requires no assent from us without sufficient arguments of conviction to any considering unprejudiced person, it is a great instance of his goodness. And these revelations of things above our reason to comprehend, as they are most powerful incitements to gratitude here, so they will be the subject of our praise and thanksgiving hereafter, when the veil is perfectly removed, and that we are enabled to apprehend them clearly.

The world is at this time so disposed for the reception of all discourses that seem to set up reason and evidence in opposition to the revealed and mysterious doctrines of Christianity that nothing less than the interpositions of authority can stop this current of infidelity and profaneness which threatens to overwhelm these nations.

How far men in power, according to their several stations, are obliged to intermeddle in point of conscience, I shall not inquire. But sure I am, in point of policy, it is become no less than necessary. For the writers of this strain have given broad hints that they are as little friends to our government as our religion. This man can say "that magistrates are made for the people," and every one knows what doctrine of rebellion men are wont to insinuate by this saying.[1] Now what would this man have said if he durst have spoke as plainly of government as he hath of religion?

Whoever observes these men's way of writing as to this one point will be convinced they deserve to be looked to. Their numbers grow formidable, they begin to speak out their infidelity and profaneness as plain as some of them do treason. They are secretly forming themselves in clubs and cabals, and have their emissaries into all parts, which are supported by contributions. And I make little doubt but that their design is at length to show us that all dominion, as well as religion, is founded in reason.

---

[1] The second edition of *Christianity Not Mysterious* is prefaced by Toland's narrative of the events which led the Irish House of Commons to condemn the book. He specifically answers Browne's charge above. Toland replies that his view of the magistrate no longer needs proof. "What dominion is not founded in reason must be doubtless unreasonable, and consequently tyrannical." The social contract was reasonable; the contract made, to agree on constitutions is reasonable; constitutions made, to honor and respect the magistrates appointed to enforce them is reasonable. "So that I fancy we must necessarily conclude that all just dominion is to be founded in reason."

CHARLES LESLIE

Leslie (1650–1722) was a widely known controversialist in matters political and ecclesiastical. He attacked not only the deists, but the Jews, Quakers (he was an acquaintance of William Penn), Whig divines (Burnet, Tillotson, etc.) and others. He was a celebrated non-Juror (i.e., one of those who, on the deposition of James II, refused to vow allegiance to William of Orange, regarding him as not divinely anointed); his "high" view of the sacraments and ministry underlie part of the method implicit in his attack on deism.

A Short and Easy Method with the Deists

You are desirous to find some one topic of reason which should demonstrate the truth of the Christian religion, and at the same time distinguish it from the impostures of Mahomet and the old pagan world, that our deists may be brought to this test, and be either obliged to renounce their reason and the common reason of mankind, or to submit to the clear proof, from reason, of the Christian religion; which must be such a proof as no imposture can pretend to, otherwise it cannot prove the Christian religion not to be an imposture.

First, then, I suppose that the truth of the doctrine of Christ will be sufficiently evinced if the matters of fact which are recorded of him in the Gospels be true; for his miracles, if true, do vouch the truth of what he delivered. The same is to be said as to Moses. If he brought the children of Israel through the Red Sea in that miraculous manner which is related in Exodus, and did such other wonderful things as are there told of him, it must necessarily follow that he was sent from God.

The method I will take is, first, to lay down such rules as to the truth of matters of fact in general that where they all meet such matters of fact cannot be false; and then, secondly, to show that all these rules do meet in the matters of fact of Moses and of Christ, and that they do not meet in the matters of fact of Mahomet, of the heathen deities, or can possibly meet in any imposture whatsoever.

The rules are these:

1. That the matters of fact be such as that men's outward senses, their eyes and ears, may be judges of it.

2. That it be done publicly, in the face of the world.

3. That not only public monuments be kept up in memory of it, but some outward actions to be performed.

4. That such monuments and such actions or observances be instituted, and do commence from the time that the matter of fact was done.

The two first rules make it impossible for any such matter of fact to be imposed upon men at the time when such matter of fact was said to be done, because every man's eyes and senses would contradict it. Therefore it only remains that such matter of fact might be invented sometime after, when the men of

that generation are all past and gone, and the credulity of after ages might be imposed on. For this, the
two last rules secure us; for whenever such a matter
of fact came to be invented, if not only monuments
were said to remain of it, but likewise that public actions and observances were constantly used ever
since the matter of fact was said to be done, the
deceit must be detected by no such monuments ap-
pearing, and by the experience of every man, woman,
and child, who must know that no such actions or
observances were ever used by them.

Let us now come to the second point, to show
that the matters of fact of Moses and of Christ have
all these rules or marks before mentioned, and that
no imposture can have them all.

As to Moses, I suppose it will be allowed me that
he could not have persuaded 600,000 men that he
had brought them out of Egypt, through the Red
Sea, fed them 4 years, without bread by miraculous
manna, and the other matters of fact recorded in his
books, if they had not been true. For the same reason, it was equally impossible for him to have made
them receive his five books as truth, and not to
have rejected them as a manifest imposture, which
told of all these things as done before their eyes, if
they had not been so done.

The utmost that even a "suppose" can stretch to
is that these books were written in some age after
Moses, and put out in his name. If this was so, it was
impossible that those books should have been received as the books of Moses, in that age wherein
they may have been supposed to have been first invented. Why? Because they speak of themselves as
delivered by Moses and kept in the ark from his
time. And there was a copy of this book to be left

likewise with the king. This book of the law speaks
of itself, not only as a history of what things were
then done, but as the standing and municipal law
and statutes of the nation of the Jews, binding the
king as well as the people. Now in whatever age
after Moses you will suppose this book to have been
forged, it was impossible it could be received as
truth because it was not then to be found, either in
the ark or with the king or anywhere else. When first
invented, everybody must know that they had never
heard of it before. And therefore they could less believe it to be the book of their statutes, and the
standing law of the land, which they had all along
received and by which they had been governed.

Could any man now at this day invent a book of
statutes, or Acts of Parliament, for England, and
make it pass upon the nation as the only book of
statutes that ever they had known?

The books of Moses have a further demonstration of their truth. They not only contain the laws,
but give an historical account of their institution, and
the practice of them from that time: as of the Pass-
over in memory of the death of the first-born in
Egypt, and the confirmation of the priesthood to the
tribe of Levi, and the sabbath, circumcision, etc.
Here are the third and fourth of the marks above-
mentioned.

Let us now descend to the utmost degree of supposition, viz., that these things were practiced before
these books of Moses were forged, and that these
books did only impose upon the nation in making them believe that they had kept these observances
in memory of such and such things as were inserted
in those books. This must suppose that the Jews kept
all these observances in memory of nothing, or with-

out knowing anything of their original or the reason why they kept them.

Let us suppose, contrary both to reason and matter of fact, that the Jews did not know any reason at all why they kept these observances; yet was it possible to put it upon them that they had kept these observances in memory of what they had never heard of before?

I come now to show that, as in the matters of fact of Moses, so likewise all these four marks do meet in the matters of fact which are recorded in the Gospel of our blessed savior. All that is said before of Moses and his books is every way applicable to Christ and his Gospel. His works and miracles are there said to be done publicly, in the face of the world, as he argued to his accusers: "I spake openly to the world, and in secret have I said nothing." (John 18:20) It is told (Acts 2:41) that three thousand at one time, and (Acts 4:4) that above five thousand at another time were converted, upon conviction of what themselves had seen, what had been done publicly before their eyes, wherein it was impossible to have imposed upon them. Therefore here were the two first of the rules before-mentioned.

Then for the two second: baptism and the Lord's Supper were instituted as perpetual memorials of these things, and they were not instituted in afterages, but at the very time when these things were said to be done, and have been observed without interruption in all ages through the whole Christian world, down all the way from that time to this. And Christ himself did ordain apostles and other ministers of his Gospel to preach and administer these sacraments and to govern his church. Accordingly they have continued by regular succession to this day. So that the Christian clergy are as notorious a matter of fact as the tribe of Levi among the Jews. And the Gospel is as much a law to the Christians as the books of Moses to the Jews.

The matters of fact of Mahomet, or what is fabled of the deities, do all want some of the aforesaid four rules whereby the certainty of matters of fact is demonstrated. Mahomet pretended to no miracles, and those which are commonly told of him pass among the Mahometans themselves but as legendary fables and as such are rejected by the wise and learned among them. Those which are told of him do all want the two first rules. His pretended converse with the moon, his night-journey from Mecca to Jerusalem and thence to heaven, etc., were not performed before anybody. We have only his own word for them. And they are as groundless as the delusions of Fox or Muggleton among ourselves. The same is to be said of the fables of the heathen gods.

It is true the heathen deities had their priests; they had likewise feasts, games, and other public institutions, in memory of them. But all these want the fourth mark, viz., that such priesthood and institutions should commence from the time that such things as they commemorate were said to be done. The Bacchanalia and other heathen feasts were instituted many ages after what was reported of these gods was said to be done, and therefore can be no proof of them. And the priests of Bacchus, Apollo, etc., were not ordained by these supposed gods, but were appointed by others, in after-ages, only in honor of them. And therefore these orders of priests are no evidence to the truth of the matters of fact which are reported of their gods.

To apply what has been said, you may challenge

all the deists in the world to show any action that is fabulous which has all the four rules or marks beforementioned. No, it is impossible. I do not say that everything which wants these four marks is false, but that nothing can be false which has them all. No manner of doubt that there was such a man as Julius Caesar, that he fought at Pharsalia, was killed in the Senate-House, and many other matters of fact of ancient times, though we keep no public observances in memory of them. But this shows that the matters of fact of Moses and of Christ have come down to us better guarded than any other matters of fact, how true soever.

SAMUEL CLARKE

Clarke (1675–1729) was regarded in his own time as a philosopher of major rank. A disciple and intimate of Sir Isaac Newton, his *a priori* method (or the "high priori road," as Pope termed it) formed a principal alternative to the views of Locke. In religion, his attempt to formulate a middle way between orthodoxy and deism caused him to be quoted by both sides, and attacked by both as well. Of his Boyle Lectures, Anthony Collins is said to have remarked that "nobody doubted the existence of God until Dr. Clarke strove to prove it." And Voltaire (who met Clarke in England in 1726) is the authority for the statement that Bishop Gibson blocked Clarke's elevation to the see of Canterbury by telling the queen that though Clarke was the most learned and honest man in her domains, he had one defect—he was not a Christian!

The Boyle Lectures, First Series

PREFACE

There being already published many and good books to prove the being and attributes of God, I have chosen to contract what was requisite for me to say upon this subject into as narrow a compass, and to express what I had to offer in as few words, as I could with perspicuity. For which reason I have also confined myself to one only method or continued thread of arguing, which I have endeavored should be as near to mathematical as the nature of such a discourse would allow.

PROPOSITIONS

I. It is absolutely and undeniably certain that something has existed from all eternity.

II. There has existed from eternity some one unchangeable and independent being.

III. That unchangeable and independent being which has existed from eternity without any external cause of its existence must be self-existent, that is, necessarily-existing.

IV. What the substance or essence of that being which is self-existent, or necessarily-existing, is, we have no idea, neither is it at all possible for us to comprehend it.

V. Though the substance or essence of the self-existent being is in itself absolutely incomprehensible to us, yet many of the essential attributes of his nature are strictly demonstrable, as well as his existence.

VI. The self-existent being must of necessity be infinite and omnipresent.

VII. The self-existent being must of necessity be but one.

VIII. The self-existent and original cause of all things must be an intelligent being.

IX. The self-existent and original cause of all things is not a necessary agent, but a being endued with liberty and choice.

X. The self-existent being, the supreme cause of all things, must of necessity have infinite power.

XI. The supreme cause and author of all things must of necessity be infinitely wise.

XII. The supreme cause and author of all things must of necessity be a being of infinite goodness, justice, and truth, and all other moral perfections such as become the supreme governor and judge of the world.

The Boyle Lectures, Second Series

I. From the eternal and necessary differences of things, there naturally and necessarily arise certain moral obligations, which are of themselves incumbent on all rational creatures, antecedent to all positive institution, and to all expectation of reward or punishment.

'Tis as absurd and blameworthy to mistake negligently plain right and wrong, that is, to understand the proportions of things in morality to be what they are not, or wilfully to act contrary to known justice and equity, as it would be absurd and ridiculous for a man in arithmetical matters ignorantly to believe that twice two is not equal to four, or that the whole is not equal in all its parts. He that wilfully refuses to honor and obey God, from whom he received his being and to whom he continually owes his preservation, is really guilty of an equal absurdity and inconsistency in practice as he that in speculation denies the effect to owe anything to its cause, or the whole to be bigger than its part. He that refuses to deal with all men equitably, and with every man as he desires they should deal with him, is guilty of the very same unreasonableness and contradiction in one case as he that in another case should affirm one number or quantity to be equal to another, and yet that other at the same time not to be equal to the first. Iniquity is the very same in action as falsity or contradiction in theory, and the same cause that makes the one absurd makes the other unreasonable.

II. The same eternal moral obligations which arise necessarily from the natural differences of things are moreover the express will, command, and law of God to all rational creatures.

III. The same eternal moral obligations which are of themselves incumbent indeed on all rational creatures, antecedent to any respect of particular reward or punishment, must yet certainly and necessarily be attended with rewards and punishments.

IV. Because these rewards and punishments are not distributed in the present state, therefore there must of necessity be a future state.

Though originally the constitution and order of God's creation was indeed such that virtue and vice are by the regular tendency of things followed with natural rewards and punishments, yet in event, through some great and general corruption and depravation, the condition of men in the present state is plainly such that this natural order of things in the world is manifestly perverted. Good men are very often afflicted and impoverished, and sometimes most cruelly and maliciously persecuted, even upon account of their goodness itself. In all which affairs, the providence of God seems not very evidently to interpose for the protection of the righteous.

But 'tis exceedingly reasonable to believe, that as the great discoveries which by the diligence and sagacity of later ages have been made in astronomy and natural philosophy have opened surprising scenes of the power and wisdom of the Creator, beyond what men could possibly have conceived or imagined in former times, so at the unfolding of the whole scheme of providence in the conclusion of this present state men will be surprised with the amazing manifestations of justice and goodness which will then appear to have run through the whole series of God's government of the moral world.

V. Though the necessity and indispensableness of all the great and moral obligations of natural religion, and also the certainty of a future state of rewards and punishments, be in general deducible from right reason, yet such is the present corrupt estate and condition of mankind in the world that very few are able, in reality and effect, to discover these things clearly and plainly for themselves, but men have great need of particular teaching and much instruction.

VI. All the teaching and instruction of the best heathen philosophers was for many reasons utterly insufficient to reform mankind.

There have indeed in almost every age been in the heathen world some wise and brave and good men, who have made it their business to study and practice the duties of natural religion themselves, and to teach and exhort others to do the like. I think it may very justly be supposed that these men were raised up and designed by providence, (the abundant goodness of God having never left itself wholly without witness—Acts 14:17) as instruments. Some of the ancient writers of the church have not scrupled to call Socrates and some others of the best of the heathen moralists by the name of Christians, and to affirm, as the law was as it were a schoolmaster to bring the Jews unto Christ, so true moral philosophy was to the

Gentiles a preparative to receive the Gospel.[1] But then, notwithstanding the most that can be made of this supposition, 'tis certain the effect of all the teaching and instruction even of the best of the philosophers in the heathen world was in comparison very small and inconsiderable.

In speculation it may perhaps seem possible that, notwithstanding it must be confessed philosophy cannot discover any complete and satisfactory remedy for past miscarriages, yet the precepts and motives offered by the best philosophers might at least be sufficient to amend and reform men's manners for the future. But in experience and practice it hath on the contrary appeared to be altogether impossible for philosophy and bare reason to reform mankind effectually, without the assistance of some higher principle.

VII. There was plainly wanting a divine revelation, to recover mankind out of their universal degenerate estate; and both the necessities of men and their natural notions of God gave them reasonable ground to hope for such a revelation.

VIII. There is no other religion now in the world but the Christian that has any just pretense or tolerable appearance of reason to be esteemed such a divine revelation.

It may perhaps be pretended by modern deists that the great ignorance and undeniable corruptness of the whole heathen world has always been owing, not to any absolute insufficiency of the light of nature itself, but merely to the fault of several particular persons in not sufficiently improving that light,

---

[1] Clarke cites Justin Martyr, and in part quotes Clement of Alexandria; the Biblical allusion is to Gal. 3:24.

and that deists now, in places where learning and right reason are cultivated, are well able to discover and explain all the obligations and motives of morality without believing anything of revelation. As to the great pretenses of modern deists, 'tis to be observed that the clearness of moral reasonings was much improved even in heathen writers after the coming of Christ. And almost all the things that are said wisely and truly by modern deists are plainly borrowed from that revelation which they refuse to embrace, and without which they could never have been able to have said the same things. Now, indeed, when our whole duty, with its true motives, is clearly revealed to us, its precepts appear plainly agreeable to reason, and conscience readily approves what is good, as it condemns what is evil. Nay, after our duty is thus made known to us, 'tis easy not only to see its agreement with reason, but also to begin and deduce its obligation from reason. But had we been utterly destitute of all revealed light, then to have discovered our duty in all points, with the true motives of it, merely by the help of natural reason, would have been a work of nicety, pains and labor, like groping for an unknown way in the obscure twilight. What ground have any modern deists to imagine that if they themselves had lived without the light of the gospel they should have been wiser than Socrates and Plato and Cicero?

IX. The Christian religion, considered in its primitive simplicity, and as taught in the Holy Scriptures, has all the marks and proofs of its being actually and truly a divine revelation that any divine revelation, supposing it was true, could reasonably be imagined or desired to have.

The necessary marks and proofs of a religion coming from God are these. First, that the duties it enjoins be all such as are agreeable to our natural notions of God, and perfective of the nature and conducive to the happiness and well-being of men. And that the doctrines it teaches be all such as may be consistent with, and agreeable to, sound and unprejudiced reason. Secondly, the motives by which it is recommended to men's belief and practice must be such as are suitable to the excellent wisdom of God, and fitted to amend the manners and perfect the minds of men. Lastly, it must moreover be positively and directly proved to come from God, by such certain signs and matters of fact as may be undeniable evidences of its author's having actually a divine commission.

X. The practical duties which the Christian religion enjoins are all such as are most agreeable to our natural notions of God, and most perfective of the nature and conductive to the happiness and well-being of men.

XI. The motives by which the Christian religion enforces the practice of the duties it enjoins are such as are most suitable to the excellent wisdom of God and most answerable to the natural expectations of men.

XII. The peculiar manner and circumstances with which the Christian religion enjoins the duties and urges the motives beforementioned are exactly consonant to the dictates of sound reason, or the unprejudiced light of nature, and most wisely perfective of it.

XIII. All the doctrines which the true, simple, and uncorrupted Christian religion requires our particular assent to are agreeable to unprejudiced reason, have every one of them a natural tendency and direct influence to reform men's manners, and do together make up the most consistent and rational scheme of belief in the world.

1. That there is only one living and true God.

2. That this supreme self-existent cause and father of all things did before all ages, in an incomprehensible manner, by his almighty power and will beget or produce a divine person, styled the Logos, the Word or Son of God. The same that is said of the Son may in like manner with little variation be, very agreeably to right reason, understood concerning the original procession or manner of derivation of the Holy Spirit likewise from the Father.

3. That the universe, the heavens and the earth, were created and made by God.

4. That, about the space of 6000 years since, the earth was without form and void, that is, a confused chaos, out of which God framed this beautiful and useful fabric we now inhabit.

5. That the same God who created all things by the Word of his power, and upholds and preserves them by his continual concourse, does also by his all-wise providence perpetually govern and direct the issues and events of things.

6. That God created man at first upright and innocent, and placed him in a happy and paradisiacal state, and that sin was the original cause that now on the contrary the very ground is cursed and barren.

7. That in process of time after the first entrance of sin into the world, men by degrees corrupted

themselves more and more till at length God brought upon them a general flood.

8. That God after the flood made particular revelation of himself and of his will to the patriarchs; and that after this God should vouchsafe by express revelation to give a law to the whole nation of the Jews cannot with any just reason be rejected as an incredible fact.

9. That all the other particulars of Scripture-history contained in the Old Testament are true relations of matter of fact.

10. That God in the fullness of time should send his only-begotten Son to take upon him our human nature, and therein to make a full and particular revelation of the will of God to mankind (who by sin had corrupted themselves and forfeited the favor of God, so that by the bare light of nature they could not discover any certain means by which they could be satisfactorily and absolutely secure of regaining that favor); to preach unto men repentance and remission of sin, and, by giving himself a sacrifice and expiation for sin, to declare the acceptableness of repentance and the certainty of pardon thereupon; to be a mediator and intercessor between God and man; to procure the particular assistance of God's Holy Spirit, which might be in men a new and effectual principle of a heavenly and divine life; in a word, to be the savior and judge of mankind, and finally to bring them to eternal life: all this, when clearly and expressly revealed, and by good testimony proved to be so revealed, is apparently agreeable and very

credible to right reason. As to the possibility of
the incarnation of the Son of God, whatever
mysteriousness there confessedly was in the
manner of it, yet as to the thing itself, there is
evidently no more unreasonableness in believing
the possibility of it than in believing the union
of our soul and body, or any other certain truth
which we plainly see implies no contradiction
in the thing itself, at the same time that we are
sensible we cannot discover the manner how it
is effected. As to the difficulty, viz., how it can
be consistent with reason to suppose God con-
descending to do so very great things for such
mean and weak creatures as men are, who in all
appearance seem to be but a very small, low
and inconsiderable part of the creation, foras-
much as the whole earth itself is but a little
spot that bears no proportion at all to the universe, the answer is very easy: that the mercy
and love of the infinitely good God is extended
equally over all his works; that, let the universe
be supposed as large, and the rational creatures
with which it is furnished as many and excellent, as anyone can imagine, yet mankind is
plainly the chief, indeed the only inhabitant, for
whose sake 'tis evident this our globe of earth
was formed into a habitable world; and this our
earth is, as far as we have any means of judging,
as considerable and worthy of the divine care
as most other parts of the system, and this our
system as considerable as any other single system in the universe; and finally that, in like
manner as the same divine providence which
presides over the whole creation does particularly govern and direct everything in this our

lower world, so there is no real difficulty to right reason in conceiving that the same divine Logos may also, for aught we know, have to other beings made different manifestations of God in ways of which we can know nothing, and in which we have no concern.

11. That the history of the life of Christ contained in the New Testament is a true relation of matters of fact.

12. That God has appointed a day wherein he will judge the world in righteousness.

13. That, in order to this final judgment not only the soul shall survive the dissolution of the body, but the body itself also shall be raised again.

14. Lastly, that after the resurrection and the general judgment, wherein every man shall be judged according to his works, they that have done well shall go into everlasting happiness, and they that have done evil into everlasting punishment.

XIV. The Christian revelation is positively and directly proved to be sent to us from God by the miracles which our savior worked, by the fulfilling of the prophecies, and by the testimony of the apostles.

XV. They who will not, by the arguments and proofs before-mentioned, be convinced of the truth and certainly of the Christian religion, would not be convinced by any other evidence whatsoever, no, not though one should rise on purpose from the dead to endeavor to convince them (Lk. 16:31).

ANTHONY COLLINS

Collins (1676–1729) was a confidant of John Locke in the philosopher's last years. A number of his skeptical works were centers of controversy in his time. Dean Swift's parody of the *Discourse of Free-Thinking* enables one to catch some of the flavor of the dispute.

A Discourse of Free-Thinking

I

By free-thinking I mean the use of the understanding in endeavoring to find out the meaning of any proposition whatsoever, in considering the nature of the evidence for or against it, and in judging of it according to the seeming force or weakness of the evidence.

If the knowledge of some truths be required of us by God; if the knowledge of others be useful to society; if the knowledge of no truth be forbidden us by God, or hurtful to us; then we have a right to know or may lawfully know any truth. And a right to know any truth whatsoever implies a right to think freely.

As in manual arts we do only by free trial, comparison, and experience of everything come to know what is best and perfect in each art, so in the sciences perfection is only to be attained by free-thinking. Let men be restrained from thinking on any science or any part of a science, they must be ignorant so

far as the restraint goes. And if a few men take now
and then a little liberty, and break through the established restraint, their thoughts will never be so
perfect as if all men were allowed and encouraged
to think of that matter, but their progress in thinking
will be only proportionate to that degree of free-
thinking which prevails. Thus before the restoration
of learning, when men were subject to the impositions of priests, a prodigious ignorance prevailed.
And when they began to think, their first notions
were rude and imperfect, and time and pains were
necessary to bring them to that degree of justness
they are at present. It was by gradual progress in
thinking that men got so much knowledge in astronomy as to know that the earth was of an orbicular
figure, and that it moves about the sun.

If men either neglect to think, or come once to be
persuaded they have no right to think freely, they
must run into the grossest absurdities imaginable
both in principle and practice. To give you the per-
fectest image I am able how unavoidable absurdities
are both in principle and practice, if thinking is
restrained, I will put the case of free-seeing and suppose the same methods made use of to prevent free-
seeing which are to prevent free-thinking.

Suppose, then, that certain men have a fancy in
their heads that it is absolutely necessary, either to
the peace of society or some other great purpose,
that all men should have the same belief with relation to certain objects of the eyes, and in order to
obtain that end will make all men under their power
subscribe the same confession of eye-sight faith. I
will suppose among the various and contradictory
forms of confession which men of different whims,
or of different interests and designs, will make at

different times, one to consist of these following articles:

That a ball can go through a table;
that two balls may be made out of one little one;
that a stone can be made to vanish out of sight;
that a knot can be undone with words;
that a thread may be burnt to pieces, and made whole with the ashes;
that one face may be a hundred or a thousand;
and, lastly, that a counter may be turned into a groat.

These propositions being drawn up in form as the standard of eye-sight faith, it will be absolutely necessary either that men should be obliged to subscribe to their truth, or that none be allowed publicly to contradict them, or at least that some encouragement be given to those who profess to believe and teach them; for otherwise no end would be served by drawing them up, and men would be as much at liberty to use their eyes as they were before.

Nor is it to be imagined that the zealous advocates for them will content themselves with the mere impositions of these absurdities. They will introduce several new absurdities by the various comments and turns which so many absurdities in eye-sight will oblige them to make. The several propositions will be said by them to be above, but not contrary to, eye-sight. Instances will be given of ten thousand mistakes in using our eyes. It will be esteemed dangerous trusting to carnal eye-sight, and be said that we ought to rely on the authority of those men who have pensions and salaries on purpose to study those things, and would not deserve what they receive should men use their own eye-sight. And as for those few men who should dare to use their own eyes, the least evil they could expect would be to be rendered odious to the multitude under the reproachful ideas of "skeptics," "Latitudinarians," "free-seers," men tied by no authority.

II

The subjects of which men are denied the right to think by the enemies of free-thinking are of all others those of which men have not only a right to think but of which they are obliged in duty to think, viz., of religious questions.

A right opinion in these matters is supposed by the enemies of free-thinking to be absolutely necessary to men's salvation, and some errors or mistakes about them are supposed to be damnable. Now where a right opinion is so necessary, there men have the greatest concern imaginable to think for themselves.

If the surest and best means of arriving at truth lies in free-thinking, then the whole duty of man with respect to opinions lies only in free-thinking. He who thinks freely does his best toward being in the right, and consequently does all that God, who can require nothing more of any man than that he should do his best, can require of him. And should he prove mistaken in many opinions, he must be as acceptable to God as if he received none but right opinions.

Superstition is an evil which, either by the means of education or the natural weakness of men, oppresses almost all mankind. Now there is no just remedy to this universal evil but free-thinking. By that alone can we understand the true causes of things, and by consequence the unreasonableness of all superstitious fears. By free-thinking alone men are

capable of knowing that a perfectly good, just, wise
and powerful being made and governs the world;
and from this principle they know that he can require nothing of men in any country or condition of
life but that whereof he has given them an opportunity of being convinced by evidence and reason
in the place where they are; and that an honest and
rational man can have no just reason to fear anything from him. Whereas superstitious men are incapable of believing in a perfectly just and good
God. Neglecting what God speaks plainly to the
whole world, they take up with what they suppose
he has communicated to a few. Wherefore I conclude
that everyone, out of regard to his own tranquillity
of mind, which must be disturbed as long as he has
any seeds of superstition, is obliged to think freely
on matters of religion.

The infinite number of pretenders in all ages to
revelations from heaven, supported by miracles, containing new notions of the deity, new doctrines, new
commands, new ceremonies, and new modes of worship, make thinking on the foregoing heads absolutely necessary. For how shall any man distinguish
between the true messenger from heaven and the
imposter but by considering the evidence produced
by the one, as freely as of the other?

As there can be no reasonable change of opinions
among men, no quitting of any old religion, no reception of any new religion, nor believing any religion
at all, but by means of free-thinking, so the Holy
Scriptures, agreeably to reason and to the design of
our blessed savior of establishing his religion throughout the whole universe, imply everywhere and press
in many places the duty of free-thinking.

The conduct of the priests, who are the chief pretenders to be guides to others in matters of religion, makes free-thinking unavoidable. Since the priests, not only of different religions and sects but of the same sect, are infinitely divided in opinion about the nature of God and the authority and meaning of Scriptures, etc., we have no way of setting ourselves in a right notion but by ceasing to rely on them, and thinking freely for ourselves.

III

I will now consider the principal objections I have met with, in the mouths of the sincere, to examination and free-thinking.

1. It is objected that to suppose men have a right to think on all subjects is to engage them in inquiries for which they are no ways qualified, the bulk of mankind really wanting a capacity to think justly about any speculations; and therefore 'tis absurd to assert that men have a right to think freely, much more that it is their duty to think freely.

To assert only a bare right in any man to do a thing implies a right in him to let it alone, if he thinks fit. To assert it is all men's duty to think freely on certain subjects engages them only in inquiries on those subjects which they who contend for the necessity of all men's assenting to certain propositions must allow all men are qualified to do. Supposing the bulk of mankind do want the capacity to think freely on matters of speculation, I do then allow that free-thinking can be no duty; and the priests must likewise allow that men can be no way concerned about truth or falsehood in speculative matters, and that the belief of no opinions can be justly required of them.

2. It is objected that to allow and encourage men to think freely will produce endless divisions in opinion, and by consequence disorder in society.

Let any man lay down a rule to prevent diversity of opinions which will not be as fertile of diversity of opinions as free-thinking, or if it prevents diversity of opinions will not be a remedy worse than the disease, and I will yield up the question.

Mere diversity of opinions has no tendency in nature to confusion in society. And it is evident matter of fact that a restraint upon thinking is the cause of all the confusion which is pretended to arise from diversity of opinions, and that liberty of thinking is the remedy for all the disorders which are pretended to arise from diversity of opinions.

3. It is objected that if free-thinking be allowed, it is possible some men may think themselves into atheism, which is esteemed the greatest of all evils in government.

Ignorance is the foundation of atheism, and free-thinking is the cure of it. And thus though it should be allowed that some men by free-thinking may become atheists, yet they will ever be fewer in number if free-thinking were permitted than if it were restrained.

4. It is objected that the priests are set apart to think freely for the laity, and are to be relied on, as lawyers, physicians, etc., are in their several faculties.

No man is excluded from studying law or physic because there are several of those professions, nor from following his own judgment when he is sick or in law; nor is there any reason why a man who is not a doctor in physic or a sergeant-at-law may not understand as much law and physic as either of them. In like manner, the setting men apart for the study of divinity does not exclude others from the study of divinity, nor from following their judgment about a point in divinity, nor from knowing as much divinity as any doctor in divinity. And by consequence there is no necessity to rely on any man's judgment, either in law, physic, or divinity.

5. It is objected that certain speculations (though false) are necessary to be imposed on men, in order to assist the magistrate in preserving the peace of society; and that it is therefore as reasonable to deceive men into opinions for their own good as it is in certain cases to deceive children; and consequently it must be absurd to engage men in thinking on subjects where error is useful and truth injurious to them.

This is an irreligious objection. I will grant the reasoning contained in the objection to be founded on a just principle, viz., that the good of society is the rule of whatever is to be allowed or restrained; and I will likewise grant that if errors are useful to human society they ought to be imposed; and consequently I must allow the inference, that thinking ought to be restrained. But then I affirm that the rule is as falsely as it is irreligiously applied, and that both experience and reason demonstrate the imposition of speculations, whether true or false, to be so far from being a benefit that it has been and must be the greatest mischief that has ever befallen or can befall mankind.

Lust, covetousness, revenge, and ambition have in all ages more or less plagued the world, and been the source of great disorders. But zeal to impose speculations has not only had the same effects in common

with those passions, but has carried men to a pitch
of wickedness which otherwise "eye had not seen, nor
ear heard, nor had entered into the heart of man to
conceive." (I Cor. 2:9) For what ancient or modern
history can parallel the brutality of religious zealots?
The most irregular of our other passions decay with
time, and their mischievous effects are restrained by
good sense and human policy; and we have some
passions in us, such as pity, good nature and humanity, which help to preserve a tolerable balance
in the human machine. But religious zeal gathers
strength with time, bears down common sense and
policy, leaps the bounds of natural humanity, and
vanquishes all the tender passions.

The peace and order of human society depending
upon, or rather consisting in, the practice of moral
duties, if you impose anything on mankind but what
is moral, the zeal to perform that must of course
abate men's zeal in the practice of moral duties, and
consequently prejudice the peace of society.

6. It is objected that free-thinkers themselves are
the most infamous, wicked, and senseless of all mankind.

I assert that free-thinkers must, as such, be the
most virtuous persons everywhere. They who have
been the most distinguished in all ages for their understanding have been free-thinkers.[1]

---

[1] Collins follows with a lengthy discussion of his list of the
saints of free-thinking, including Socrates, Plato, Aristotle,
Epicurus, Plutarch, Varro, Cato the Censor, Cicero, Cato
of Utica, Seneca, Solomon, the Jewish prophets, Josephus,
Origen, Minucius Felix, Synesius, Francis Bacon, Hobbes,
and Tillotson. He then adds: "I might in like manner have
instanced in Erasmus, Father Paul, Joseph Scaliger, Car-
tesius, Gassendus, Grotius, Hooker, Chillingworth, Lord

As I take it to be a difficult, if not impossible, task to name a man distinguished for his sense and virtue, and who has left anything behind him to enable us to judge of him, who has not given us some proofs of his free-thinking, by departing from the opinions commonly received, so I look upon it as impossible to name an enemy to free-thinking, however dignified or distinguished, who has not been either crack-brained and enthusiastical, or guilty of the most dia-bolical vices, malice, ambition, inhumanity, and stick-ing at no means (though ever so immoral) which he thought tended to God's glory and the good of the church; or has not left us some marks of his profound ignorance and brutality.

Falkland, Lord Herbert of Cherbury, Selden, Hales, Mil-ton, Wilkins, Marsham, Spencer, Whitchcot, Cudworth, More, Sir W. Temple, and Locke, but that I am afraid I have been already too tedious, and besides, they are all already known for their penetration, virtue, and free-think-ing, to those who apply themselves to the reading of the best modern authors."

THOMAS WOOLSTON

Woolston (1670–1733) gained an early reputation for scholarship. His defense of the allegorical method of Biblical interpretation developed very early in his career, but culminated in his treatment of the miracle stories. The government had begun to prosecute Woolston for blasphemy prior to these essays, and revived the suspended case after the fourth discourse was published. Found guilty, he was sentenced to a fine and prison term; a portion of his defense follows the excerpts from the *Discourses*.

Discourses on the Miracles

If ever there was a useful controversy started or revived in this age of the church, it is this about the Messiahship of the holy Jesus. I believe this controversy will end in the absolute demonstration of Jesus' Messiahship from prophecy. And though this way of proof from prophecy seems to labor under many difficulties at present, and though some writers are for seeking refuge in the miracles of our savior, yet we must persist in it till, what I have no doubt of, his Messiahship shall be clearly made out of it.

And the way in prophecy that I would take for the proof of Jesus' Messiahship should be by an allegorical interpretation and application of the law and the prophets to him, the very same way that all the fathers of the church have gone in. But this way does not please our ecclesiastical writers in this controversy. To show that there's no sanctuary for them

in the miracles of our savior, I write this *Discourse*.
And this I do, not for the service of infidelity, which
has no place in my heart, but for the honor of the
holy Jesus, and to reduce the clergy to the good old
way of interpreting prophecies, which the church
has unhappily apostatized from, and which, upon the
testimony of the fathers, will, one day, be the conversion of Jews and Gentiles. I take this method
following:

1. I will show that the miracles of healing all manner of bodily diseases, which Jesus was justly famed
for, are none of the proper miracles of the Messiah,
neither are they so much as a good proof of his
divine authority to found a religion.

2. That the liberal history of many of the miracles
of Jesus, as recorded by the evangelists, does imply
absurdities, improbabilities, and incredibilities; consequently they, either in whole or in part, were never
wrought, as they are commonly believed nowadays,
but are only related as prophetical and parabolical
narratives of what would be mysteriously and more
wonderfully done by him.

3. I shall consider what Jesus means when he appeals to his miracles as to a testimony and witness of
his divine authority, and show that he could not properly and ultimately refer to those he then wrought
in the flesh, but to those mystical ones, which he
would do in the Spirit, of which those wrought in the
flesh are but mere types and shadows.

In treating on these heads, I shall not confine myself only to reason, but also to the express authority
of the fathers, those holy, venerable and learned
preachers of the Gospel in the first ages of the
church; who took our religion from the hands of the
apostles, and of apostolical men, who died, some of

them, and suffered for the doctrine they taught, who professedly and confessedly were endued with divine and extraordinary gifts of the Spirit; who consequently can't be supposed to be corrupters of Christianity, or teachers of false notions about the miracles of our savior, or so much as mistaken about the apostolical and evangelical sense and nature of them.

Let us consider first, in general, what was the opinion of the fathers about the writings of the evangelists, in which the life of Christ is recorded. Eucherius says "that the scriptures of the New as well as Old Testament, are to be interpreted in an allegorical sense," and this his opinion is no other than the common one of the first ages of the church. Origen says that "whatsoever Jesus did in the flesh was but typical and symbolical of what he would do in the Spirit," and that "the several bodily diseases which he healed were no other than figures of the spiritual infirmities of the soul, that are to be cured by him." St. Irenaeus says that if "we consider only the then temporal use of Jesus' power of healing, he did nothing grand and powerful." Nay, the fathers say, what I believe, that anti-Christ will imitate and equal Jesus in all his miracles which he wrought of old.

The power of doing miracles is no certain nor rational seal of the commission and authority of a divine lawgiver. St. Paul says there is a "diversity of the gifts of the Spirit." (I Cor. 12:4) We may as well say that the strongest man is the wisest, or that a good physician must needs be a good casuist, as that Jesus, because he was a worker of miracles, ought to be received as the guide of our consciences, the director of our understandings, the ruler of our hearts, and the author of a religion.

Our divines may admire and adore Jesus as much as they please for his miracles of healing bodily distempers, but I am for the spiritual Messiah that cures those distempers of the soul that metaphorically pass under the names of blindness, lameness, deafness, etc. The cure of spiritual infirmities is a God-like work, above the imitation of man or of the anti-Christ, infinitely more miraculous than the healing any bodily distempers can be.

I come now to a particular consideration of that miracle of Jesus' driving the buyers and sellers out of the temple. (Matt. 21; Mk. 11; Lk. 19; Jn. 2) I have read in some modern author that this was the most stupendous miracle that Jesus wrought. It is hard to conceive how any one in the form of a man, and of a despised one too, with a whip in his hand, could execute such a work upon a great multitude of people who were none of his disciples nor had any regard for him. Supposing he could, by his divine power, infuse a panic fear into the people, yet what was the reason that he was so eaten up with zeal against the profanation of that house which he himself came to destroy? But let's hear what the fathers say to it.

Origen makes the whole but a parable. By the temple, he understands the church; by the sellers in the temple, he means such preachers who make merchandise of the Gospel, whom the Spirit of Christ, some time or other, would rid his church of. St. Hilary is of the same mind with Origen. And he admonishes us to search into the profound and mystical import of every part of it; particularly he hints that by "the seats of those who sell doves" may be understood the pulpits of preachers who make sale of the gifts of the spirit. St. Augustine is very positive that ecclesiastics who are selfish and make worldly gain of the Gospel are here meant. Behold what a wonderful harmony among the fathers in their rejection of the literal, and espousal of the mystical sense of this miracle, favoring an enmity to a hireling priesthood.

I begin to speak of that miracle of Jesus' healing a woman diseased with an issue of blood, twelve years. (Matt. 9; Lk. 8; Mk. 5). How shall we come to the knowledge of the greatness of this miracle?

First, as to the nature of the disease, we are much in the dark about it, and very uncertain of what kind and degree it was. How will they make a grievous distemper of it in order to a miracle? The woman subsisted too long under her issue of blood, and bore it too well, for any to make her case very grievous.

Secondly, consider the manner of the cure. I can't but commend her, at this distance of time, for the power of her faith, persuasion or imagination in the case, which was a good preparative for relief, and without which, it's certain, she had continued under her disease. As despair and dejection of mind sometimes kills, where otherwise, reasonably speaking, proper medicines would cure; so a good conceit in the patient at other times, whether the medicine be pertinent or not, is almost all in all. And if infields should say that this was the case of this woman; if they should say as St. John of Jerusalem did, "that her own imagination cured herself," and should urge the probability of it because Jesus could do no cures nor miracles against unbelief (Matt. 13:58), who can help it?

It is said of the pope, when he was last at Benevento, that he wrought three miracles, which our Protestant clergy, I dare say, believe nothing at all of.

But, for all that, it is not improbable but that some diseased people, considering their superstitious veneration for the pope, might be persuaded of his gift of miracles; and if they fancifully or actually received benefit by his touch, I don't wonder, without a miracle. And what if we had been told of the pope's curing a hemorrhage like this before us, what would Protestants have said to it? Why, "that a foolish, credulous, and superstitious woman had fancied herself cured of some slight indisposition, and the crafty pope and his adherents, aspiring after popular applause, magnified the presumed cure into a miracle. If they would have us Protestants to believe the miracle, they should have given us an exacter description of her disease, and then we could better have judged of it."

My design in what I have done is not to do service to infidelity, but, upon the command and encouragement of the fathers, to turn men's thoughts to the mystical meaning of the miracle, which I come now to give an account of. They tell us that this woman is a type of the church of the Gentiles in after times. As to her hemorrhage or issue of blood, they understand it of the impurity and corruption of the church by ill principles and bad morals. The twelve years of the woman's affliction is a typical number of the church's impure state for above twelve hundred years. It is the opinion of the fathers that the church universal, after twelve hundred years, will be purified and sanctified by the gifts of the Spirit of Christ, and enter upon a more holy, peaceable, and happy condition, absolutely freed from her issue of blood which, through persecution and war, she has for many ages labored under.

But who are meant by the physicians of the

woman, that have had the mystical hemorrhage and diseases of the church under cure all this while? Who but pretended ministers of the Gospel? The woman of the Gospel is said to "suffer many things of many physicians, and was nothing bettered, but rather grew worse." So the diseases of the church in time have increased, for all the use she has made of her spiritual physicians, the clergy. In every age has the church been degenerating in morals and principles; and all along have her ecclesiastical quack doctors contributed to her ill state of health. The woman "spent all her living" upon her physicians, and, as it seems, to a bad purpose; so very great and large revenues of the church are expended on her ecclesiastical doctors in spiritual physic. And to what end and purpose? Why, to open and widen the bleeding wounds of the church, which they should heal and salve up.

I come to the consideration of the miracle of his giving sight to a man who was born blind, by the means of eye-salve made of dirt and spittle. (Jn. 9) There is no doubt to be made but he healed many of one weakness or other in their eyes, but whether he wrought any miracle upon any is uncertain. There are many kinds of blindness that are incurable by art or nature, and there are other kinds of it that nature and art will relieve a man in. Unless we knew of a certainty that the sore or blind eyes Jesus cured were absolutely out of the reach of art and nature, infidels will imagine and suggest that he was only master of a good ointment for sore eyes. Our surgeons, with their ointments and washings, can cure sore and blind eyes of one sort or another, and Jesus did no more here. Where's the sense and reason of difference between them? A miracle, if I mistake not the notion of our divines about it, is a supernatural event, or a work out of the power of nature or art to effect. But we know nothing of the nature of this poor man's blindness, without which knowledge it is impossible and unreasonable to assert that there was a miracle wrought in the cure of him. There are grounds enough to suspect that it was not divine power which healed this man, or Jesus would never have prepared and ordered an ointment and wash for him. But Jesus' eye-salve, for absurdity, whim, and incongruity, was never equalled, either in jest or in earnest, by any quack doctor. I am puzzled to think how our divines will extricate themselves out of this strait, and account for the use of this eye-salve without any diminution of the miracle.

If I was, what I am not, an infidel, I should think, from the letter of this story, that Jesus was a juggling impostor, who would pass for a miraculous healer of diseases, though he used underhand proper medicines. The clay and the spittle he made an open show of, as what, to admiration, he would cure the blind man with; but in reserve he had a more sanative balsam, that he subtly flipped in the room of the clay, and repeatedly to good purpose anointed the man's eyes with it. I would gladly know upon what bottom the faith of our divines can stand as to this miracle, and Jesus' divine power in it. The miracles of Jesus are, as our divines own, appeals to our reason and senses for his authority; and by our reason and senses they are to be tried, condemned or approved of. We must go to the fathers for a mystical and allegorical interpretation of the story of this eye-salve, or the miracle will fall to the ground.

Who is this blind man mystically? This blind man is a type of mankind of all nations, who in the perfection of time, signified by the sabbath in the story, is to be cured of this blindness in understanding. What is mankind's blindness here signified? It is ignorance, error and infidelity, or the want of the intellectual sight and knowledge of God and his providence. Origen, St. John of Jerusalem, and St. Theophylact tell us the reason of this spiritual blindness of mankind, that is, because they adhere to the letter of the Scriptures.

And how will Jesus, or right reason and truth, which are his mystical names, cure mankind of this his spiritual blindness? By his mystical spittle tempered with mystical dirt. By the spittle of Jesus must be understood the water of the Spirit, instilled into the earth of the letter of the Scriptures, which tempered together does, in the judgment of them all, make perfect doctrine to the opening of the eyes of our understanding in the knowledge of the providence of God of all ages, which knowledge, light, sight, or illumination mankind has hitherto wanted.

I am now to take into examination the three miracles of Jesus' raising the dead, viz., of Jairus' daughter (Matt. 9; Mk. 5; Lk. 8); of the widow of Naim's son (Lk. 7); and of Lazarus (Jn. 11), the literal stories of which I shall show to consist of absurdities, improbabilities and incredibilities, in order to the mystical interpretation of them. These three miracles are reputed the greatest that Jesus wrought. And I believe it will be granted on all hands that the restoring a person, indisputably dead, to life again, is a stupendous miracle; and that two or three such miracles, well circumstanced and credibly reported, are enough to conciliate the belief of mankind that the author of them was a divine agent and invested with the power of God, or he could not do them.

But God knows this is far from the case of these three miracles before us, or of any one of them.

1. Observe that the unnatural and preposterous order of time in which these miracles are related justly brings them all under suspicion of fable and forgery. The greatest of the three is indisputably that of Lazarus' resurrection; but since this is only mentioned by St. John, who wrote his Gospel after the other evangelists, and above sixty years, according to the best computation, after our Lord's ascension, here is too much room for cavil and question whether this story be not entirely his invention. What could be the reason that Matthew, Mark, and Luke, who all wrote their Gospels before John, and many years nearer to the death of our savior, should omit to record this most remarkable and illustrious miracle of Lazarus? They could not forget it, nor be ignorant of it, if the story had been really true; and to assign any other reason than ignorance or forgetfulness is hard and impossible. And why too did not Matthew and Mark mention the story of the Widow of Naim's son? They tell us the story of Jairus' daughter, that is an imperfect and disputable miracle, in comparison with the other two, which consequently they knew nothing at all of.

2. What became of these three persons after their resurrection? Of what use and advantage were their restored lives to the church or to mankind? The evangelical and ecclesiastical history is entirely silent as to these questions, which is enough to make us suspect their stories to be merely romantic or parabolical, and that there were no such persons raised from the dead, or we must have heard somewhat of their station and conversation in the world afterwards.

3. Let us consider the condition of the persons raised from the dead, and whether they were at all proper persons for Jesus to work such a miracle upon, in testimony of his divine power. Jairus' daughter was an insignificant girl of twelve years old. The widow of Naim's son too was but a youth, but his life certainly was of no more importance to the world after than before his resurrection. Lazarus indeed was Jesus' friend, but even this reason, supposing Jesus was to raise but three persons, is not sufficient against the cases of many others that may be put for the manifestation of his power, for the illustration of his wisdom and goodness, and for the conversion of unbelievers. I should think Jesus ought to have raised a useful magistrate, whose death was a public loss; a father of a numerous family, which for a comfortable subsistence depended on him.

4. None of these three raised persons had been long enough dead to amputate all doubt of Jesus' miraculous power in their resurrection. As to Jairus' daughter, she was but newly expired, if at all dead; Jesus himself says she was but asleep. The widow of Naim's son was carried forth to his burial, and so may be presumed to be really a dead corpse. But might not here be fraud or mistake in the case? History affords instances of the mistaken deaths of persons who sometimes have been unfortunately buried alive. Who knows but Jesus might suspect this youth to be in a lethargic state? Or might not a piece of fraud be here concerted between Jesus, a subtle youth, and his mother and others, and all the formalities of a death and burial contrived, that Jesus, whose fame for a worker of miracles was to be raised, might here have an opportunity to make a show of a grand one? Lazarus' case seems to be the

less exceptionable of the three. He had been buried four days. Whether Lazarus would not come into measures with his Lord, for the defense of his honor and propagation of his fame, infidels, who take Christianity for an imposture, will not question. And whether he would not consent to be interred alive, in a hollow cave, where there was only a stone laid at the mouth of it, as long as a man could fast, none of them will doubt. As to the stinking of Lazarus' carcass, that, infidels will say, was but the assertion of his sisters beforehand, like a prologue to a farce. And what's worst of all, his face was bound about with a napkin, so that the spectators could not discern what was of the essence of the miracle, the change of his countenance from a dead to a live one.

5. None of these raised persons did or could, after the return of their souls to their bodies, tell any tales of their separate existence.

6. Lastly, let us consider the intrinsic absurdities and incredibilities of the stories of these miracles. Observe that Jesus is said to have wept for the death of Lazarus. Was not this an absurdity to weep at all for the death of him whom he could and was about to recover to life again? John says it was with a loud voice that Jesus called Lazarus forth out of his cave. Why, I pray, a louder voice than ordinary? Was Lazarus deafer than Jairus' daughter? Or was his soul at so great a distance from his body, as he could not hear a still and low voice? The dead can hear the whisper of the Almighty, if power go along with it, as soon as the sound of a trumpet.

Thus have I done with my objections against the letter of these three miracles. I think it impossible satisfactorily to reply to them, without having recourse to the opinions of the fathers that these miracles, whether they were ever literally transacted or not, are now but emblematical representations of mysterious and more wonderful operations to be performed by Jesus. St. Augustine says: "There are some so silly as to stand amazed at the corporal miracles of Jesus, and have no consideration of his greater and spiritual miracles, signified by them." There are two ways that the fathers took in the moral and mystical interpretation of these miracles.

One was from the number three, and their difference in magnitude. According to which they said with St. Augustine that "these three sorts of dead persons, so raised to life, are figures of three sorts of sinners, whom Jesus raised from the death of sin to the life of righteousness. They who have conceived sin in their hearts, and have not brought it forth into act, are figured by Jairus' daughter. Others who after cogitation and consent pass into actual sin are figured by the young man. But those sinners who are habituated and long accustomed to sin, are like Lazarus buried and in a stinking condition under the corruption of it."

The other mystical way of interpreting these miracles is by making them types of three great events at the time of Christ's spiritual advent. The raising of Jairus' daughter is a type of the conversion of the Jews at this day; by Jairus, the ruler of a synagogue, is meant Moses, and by his daughter is to be understood the Jewish church. Among all the miracles recorded, the fathers are most scanty in their interpretations of the widow of Naim's son. But if Origen's comments on this miracle had been extant, I dare say he would have given us this following interpretation of it. This widow he would have called the church; and her only son he would have called the spiritual sense of the Scriptures, which is now dead; and that the ministers of the letter, who are his bearers, are for interring him within the earth of the letter; but Jesus, upon his spiritual advent, will revive the spiritual sense of the Scriptures. As to Lazarus' resurrection, it is in the opinion of the fathers a type of the general and mystical resurrection of mankind in the perfection of time.

[Woolston's sixth discourse deals with the narratives of the resurrection of Jesus; because their content is assumed in Sherlock's *Trial*, and because Woolston professed that the depiction there of his position was a fair one, no excerpts from that discourse are here presented.]

Defense, I (1729)

It is not because I am an infidel that the clergy so exclaim against me and my *Discourses*, but because, as a Christian, I have particular designs in view which, if I can compass, will tend to their dishonor and the ruin of their interests; and therefore, by defamations and prosecutions, they will, if they can, in time to put a stop to them. The designs that, for the truth of religion and good of mankind, I have in view, and which, maugre all opposition, terrors, and sufferings, I will pursue to the utmost of my power, are these three.

1. To restore the allegorical interpretation of the Old and New Testament that is called, say the fathers, the sublime mountain of vision, on which we shall contemplate the wisdom and beauty of the providence of God. It is plain enough, and wants no proof, that the revival of the allegorical scheme

portends ruin to the ministry of the letter, and will be such an argument of the ignorance and apostasy of our clergy that it's no wonder they defame, calumniate, and persecute me for my attempts toward it.

2. The second design which, as a Christian, I have in view, and which occasionally I write for, is a universal and unbounded toleration of religion without any restrictions or impositions on men's consciences; for which design the clergy will hate and defame me, and, if possible, make an infidel of me. Upon a universal toleration the world would be at quiet. That hatred of one another, which is now so visible among different sects, would then be terminated by a unity of their interests, when they are all upon a level in the eye of the civil magistrate, who would choose men to places of trust, not for their faith and affection to theological doctrines, but for their abilities to serve the public. In this case, ten thousand different notions in religion would no more obstruct the welfare of the community than so many different noses do the happiness of this city. But the clergy will never hearken to such a toleration because it would be the downfall of ecclesiastical power; for which reason, among others, I am,

3. For the abolition of a hired and established priesthood. Why should not the clergy of the Church of England be turned to grass, and be made to seek their fortune among the people, as well as preachers of other denominations? Where's the sense and reason of imposing parochial priests upon the people to take care of their souls, more than parochial lawyers to look to their estates, or parochial physicians to attend their bodies, or parochial tinkers to mend the'r kettles?

Defense, II (1730)

From the Dedication to Robert Raymond, Lord Chief Justice:

That it is a transgression of the law of the land to write against Christianity, established in it, I'll not question, since I have your Lordship's word for it. But for all that, I would wish, for the sake of Christianity, that such a liberty was indulged to infidels. Whatever our zealous clergy may think, one persecution of an infidel does more harm to religion than the publication of the worst book against it.

Liberty is so essential to the inquiry after truth that where it is wanted, truth will want that splendor which it receives from disputation. And Christianity would be the more triumphant over its enemies for that unbounded liberty they may enjoy to contest it from the press.

Ever since the Reformation, which was founded on our natural and Christian rights to liberty of conscience, has this great blessing of liberty at times been interrupted by persecutions; but whether any of them hitherto have done any service to church or state, your Lordship is a good judge.

THOMAS SHERLOCK

Sherlock (1678–1761) was a widely known and generally popular English cleric. He entered the controversy with the deists in 1725 through six sermons entitled *The Use and Intent of Prophecy*. Between that work and the publication of the *Trial*, he became Bishop of Bangor, and later (1748) he was named Bishop of London.

The Trial of the Witnesses
of the Resurrection of Jesus

We were, not long since, some gentlemen of the inns of court, together. Among other things we fell on the subject of Woolston's trial and conviction, which had happened some few days before. It may easily be imagined that this opened a door to much dispute, and determined the conversation for the remainder of the evening. At length one of the company said, pleasantly, "Gentlemen, you do not argue like lawyers; if I were judge in this cause I would hold you better to the point." The company took the hint, and cried they should be glad to have the cause re-heard, and him to be the judge.

To bring the matter within bounds and under one view, it was agreed that the evidence of Christ's resurrection, and the exceptions taken to it, should be the only subject of the conference.

The company met at the time appointed, and the judge called on the counsel for Woolston to begin.

Mr. A., counsel for Woolston. May it please your lordship, I conceive the gentleman on the other side ought to begin, and lay his evidence, which he intends to maintain, before the court; till that is done, it is to no purpose for me to object. I may perhaps object to something which he will not admit to be any part of his evidence, and therefore, I apprehend, the evidence ought in the first place to be distinctly stated.

Judge. Mr. B., what say you to that?

Mr. B., counsel on the other side. My lord, if the evidence I am to maintain were to support any new claim, if I were to gain anything which I am not already possessed of, the gentleman would be in the right; but the evidence is old, and is matter of record, and I have been long in possession of all that I claim under it. This I take to be the known method of proceeding in such cases; no man is obliged to produce his title to his possession; it is sufficient if he maintains it when it is called in question.

Mr. A. Surely, my lord, the gentleman mistakes the case. I can never admit myself to be out of possession of my understanding and reason; and since he would put me out of this possession, and compel me to admit things incredible, in virtue of the evidence he maintains, he ought to set forth his claim, or leave the world to be directed by common sense.

Judge. Sir, you say right, on supposition that the truth of the Christian religion were the point in judgment. But the matter now before the court is whether the objections produced by Mr. Woolston are of weight to overthrow the evidence of Christ's resurrection.

Mr. A. I cannot but observe that the gentleman on the other side did not forget to lay in his claim to prescription, which is, perhaps, in truth the very strength of his cause. I do allow that the gentleman maintains nothing but what his father and grandfather, and his ancestors, beyond time of man's memory, maintained before him. I allow too that prescription in many cases makes a good title, but it must always be with this condition, that the thing is capable of being prescribed for, and I insist that prescription cannot run against reason and common sense. Besides, if prescription must be allowed in this case, how will you deal with it in others? What will you say to the ancient Persians, and their fire-altars? Nay, what to the Turks . . .

Mr. B. I beg pardon for interrupting the gentleman, but it is to save him trouble. He is going into his favorite commonplace, and has brought us from Persia to Turkey already; and if he goes on, I know we must follow him round the globe. To save us from this long journey, I will waive all advantage from the antiquity of the resurrection, and the general reception the belief of it has found in the world, and am content to consider it as a fact which happened but last year.

Mr. A. Yet I suspect some art even in this concession. For I am persuaded that one reason why men believe this history of Jesus is that they cannot conceive that anyone should attempt, much less succeed in such an attempt as this, on the foundation of mere human cunning and policy; and it is worthwhile to go round the globe to see various instances of the like kind, in order to remove this prejudice.

Mr. B. My lord, the gentleman in justification of his first argument has entered on another of a very different kind. The mere antiquity of the resurrection I gave up; for if the evidence was not good at first, it cannot be good now. The gentleman is willing, he says, to spare us his history of ancient errors, and intimates that on this account he passes over many instances of fraud that were like in circumstances to the case before us. By no means, my lord, let them be passed over. Nothing can be more material than to show a fraud of this kind that prevailed universally in the world.

MR. A. My lord, there has hardly been an instance of a false religion in the world but it has also afforded a like instance to this before us. Have they not all pretended to inspiration? On what foot did Pythagoras, Numa, and others set up? Did they not all converse with the gods, and pretend to deliver oracles? I suppose it will be allowed to be as great a thing to go to heaven and converse with angels and with God, and to come down to the earth again, as it is to die and rise again. Now this very thing Mahomet pretended to do, and all his disciples believed it.

MR. B. But tell us who went with Mahomet? Who were his witnesses? I expect, before we have done, to hear of the guards set over the sepulchre of Christ, and the seal of the stone; what guard watched Mahomet in his going or returning? What seals and credentials had he? We are now to consider the evidence of Christ's resurrection, and you think to parallel it by producing a case for which no one ever pretended there was any evidence.

JUDGE. Gentlemen, you forget that you are in a court, and are falling into dialogue. Look ye, the evidence of the resurrection of Jesus is before the court, recorded by Matthew, Mark, and others. You must take it as it is; you can neither make it better nor worse. These witnesses are accused of giving false evidence. Come to the point, and let us hear what you have to offer to prove the accusation.

Mr. A. I am now to disclose to you a scene, of all others the most surprising. "The resurrection has been long talked of, and to the amazement of everyone who can think freely, has been believed through all ages of the church." [1] This general and constant belief creates in most minds a presumption that it was founded on good evidence. In other cases the evidence supports the credit of the history; but here the evidence itself is presumed only on the credit which the story has gained. I wish the books dispersed against Jesus by the ancient Jews had not been lost; for they would have given us a clear insight into this contrivance. But it is happy for us that the very account given by the pretended witnesses of this fact is sufficient to destroy the credit of it.

The resurrection was not a thing contrived for its own sake. No! It was undertaken to support great views, and for the sake of great consequences that were to attend it. It will be necessary therefore to lay before you these views, that you may be the better judge of this part of the contrivance when you have the whole scene before you.

From old books and traditions the Jews formed many extravagant expectations; and among the rest one was that some time or other a great victorious prince should arise among them, and subdue all their enemies, and make them lords of the world. In Augustus' time the eagerness of this hope turned into a firm expectation that he would soon come. This proved a temptation to some bold and to some cunning men, to personate the prince so much expected. Accordingly many such impostors rose, pretending to be the victorious prince expected; and they and

---

[1] From Woolston's *Sixth Discourse*.

the people who followed them perished in the folly of their attempt.

But Jesus, knowing that victories and triumphs are not things to be counterfeited, that the people were not to be delivered from the Roman yoke by sleight of hand, and having no hope of being able to cope with the emperor of Rome in good earnest, took another and more successful method to carry on his design. He took on him to be the prince foretold in the ancient prophets; but then he insisted that the true sense of the prophecies had been mistaken; that they related not to the kingdoms of this world, but to the kingdom of heaven; that the Messiah was not to be a conquering prince, but a suffering one, that he was not to come with horses of war and chariots of war, but was to be meek and lowly, and riding on an ass. By this means he got the common and necessary foundation for a new revelation, which is to be built and founded on a precedent revelation.

To carry on this design, he made choice of twelve men of no fortunes or education, and of such understandings as gave no jealousy that they would discover the plot. And what is most wonderful, and shows their ability, whilst the master was preaching the kingdom of heaven, these poor men, not weaned from the prejudices of their country, expected everyday that he would declare himself a king, and were quarrelling who should be his first minister. This expectation had a good effect on the service, for it kept them constant to their master.

Now as something extraordinary was necessary to support the pretensions of Jesus, he dexterously laid hold on the weakness of the people, and set up to be a wonder-worker. This conduct had the desired success. The whole country was alarmed, and full of the news of a great prophet's being come among them. They were too full of their own imagination to attend to the notion of a kingdom of heaven; here was one mighty in deed and in word, and they concluded he was the very prince their nation expected. Accordingly they once attempted to set him up for a king, and at another time attended him in triumph to Jerusalem. This natural consequence opens the natural design of the attempt. If things had gone on successfully to the end, it is probable the kingdom of heaven would have been changed into a kingdom of this world. The design indeed failed, by the impatience and over-hastiness of the multitude, which alarmed not only the chief of the Jews, but the Roman governor also.

The case being come to this point, and Jesus seeing that he could not escape being put to death, he declared that the ancient prophets had foretold that the Messiah should die on a cross, and that he should rise again on the third day. Here was the foundation laid for the continuing this plot, which otherwise had died with its author. This was his legacy to his followers, which, having been well managed by them and their successors, has at least produced a kingdom indeed, a kingdom of priests, who have governed the world for many ages, and have been strong enough to set kings and emperors at defiance. As he expected, so it happened that he died on a cross; and the prosecuting of this contrivance was left to the management of his disciples and followers.

Mr. B. My lord, this court sits to examine evidence, and not to be entertained with fine imaginations. You have had a scheme laid before you, but not one bit of evidence to support any part of it. The gentleman was very sorry that the old books of the Jews were lost, which would, as he supposes, have set forth all this matter; and I agree with him that he has much reason to be sorry, considering his great scarcity of proof. I would ask the gentleman now, how he knows there ever were such books? And since if ever there were any they are lost, how he knows what they contained?

The gentleman's observation that the general belief of the resurrection creates a presumption that it stands on good evidence, and therefore people look no further, but follow their fathers, as their fathers did their grandfathers before them, is in great measure true; but it is a truth nothing to his purpose. He allows that the resurrection has been believed in all ages of the church, that is, from the very time of the resurrection; what then prevailed with those who first received it? They certainly did not follow the example of their fathers. Here then is the point, how did this fact gain credit in the world at first? And it cannot be denied but that truth may be received through prejudice, as it is called, that is, without examining the proof or merits of the cause, as well as falsehood. What general truth is there the merits of which all the world, or the hundredth part, has examined?

The gentleman thought proper to begin with an account of the Jews. They were, he says, a weak superstitious people, and lived under the influence of certain pretended prophecies and predictions; that on this ground they had, some time before the appearance of Christ Jesus, conceived great expectations of the coming of a victorious prince, who should deliver them from the Roman yoke, and make them all kings and princes. This foundation being laid, it was natural to expect that the gentleman

would go on to show that Jesus laid hold of this opportunity, struck in with the opinion of the people,
and professed himself to be the prince who was to
work their deliverance. But so far, it seems, is this
from being the case, that the charge on Jesus is that
he took the contrary part, and set up in opposition
to all the popular notions and prejudices of his country; that he interpreted the prophecies to another
sense and meaning than his countrymen did; and by
his expositions took away all hopes of their ever seeing the victorious deliverer so much wanted and
expected.

I know not how to bring the gentleman's premises
and his conclusion to any agreement; they seem to
be at a great variance at present. If it be the likeliest
method for an impostor to succeed, to build on the
popular opinions, prejudices, and prophecies of the
people, then surely an impostor cannot possibly take
a worse method than to set up in opposition to all
the prejudices and prophecies of the country. Where
was the art and cunning then of taking this method?
Could anything be expected from it but hatred, contempt, and persecution? And did Christ in fact meet
with any other treatment from the Jews?

But it seems Jesus dared not set up to be the victorious prince expected, for victories are not to be
counterfeited. I hope it was no crime in him that
he did not assume this false character, and try to
abuse the credulity of the people. No, he wanted,
we are told, the common and necessary foundation
for a new revelation, the authority of an old one, to
build on. You see the reason of the necessity of this
foundation; it is that the new teacher may have the
advantage of old popular opinions, and fix himself
on the prejudices of the people. Had Christ any such

advantages, or did he seek any such? The people expected a victorious prince; he told them they were mistaken. They held as sacred the traditions of the elders; he told them those traditions made the law of God of none effect. They valued themselves for being the peculiar people of God; he told them that people from all quarters of the world should be the people of God, and sit down with Abraham, Isaac, and Jacob in the kingdom. They thought God could be worshipped only at Jerusalem; he told them God might and should be worshipped everywhere. They were superstitious in the observance of the sabbath; he broke it frequently. The cry ran strongly against him that he came to destroy the law and the prophets. Now, now, sir, what advantage had Christ of your common and necessary foundation? What sufficient number of principles, owned by the people, did he build on?

But what design, what real end was carrying on all this while? Why, the gentleman tells us that the very thing disclaimed, the temporal kingdom, was the real thing aimed at under this disguise. He told the people there was no foundation to expect a temporal deliverer, warned them against all who should set up those pretensions, declared there was no ground from the ancient prophecies to expect such a prince, and yet by these very means he was working his way to an opportunity of declaring himself to be the very prince the people wanted. Let us see then what follows.

The government was alarmed, and Jesus was looked on as a person dangerous to the state; and he had discernment enough to see that his death was determined and inevitable. What does he do then? Why, to make the best of a bad case, and to save

the benefit of his undertaking to those who were to
succeed him, he pretends to prophesy of his death,
which he knew could not be avoided; and further,
that he should rise again the third day. The gentleman tells us a kingdom has arisen out of this plot, a
kingdom of priests. But when did it arise? Some
hundred years after the death of Christ, in opposition
to his will, and almost to the subversion of his religion. And yet we are told this kingdom was the
thing he had in view.

It is allowed that Christ foretold his own death
and resurrection; if the resurrection was managed by
fraud, Christ was certainly in the fraud himself, by
foretelling the fraud that was to happen. Disprove
therefore the resurrection, and we shall have no
further occasion for prophecy. On the other side, by
foretelling the resurrection, he certainly put the proof
of his mission on the truth of the event. Without
doubt Jesus is not the Messiah if he did not rise
again; for by his own prophecy he made it part of
the character of the Messiah. If the event justified
the prediction, it is such an evidence as no man
of sense and reason can reject. There must of necessity have been either a real miracle or a great fraud
in this case. There is here no medium; you must
either admit the miracle, or prove the fraud.

MR. A. Jesus is his lifetime foretold his death, and
that he should rise again the third day. The first part
of his prediction was accomplished; he died on the
cross, and was buried. I will not trouble you with the
particulars of his crucifixion, death, and burial. It is a
well known story.

MR. B. My lord, I desire to know whether the
gentleman charges any fraud on this part of the history; perhaps he may be of opinion by and by that

there was a sleight of hand in the crucifixion, and that Christ only counterfeited death.

MR. A. No, no, have no such fears. He was not crucified by his disciples, but by the Romans and the Jews, and they were in very good earnest. I will prove beyond contradiction that the dead body was fairly laid in the tomb, and the tomb sealed up; and it will be well for you if you can get it as fairly out again.

The crucifixion being over, the dead body was conveyed to a sepulchre; and in the general opinion there seemed to be an end of the whole design. But the governors of the Jews, watchful for the safety of the people, called to mind that Jesus in his lifetime had said that he would rise again on the third day. They had warning to be watchful. It was not long before that the people "had like to have been fatally deluded, and imposed on by him, in the pretended resuscitation of Lazarus." They had fully discovered the cheat in the case of Lazarus, and had narrowly escaped the dangerous consequences of it. On this account they addressed themselves to the Roman governor, told him how the case was, and desired that he would grant them a guard to watch the sepulchre; that the service would not be long, for the prediction limited the resurrection to the third day. Pilate granted the request, and a guard was set to watch the sepulchre.

This was not all. The chief priests took another method to prevent all frauds, and it was the best that could possibly be taken, which was to seal up the door of the sepulchre. A seal thus used imports a covenant. Should the seal be broken, it would be a manifest fraud and breach of trust. On one side there was a concern to see the prediction fulfilled; on the other, to prevent fraud in fulfilling it. The sum of their agreement was naturally this: that the seals should be opened at the time appointed for the resurrection, that all parties might see and be satisfied whether the dead body was come to life or no.

What now would any reasonable man expect from these circumstances? Do you not expect to hear that the chief priests and the apostles met at the time appointed, opened the seals, and that the matter in dispute was settled beyond all controversy one way or other? But see how it happened. The seals were broken, the body stolen away in the night by the disciples; none of the chief priests present, or summoned to see the seals opened. The guards, when examined, were forced to confess the truth, though joined with an acknowledgement of their guilt, which made them liable to be punished by Pilate. They confessed that they were asleep, and in the meantime that the body was stolen away by the disciples.

Mr. B. The gentleman seems to be at a great loss to account for the credit which the chief priests gave to the prediction of the resurrection, by the care they took to prevent it. He thinks the thing in itself was too extravagant and absurd to deserve any regard, and that no one would have regarded such a prediction in any other time or place. I agree with the gentleman entirely; but then I demand of him a reason why the chief priests were under any concern about this prediction. Was it because they had plainly discovered him to be a cheat and an impostor? It is impossible. This reason would have convinced them of the folly and presumption of the prediction. It must therefore necessarily be that they had discovered something in the life and actions of Christ which raised this jealousy, and made them listen to a prophecy in his case which in any other case they would have despised. And what could this be but the secret conviction they were under, by his many miracles, of his extra-ordinary powers? This care therefore of the chief priests over his dead, helpless body, is a lasting testimony of the mighty works which Jesus did in his lifetime.

But the gentleman is of another mind. He says they had discovered a plain cheat in the case of Lazarus, whom Christ had pretended to raise from the dead; and therefore they took all this care to guard against a like cheat.

I begin now to want evidence; I am forbid to call this imagination; what else to call it I know not. There is not the least intimation given from history that there was any cheat in the case of Lazarus, or that anyone suspected a cheat. The rulers had Christ in their possession when they brought him to a trial; why did they not then object this cheat to Christ? It would have been much to their purpose. Instead of that, they accuse him of a design to pull down their temple, to destroy their law, and of blasphemy; but not one word of any fraud in the case of Lazarus or any other case.

But let us take the case to be as the gentleman states it, that the cheat, in the case of Lazarus, was detected. What consequence is to be expected? In all other cases, impostors, once discovered, grow odious and contemptible, and quite incapable of doing further mischief; so little are they regarded that even when they tell the truth they are neglected. Was it so in this case? No, says the gentleman, the Jews were the more careful that Christ should not cheat them in his own resurrection. Surely this is a most singular case: when the people thought him a prophet, the chief priests sought to kill him, and thought his death

would put an end to his pretensions; when they and
the people had discovered him to be a cheat, then
they thought him not safe even when he was dead,
but were afraid he should prove a true prophet, and,
according to his own prediction, rise again. A needless, a preposterous fear!

On this occasion, the gentleman has explained the
use of seals when applied to such purposes. They
imply, he says, a covenant that the things sealed shall
remain in the condition they are, till the parties to
the sealing are agreed to open them. Why then, it
seems, the apostles and chief priests were in a covenant that there should be no resurrection, at least no
opening of the door, till they met together at an
appointed time to view and unseal the door.

Your lordship and the court will now consider the
probability of this supposition. When Christ was
seized and carried to his trial, his disciples fled, and
hid themselves for fear of the Jews. After the death
of Christ, his disciples were so far from being ready
to engage for his resurrection, or to enter into terms
and agreements for the manner in which it should be
done, that they themselves did not believe it ever
would be. They gave over all hopes and thoughts of
it; and far from entering into engagements with the
chief priests, their whole concern was to keep themselves concealed from them.

The simple plain account of this matter will best
answer all these suspicions. The Jews, it is plain,
were exceedingly solicitous about this event. For
this reason they obtained a guard from Pilate; and
when they had, they were still suspicious lest their
guards should deceive them, and enter into combination against them. To secure this point they sealed
the door, and required of the guards to deliver up

the sepulchre to them sealed as it was. This is a natural and true account of the matter.

The guards, the gentleman says, have confessed the truth, and owned that they were asleep, and that the disciples in the meantime stole away the body. I wish the guards were in court; I would ask them how they came to be so punctual in relating what happened when they were asleep; what induced them to believe that the body was stolen at all; what, that it was stolen by the disciples; since by their own confession they were asleep and saw nothing, saw nobody.

As this story has no evidence to support it, so neither has it any probability. What good could the dead body do the apostles? Or if it could have done them any, what hope had they to succeed in their attempt? A dead body is not to be removed by sleight of hand; it requires many hands to move it. Besides, the great stone at the mouth of the sepulchre was to be removed, which could not be done silently, or by men walking on tiptoes to prevent discovery; so that if the guards had really been asleep, yet there was no encouragement to go on this enterprise, for it is hardly possible to suppose but that rolling away the stone, moving the body, the hurry and confusion in carrying it off, must awaken them.

But supposing the thing practicable, yet the attempt was such as the disciples consistently with their own notions could not undertake. The gentleman says they continued all their master's lifetime to expect to see him a temporal prince. Consider now their case. Their master was dead; and they are to contrive to steal away his body. For what? Did they expect to make a king of the dead body, if they could get it into their power? Or did they think, if they had it, they could raise it to life again? If they trusted so far to their master's prediction as to expect his resurrection (which I think is evident they did not), could they yet think the resurrection depended on their having the dead body? It is in all views absurd.

But let us see how the true evidence in this case stands. Guards were placed, and they did their duty. But what are guards and sentinels against the power of God! An angel of the Lord opened the sepulchre; the guards saw him, and became like dead men. This account they gave to the chief priests who, still persisting in their obstinacy, bribed the guards to tell the contradictory story of their being asleep and the body stolen.

I cannot but observe to your lordship that all these circumstances, so much questioned and suspected, were necessary circumstances, supposing the resurrection to be true. It is surprising to hear these circumstances made use of to prove the resurrection to be a fraud, which yet could not but happen, supposing the resurrection to be true.

I have now gone through the several objections on this head; what credit they may gain in this age I know not, but it is plain they had no credit when they were first spread abroad. Nay, it is evident that the very persons who set abroad this story of the body being stolen did not believe it themselves. And not to insist here on the plain fact, which was that the guards were hired to tell this lie by the chief priests, it will appear from the after-conduct of the chief priests themselves that they were conscious that the story was false. Not long after the resurrection, the disciples, having received new power from above, appeared publicly in Jerusalem and testified the resurrection of Christ, even before those who had murdered him. What now do the chief priests do? They seize on the apostles, they threaten them, they beat them, they scourge them, and all to stop their mouths, insisting that they should say no more of the matter. But why did they not, when they had the disciples in their power, charge them directly with their notorious cheat in stealing the body, and expose them to the people as impostors? But of this not one word is said.

But let us see what the council and senate of the children of Israel thought of the matter. Not long after the resurrection the apostles were taken; the high priest thought the matter of that weight that he summoned the council and senate of the children of Israel. The apostles are brought before them and make their defense. Part of their defense is in these words: "the God of our fathers raised up Jesus, whom ye slew and hanged on a tree." (Acts 5:30) The defense was indeed a heavy charge on the senate, and in the warmth of their anger their first resolution was to slay them all. But Gamaliel, one of the council, stood up and told them that the matter deserved more consideration. He concluded: "if this work be of men, it will come to nought; but if it be of God, ye cannot overthrow it, lest haply ye be found to fight against God." The council agreed to this advice, and after some ill treatment the apostles were discharged. I ask now, could Gamaliel possibly have given this advice, and supposed that the hand of God might be with the apostles, if he had known that there was a cheat discovered in the resurrection of Jesus? Could the whole senate have followed this advice, had they believed the discovery of the cheat?

MR. A. I shall trouble you, Sir, with but one obser-

vation more, which is this: that although in common
life we act in a thousand instances on the faith and
credit of human testimony, yet the reason for so
doing is not the same in the case before us. In common affairs, where nothing is asserted but what is
probable and possible, and according to the usual
course of nature, a reasonable degree of evidence
ought to determine every man; for the very probability or possibility of the thing is a support to the
evidence; and in such cases we have no doubt but a
man's senses qualify him to be a witness. But when
the thing testified is contrary to the order of nature,
and, at first sight at least, impossible, what evidence
can be sufficient to overturn the constant evidence of
nature, which she gives us in the uniform and regular
method of her operations? In the case before us, since
the body raised from the grave differed from common natural bodies, how can I be assured that the
apostles' senses qualified them to judge at all of this
body, whether it was the same or not the same which
was buried? They handled the body, which yet could
pass through doors and walls; they saw it, and sometimes knew it, at the other times knew it not. In a
word, it seems to be a case exempt from human evidence. Men have limited senses and a limited reason;
when they act within their limits, we may give credit
to them; but when they talk of things removed beyond
the reach of their senses and reason, we must quit
our own if we believe theirs.

Mr. B. My lord, the gentleman seemed to argue as
if evidence would have put the matter in question out
of all doubt; but he concluded with an observation to
prove that no evidence in this case can be sufficient;
that a resurrection is a thing in nature impossible, at
least impossible to be proved to the satisfaction of a

rational inquirer. If this be the case, why does he require more evidence, since none can be sufficient? Or to what purpose is it to vindicate the particular evidence of the resurrection of Christ so long as this general prejudice, that a resurrection is incapable of being proved, remains unremoved?

The gentleman allows it to be reasonable in many cases to act on the testimony and credit of others; but he thinks that the testimony of others ought not to be admitted, but in such matters as appear probable, or at least possible to our conceptions. For instance: a man who lives in a warm climate, and never saw ice, ought on no evidence to believe that rivers freeze and grow hard in cold countries; for this is improbable, contrary to the usual course of nature, and impossible according to his notion of things. And yet we all know that this is a plain manifest case, discernible by the senses of men, of which therefore they are qualified to be good witnesses. And what has the gentleman said against the resurrection more than any man who never saw ice might say against a hundred honest witnesses who assert that water turns to ice in cold climates?

It is very true that men do not so easily believe on testimony of others things which to them seem improbable or impossible; but the reason is not because the thing itself admits no evidence, but because the hearer's preconceived opinion outweighs the credit of the reporter, and makes his veracity to be called in question. For instance, it is natural for a stone to roll down hill, it is unnatural for it to roll up hill. But a stone moving up hill is as much the object of sense as a stone moving down hill; and all men in their senses are as capable of seeing and judging and reporting the fact in one case as in the other. Should a man then tell you that he saw a stone go up hill of its own accord, you might question his veracity, but you could not say the thing admitted no evidence because it was contrary to the law and usual course of nature; for the law of nature formed to yourself from your own experience and reasoning is quite independent of the matter of fact which the man testifies. And whenever you see facts yourself which contradict your notions of the law of nature, you admit the facts, because you believe yourself; when you do not admit like facts on the evidence of others, it is because you do not believe them, and not because the facts in their own nature exclude all evidence.

Suppose a man should tell you that he was come from the dead; you would be apt to suspect his evidence. But what would you suspect? That he was not alive, when you heard him, saw him, felt him, and conversed with him? You would question whether the man had ever been dead. But would you say that it is incapable of being made plain by human testimony that this or that man died a year ago?

A resurrection considered only as a fact to be proved by evidence is a plain case; it requires no greater ability in the witnesses than that they be able to distinguish between a man dead and a man alive. I do allow that this case and others of like nature require more evidence to give them credit than ordinary cases do. But it is absurd to say that such cases admit no evidence, when the things in question are manifestly objects of sense.

The gentleman has rightly stated the difficulty on the foot of common prejudice, and that it arises from hence that such cases appear to be contrary to the course of nature. It appears that when men talk of the course of nature, they really talk of their own prejudices and imaginations, and that sense and reason are not so much concerned in the case as the gentleman imagines. For I ask, is it from the evidence of sense or the evidence of reason that people in warm climates think it contrary to nature that water should grow solid and become ice? Our senses inform us rightly what the usual course of things is; but when we conclude that things cannot be otherwise, we outrun the information of our senses, and the conclusion stands on prejudice and not on reason. And yet such conclusions form what is generally called the course of nature. And when men on proper evidence and information admit things contrary to this presupposed course of nature, they do not quit their own sense and reason, but in truth they quit their own mistakes and prejudices.

In the case before us, the case of the resurrection, the great difficulty arises from the like prejudice. We all know by experience that all men die and rise no more; therfore we conclude that for a dead man to rise to life again is contrary to the course of nature; and certainly it is contrary to the uniform and settled course of things. But if we argue from hence that it is contrary and repugnant to the real laws of nature, and absolutely impossible on that account, we argue without any foundation to support us either from our senses or our reason. We cannot learn from our eyes, or feeling, or any other sense, that it is impossible for a dead body to live again; if we learn it at all, it must be from our reason. And yet what one maxim of reason is contradicted by the supposition of a resurrection? For my own part, when I consider how I live—that all the animal motions necessary to my life are independent of my will, that my heart beats without my consent and without my direction, that digestion and nutrition are performed by methods to which I am not conscious, that my blood moves in a perpetual round, which is contrary to all known laws of motion—I cannot but think that the preservation of my life, in every moment of it, is as great an act of power as is necessary to raise a dead man to life. And whoever so far reflects on his own being as to acknowledge that he owes it to a superior power must needs think that the same power which gave life to senseless matter at first, and set all the springs and movements a-going at the beginning, can restore life to a dead body. For surely it is not a greater thing to give life to a body once dead than to a body that never was alive.

I will not spend your time in enumerating witnesses, or in setting forth the demonstration they had of the truth which they report. These things are well known. If you question their sincerity, they lived miserably and died miserably, for the sake of this truth. And what greater evidence of sincerity can man give or require? And what it still more, they were not deceived in their expectation by being ill treated; for he who employed them told them beforehand that the world would hate them, and treat them with contempt and cruelty.

But I beg leave to lay before you another evidence, passed over in silence by the gentleman on the other side. He took notice that a resurrection was so extraordinary a thing that no human evidence could support it. I am not sure that he is not in the right. If twenty men were to come into England with such a report from a distant country, perhaps they might not find twenty more here to believe their story. And I rather think the gentleman may be in the right, because in the present case I see clearly that the credit of the resurrection of Christ was not trusted to mere human evidence. To what evidence it was trusted we find by his own declaration: "The Spirit of truth which proceedeth from the Father, he shall testify of me; and ye also shall bear witness, because ye have been with me from the beginning." (John 15:26f.) And therefore though the apostles had conversed with him forty days after his resurrection, and had received his commission to go teach all nations, yet he expressly forbids them entering on the work till they should receive powers from above. (Acts 1:14)

Now what were the powers received by the apostles? Were they not the powers of wisdom and courage; the power of miracles; and a power to communicate these gifts to believers? Can you wonder that men believed the reality of those powers of which they were partakers, and became conscious to themselves? With respect to these communicated powers St. John speaks, when he says: "He that believeth on the Son of God hath the witness in himself." (I John 5:10)

If the same thing were to happen in our own time; if one or two were to come into England, and report that a man was raised from the dead, and in consequence of it teach nothing but that we ought to love God and our neighbors; if to confirm their report they should before our eyes cure the blind, the deaf, the lame, and even raise the dead to life; if endowed with all these powers they should live in poverty and distress, and patiently submit to all that scorn, contempt, and malice could contrive to distress them, and at last sacrifice even their lives in justification of their report; if on inquiry we should find that all the countries of Europe had received the same account, supported by the same miraculous powers, attested in like manner by the sufferings, and confirmed by the blood of the witnesses—I would fain know what any reasonable man would do in this case? Would he despise such evidence? I think he would not; and whoever thinks otherwise must say that a resurrection, though in its own nature possible, is yet such a thing in which we ought not to believe either God or man.

Mr. A. Allowing the gentleman all he demands, what is it to us? They who had the witness within them, did perhaps very well to consult him and to take his word; but how am I, or others, who have not this witness in us, the better for it? If the first ages of the church saw all the wonders related by the gentleman, and believed, it shows at least, in his opinion, that this strong evidence was necessary to create the belief he requires; why then does he require this belief of us who have not this strong evidence?

Judge. Very well. Gentlemen of the jury, you have heard the proofs and arguments on both sides, and it is now your part to give a verdict.

The jury consulted together, and the foreman rose up.

Judge. What say you? Are the apostles guilty of giving false evidence in the case of the resurrection of Jesus, or not guilty?

Foreman. Not guilty.

MATTHEW TINDAL

Tindal (1657–1733) was educated as a lawyer; indeed he was fellow of All Souls', Oxford, from 1678 until his death. *Christianity as Old as the Creation* became, very soon after its publication, the focal center of the deist controversy. Because almost every argument, quotation and issue raised for decades can be found here, the work is often termed "the deist's Bible." Tindal promised a second volume, but its publication was apparently prevented by Bishop Gibson of London.

Christianity as Old as the Creation

I

That God, at all times, has given mankind suf-
ficient means of knowing whatever He requires
of them; and what those means are.

B. I was yesterday in company with a great many clergymen, where the complaint was general of the coldness and indifference with which people received the speculative points of Christianity, and all its holy rites. This coldness they chiefly imputed to those Low Churchmen who lay the main stress on natural religion, and withal so magnify the doctrine of sincerity as in effect to place all religions on a level, where the professors are alike sincere. I would be glad to know the sentiments of so good a judge

on these two important points, viz., sincerity and
natural religion.

A. I think a sincere examination into religious
matters can't be too much pressed, this being the
only way to discover true Christianity. The apostles
thought themselves obliged, in making proselytes, to
recommend an impartial search; they both desired
and required men to "judge for themselves, to prove
all things," etc. (I Cor. 10:15; I Thess. 5:21) Nay,
even those very men who most ridicule the doctrine
of sincerity never fail on other occasions to assert
that infidelity is owing to the want of a sincere examination, and that whosoever impartially considers
Christianity must be convinced of its truth. I might
add that, could we suppose a sincere examination
would not always produce this effect, yet must it
always make men acceptable to God, since that is all
God can require, all that it is in their power to do for
the discovery of his will. And I think too great a
stress can't be laid on natural religion, which, as I
take it, differs not from revealed but in the manner
of its being communicated, the one being the internal, as the other the external revelation of the
same unchangeable will of a being who is alike at
all times infinitely wise and good.

I advance nothing in either of these points without reason. I desire to be informed whether God has
not, from the beginning, given mankind some rule,
or law, for their conduct? And whether the observing
that did not make them acceptable to him? What
more can any external revelation do, than render men
acceptable to God? Again, if God from the beginning gave men a religion, I ask, was that religion
imperfect, or perfect?

B. Most perfect, without doubt, since no religion

can come from a being of infinite wisdom and perfection, but what is absolutely perfect.

A. Can, therefore, a religion absolutely perfect admit of any alteration, or be capable of addition, or diminution, and not be as immutable as the author of it? Can revelation, I say, add any thing to a religion thus absolutely perfect, universal, and immutable? Besides, if God at all times was willing all men should come to the knowledge of his truth, could not his infinite wisdom and power at all times find sufficient means for making mankind capable of knowing what his infinite goodness designed they should know?

B. I grant you that God was always willing that all men should come to the knowledge of true religion; and we say that the Christian religion, being the only true and absolutely perfect religion, was what God from the beginning designed for all mankind.

A. If so, it follows that the Christian religion has existed from the beginning; and that God, both then and ever since, has continued to give all mankind sufficient means to know it. So that Christianity, though the name is of a later date, must be as old, and as extensive, as human nature, and as the law of our creation must have been then implanted in us by God himself.

If God never intended mankind should at any time be without religion, or have false religions; and there be but one true religion, which all have been ever bound to believe and profess; I can't see any heterodoxy in affirming that the means to effect this end of infinite wisdom must be as universal and extensive as the end itself; or that all men, at all times, must have had sufficient means to discover whatever God designed they should know and practice. I do not mean by this that all should have equal knowledge, but that all should have what is sufficient for the circumstances they are in.

B. What are those means which, you suppose, God has at all times given the whole race of mankind to enable them to discover what he wills?

A. I freely declare, that the use of those faculties by which men are distinguished from brutes is the only means they have to discern whether there is a God, and whether he concerns himself with human affairs, or has given them any laws, and what those laws are. And as men have no other faculties to judge with, so their using these after the best manner they can must answer the end for which God gave them, and justify their conduct.

If God will judge mankind as they are accountable, that is, as they are rational, the judgment must hold an exact proportion to the use they make of their reason. If God designed all mankind should at all times know what he wills them to know; and has given them no other means for this but the use of reason; reason, human reason, must then be that means. For as God has made us rational creatures, and reason tells us that 'tis his will that we act up to the dignity of our natures, so 'tis reason must tell us when we do so. As the eye is the sole judge of what is visible, the ear of what is audible, so reason of what is reasonable.

B. If men, having done all in their power to find out his will, should fall into opposite sentiments, must it not be the will of God that it should be so?

A. There is, I think, no way to avoid this objection, of God's willing contrarieties, but by supposing he requires nothing of men but what is founded on the nature of things, and the immutable relations they bear to one another.

B. This seems to my bewildered reason to imply that there was from the beginning but one true religion, which all men might know was their duty to embrace; and if this is true, I can't well conceive how this character can consist with Christianity, without allowing it, at the same time, to be "as old as the Creation." [1]

A. I shall attempt to show you that men, if they sincerely endeavor to discover the will of God, will perceive that there's a law of nature, or reason, which is so called as being a law which is common, or natural, to all rational creatures; and that this law, like its author, is absolutely perfect, eternal, and unchangeable; and that the design of the Gospel was not to add to, or take from this law, but to free men from that load of superstition which had been mixed with it. So true Christianity is not a religion of yesterday, but what God at the beginning dictated, and still continues to dictate to Christians as well as others. If I am so happy as to succeed in this attempt, I hope greatly to advance the honor of external revelation, by showing the perfect agreement between that and internal revelation.

But first, I must premise that, in supposing an external revelation, I take it for granted that there is

---

[1] The phrase is taken from Bishop Thomas Sherlock's sermon before the Society for the Propagation of the Gospel in Foreign Parts. On the title page, Tindal cites Sherlock's words: "The religion of the gospel is the true original religion of reason and nature, . . . and its precepts declarative of that original religion which was as old as the creation."

sufficient evidence of a person being sent from God
to publish it; nay, I further own that this divine person by living up to what he taught has set us a noble
example; and that as he was highly exalted for so
doing, so we, if we use our best endeavors, may
expect a suitable reward.

B. In order to succeed, you are to prove two things;
first, that the supreme governor of mankind has given
his subjects a universal law, which they, when they
come to the use of reason, are capable of knowing;
secondly, that the divine precepts must be the same,
whether internally or externally revealed.

A. If it be absurd to suppose that men, though
they lived ever so impiously and immorally, could do
nothing which God has forbid them; or if ever so
piously and virtuously, could not do any thing God
has commanded them; must there not always have
been a universal law so fully promulgated to mankind that they could have no just plea from their
ignorance not to be tried by it? Consequently, nothing less than its being founded on the nature of
things, and the relation they stand in to God and one
another, visible at all times to all mankind, could
make it thus universally promulgated. Can it be imagined, that if God has been so good to all other
animals as to give them, in all places whatsoever, sufficient means to act for their own preservation, that
he has had less kindness for the immortal souls of
those made after his own image, and has not given
them sufficient means to provide for their eternal
happiness? Can it be supposed an infinitely good and
gracious being, which gives men notice by their
senses what does good or hurt to their bodies, has
had less regard for their immortal parts, and has not
given them at all times by the light of their under-

standing sufficient means to discover what makes for the good of their souls?

To press this matter further, let me ask you whether there's not a clear and distinct light that enlightens all men; which, the moment they attend to it, makes them perceive those eternal truths which are the foundation of all our knowledge? And is it not God himself who immediately illuminates them? What better reason can you assign why infinite wisdom should act thus, except it be to give mankind standing rules to distinguish truth from falsehood, especially in matters of the highest consequence to their eternal as well as temporal happiness? This light of nature, like that of the sun, is universal, and would, did not men shut the eyes of their understanding, or suffer others to blind them, soon disperse all these mists and fogs which arise from false traditions or false interpretations of the true tradition.

II

That the religion of nature consists in observing those things which our reason, by considering the nature of God and man, and the relation we stand in to him and one another, demonstrates to be our duty; and that those things are plain; and likewise what they are.

A. By natural religion, I understand the belief of the existence of a God, and the sense and practice of those duties which result from the knowledge we, by our reason, have of him and his perfections; and of ourselves, and our own imperfections, and of the relation we stand in to him, and to our fellow-creatures; so that the religion of nature takes in everything that is founded on the reason and nature of things.

I suppose you will allow that it is evident by the light of nature that there is a God, or in other words, a being absolutely perfect, and infinitely happy in himself, who is the source of all other beings; and that what perfections soever the creatures have, they are wholly derived from him. It is equally demonstrable that the creatures can neither add to, or take away from, the happiness of that being; and that he could have no motive in framing his creatures, or in giving laws to such of them as he made capable of knowing his will, but their own good. It unavoidably follows, nothing can be a part of the divine law, but what tends to promote the common interest and mutual happiness of his rational creatures; and everything that does so must be a part of it.

As God can require nothing of us, but what makes for our happiness; so he, who can't envy us any happiness our nature is capable of, can forbid us those things only which tend to our hurt. From the consideration of these perfections, we cannot but have the highest veneration, nay, the greatest adoration and love for this supreme being, who, that we may not fail to be as happy as possible for such creatures to be, has made our acting for our present, to be the only means of obtaining our future happiness; and that we can't sin against him, but by acting against our reasonable natures.

Our reason, which gives us a demonstration of the divine perfections, affords us the same concerning the nature of those duties God requires, not only with relation to himself, but to ourselves, and one another.

With relation to ourselves, we can't but know how

we are to act, if we consider that God has endowed
man with such a nature as makes him necessarily
desire his own good; and, therefore, he may be sure
that God, who has bestowed this nature on him,
could not require anything of him in prejudice of it;
but on the contrary, that he should do everything
which tends to promote the good of it. The health of
the body and the vigor of the mind being highly
conducing to our good, we must be sensible we offend our maker if we indulge our senses to the
prejudice of these. We can't but know we ought to
use great moderation with relation to our passions,
or, in other words, govern all our actions by reason,
that and our true interest being inseparable. And,
in a word, whoever so regulates his natural appetites as will conduce most to the exercise of his
reason, the health of his body, and the pleasure of his
senses, taken and considered together (since herein
his happiness consists), may be certain he can never
offend his maker.

As to what God expects from man with relation
to each other, everyone must know his duty who
considers that the common parent of mankind has
the whole species alike under his protection, and will
equally punish him for injuring others, as he would
others for injuring him; and consequently that it is
his duty to deal with them, as he expects they
should deal with him in the like circumstances. Considering the variety of circumstances men are under,
and these continually changing, as well as being for
the most part unforeseen, it is impossible to have
rules laid down by any external revelation for every
particular case. Therefore, there must be some standing rule, discoverable by the light of nature, to direct
us in all such cases. And we can't be more certain

that it is the will of God that those effects which flow from natural causes should so flow, than we are that it is the will of God that men should observe whatever the nature of things, and the relation they have to one another, make fit to be observed, should be so observed.

And I may add that the better to cause men to observe those rules which make for their mutual benefit, infinite goodness has sown in their hearts seeds of pity, humanity and tenderness, which, without much difficulty, cannot be eradicated; but nothing operates more strongly than that desire men have of being in esteem, credit, and reputation with their fellow creatures, not to be obtained without acting on the principles of natural justice, equity, benevolence, etc. In a word, as a most beneficent disposition in the supreme being is the source of all his actions in relation to his creatures, so he has implanted in man, whom he has made after his own image, a love for his species; the gratifying of which in doing acts of benevolence, compassion and good will, produces a pleasure that never satiates, as on the contrary actions of ill nature, envy, malice, etc., never fail to produce shame, confusion, and everlasting self-reproach.

From these premises, I think, we may boldly draw this conclusion, that if religion consists in the practice of those duties that result from the relation we stand in to God and man, our religion must always be the same. If God is unchangeable, our duty to him must be so too; if human nature continues the same, and men at all times stand in the same relation to one another, the duties which result from those relations must always be the same. And consequently, our duty to God and man must, from the beginning of the world to the end, always be the same, always alike plain and perspicuous, and can neither be changed in whole or part. Consequently, whoever acts what is best for himself, both in a public and private capacity, does all that either God or man can require. Hence I think we may define true religion to consist in a constant disposition of mind to do all the good we can, and thereby render ourselves acceptable to God in answering the end of his creation.

III

That the perfection and happiness of all rational beings, supreme as well as subordinate, consists in living up to the dictates of their nature.

A. The principle from which all human actions flow is the desire of happiness. The happiness of all beings whatever consists in the perfection of their nature; and the nature of a rational being is most perfect when it is perfectly rational, that is, when it governs all its actions by the rules of right reason. A man's happiness and duty must consist in the same things, since no one can be obliged to do anything that does not some way or another contribute to his happiness.

By living according to the rules of right reason we more and more implant in us the moral perfections of God. We then, if I may say so, "live the life of God" (cf. Rom. 6:10f.); that is, we, in our place and station, live after the same manner, and by the same rules as he does in his. Hence we may contemplate the great dignity of our rational nature, since our reason for kind, though not for degree, is of the same nature with that of God's; nay, it is our reason which makes us the image of God himself, and is the common bond which unites heaven and earth, the creatures and the creator.

Herein appears the great wisdom of God, in making men's misery and happiness the necessary and inseparable consequence of their actions, and that rational actions carry with them their own reward, and irrational their own punishment. This, I think, can't be denied as long as there are some actions naturally beneficial to us, and others as hurtful, and that there is no virtue but what has some good inseparably annexed to it, and no vice but what as necessarily carries with it some evil.

In this life, it is true, we can't be perfectly happy, as subject to diseases and disasters. We are imperfect ourselves, and have none to converse with but imperfect creatures. And yet if we act according to the dictates of right reason, we shall receive, even here, true inward comfort and satisfaction; and hereafter, when we are freed from those imperfections, complete happiness. How can it be otherwise, since good and evil have their foundation in the essential difference of things, and their nature is fixed and immovable.

Had God, from time to time, spoke to all mankind in their several languages, and his words had miraculously conveyed the same ideas to all persons, yet he could not speak more plainly than he has done by the things themselves, and the relation which reason shows there is between them. And I may add that most of the particular rules laid down in the Gospel for our direction are spoken after such figurative manner, that except we judge of their meaning, not merely by the letter, but by what the law of nature antecedently declares to be our duty, they are apt to lead us wrong. But God's will is so clearly and fully manifested in the book of nature that he who runs may read it.

B. Do divines always give this character of Christianity; do they never distinguish it from the religion of nature, by supposing it contains certain arbitrary precepts?

A. When they consider how repugnant it is to the nature of God to give any arbitrary commands, then indeed the force of truth obliges them to declare there's nothing in religion but what tends to the good of mankind; but if at any time they talk otherwise, it is for the sake of such things as either directly or indirectly serve their interest.

IV

That not only the matter of all God's laws, but the penalties annexed to them are for the good of mankind, even of those who suffer for the breach of them.

B. Though it be allowed that God framed his laws and, consequently, the sanctions that make them laws, for the good of man, yet a due regard to his own honor, the dignity of his laws and government, will oblige him to punish those who violate his laws, as for an injury done to himself, distinct from the harm that by the breach of them accrues to his creatures.

A. As it was for the sake of man that he gave him

laws, so he executes them purely for the same reason, since upon his own account he can't be in the least affected whether his laws be, or be not, observed. Consequently in punishing, no more than rewarding, does he act as a party, much less an injured party, who wants satisfaction or reparation of honor. Indeed, to suppose it is highly to dishonor him, since God, as he never can be injured, so he can never want reparation, and he who is infinitely satisfied in himself can gain no addition of satisfaction by his creatures observing his laws. Even among men none ought to be punished, (since what is past can't be helped) but to prevent a future breach of the law.

Our greatest felicity consists in having such an impartial and disinterested judge as well as legislator that, whether he punishes or rewards, he acts alike for our good, that being the end of all his laws and consequently of the penalties as well as rewards which make them laws; whereas your common systems of divinity represent him full of wrath and fury, ready to glut himself with revenge for the injuries he has suffered by the breach of his laws.

The greatest difference in this case between God and man is that the most powerful monarch on earth is of the same nature with his subjects, and his good involved in the good of the whole, and by the breach of his laws may be injured, and as a party injured may exact reparation and satisfaction. But this without blasphemy can't be said of God, whose nature is infinitely superior to that of man. Therefore, in doing acts of justice he can't, like the monarchs of this world, propose any security to himself, but acts purely for the good of his creatures. And the effects of his justice (they never extending to annihilation) must not only be for the good of others, but even of the persons punished, because God, whose love infinitely exceeds that of mortal parents, chastises his children (and all mankind are alike his offspring) because he loves them, and designs their amendment. Consequently, whatever punishment he inflicts must be a mark of his love, in not suffering his creatures to remain in that miserable state which is inseparable from sin and wickedness. As God's infinite goodness appears in the sanctions as well as matter of his laws, so his infinite wisdom knows how to adjust the punishment to the offense, that it may be exactly fitted to produce the desired amendment.

V

That God requires nothing for his own sake, no, not the worship we are to render him, nor the faith we are to have in him.

B. Your arguing from the nature of God that everything, consequently faith in him, and even the worship and service we render to him, is wholly for our own sake, will hardly go down with the bulk of mankind, who imagine they by those acts do him some real service.

A. If they think so, it is a sign they have not been well instructed; the most eminent of our divines would teach them that prayer itself, God knowing before-hand what we will ask, chiefly becomes a duty as it raises in us a due contemplation of the divine attributes, and an acknowledgement of his great and constant goodness, and serves to keep up a constant sense of our dependence on him, and as it disposes us to imitate those perfections we adore in him, in being kind and beneficent to one another. There are few so gross as to imagine we can direct infinite wisdom in the dispensation of providence, or persuade him to alter those laws he contrived before the foundation of the world for putting things in a regular course.

Therefore, if from excess of devotion, a man neglects the duties of civil life, he is so far from doing a thing acceptable to God that he mistakes the end of religion, which is to render him as perfect as may be in all moral duties whatever.

B. There's one difficulty which to me seems insuperable, how to make the faith required by the religion of nature and of the Gospel to have the same views, and tend to the same end.

A. If faith in God himself, no more than in any other act of religion, is required not for God's sake, but our own, can faith in one sent by God be required for any other end? Especially considering, that no person is ever the more known to posterity because his name is transmitted to them. When we say "Caesar" conquered "Pompey," we having no idea of either can only mean, somebody conquered somebody. And have we more distinct ideas of "Jesus" and "Pilate"? And though we had a personal idea of the former, he could receive no advantage or disadvantage by what we thought of him. And if faith in him was required for a cause antecedent to his being so sent, founded in his and our nature, and the relation we always stood in to him, would not the eternal reason of things have made it manifest? That which concerned all must be knowable by all, for which reason the apostle says, "that which may be known of God" (and none can know that which may not be known) "was manifest in the Gentiles." (Rom. 1:19)

The end of Christ's coming seems not to teach men new duties, but (repentance being the first thing preached by him and his apostles both to Jews and Gentiles) to repent of the breach of known duties. And Jesus does not say he was "sent" to all "Israel, but to the lost sheep of the house of Israel" (Matt. 15:24); and that the "Son of Man is come to save that which is lost." (Matt. 18:11) And his parable about the lost sheep (Lk. 15:7) supposed all were not lost. And when it was objected to him that he kept company with sinners, he owns the charge and says, "the whole need no physician, but they that are sick" (Matt. 9:12); which would have been an improper answer if he thought that all stood in need of him and his spiritual physic. And to confirm this, he adds, "I am not come to call the righteous, but sinners to repentance." (Matt. 9:13) Which is dividing mankind into two parts, the whole or righteous, and the sick or sinners, and that his business was entirely with the latter. In religion there are no nostrums, or secrets, but all may know what God requires of all; and there is but one universal remedy for all sick persons, repentance and amendment. They, certainly, are whole, and need no physician, who do of themselves what will make them acceptable to him, living as those whom Christ came to reform were taught to live. Is it not absurd to suppose that till then none had sufficient means given them to answer the end for which all were created?

What can be more required than those qualifications as will make Jesus in the last day declare, "Come ye blessed of my Father, inherit the Kingdom prepared for you from the beginning of the world?"

(Matt. 25:34) And what are those qualifications, but living up to the law of reason, in exercising acts of benevolence, goodness, etc.? St. Paul in the first chapter to the Romans is very large in showing that the Gentiles could not plead ignorance of their duty, either to God or man, and as sinning against knowledge were inexcusable. And pursuing the same subject in the second, he says that "God who is no respecter of persons" (Rom. 2:11) will deal with every one both Jew and Gentile according to their deeds. And does not St. Paul in another place put our future state on the same foot, in supposing we shall be dealt with at the last day "according to what we have done in the body, whether good or bad." (II Cor. 5:10) In short, if the tree is to be known by its fruit, and it brings forth good fruit, the means by which this good fruit is produced are not material; but if it does not, no means whatever can hinder it from being "hewn down, and cast into the fire." (Matt. 7:19f.)

Faith considered in itself can neither be a virtue or a vice, because men can no otherwise believe than as things appear to them. Nay, can there be a higher affront to God than to suppose he requires men to judge otherwise than the faculties he has given them enable them to do? Therefore faith is only to be esteemed by the works it produces, for the strongest faith may be worse than no faith at all.

If charity, which comprehends doing all possible good to our fellow-creatures, is to be destroyed for the sake of faith; or if incapacities, fines, imprisonments, rods, gibbets, racks, and fire, are marks of charity, the Christian world has outdone all mankind in acts of charity. But the description St. Paul gives of charity is so far from requiring us to make others suffer that itself "suffers long, seeks not her own, bears all things, endures all things," (I Cor. 13) and strictly enjoins us so to do. Here is the practice of the Christian world on the side of faith, sacrificing charity and all that is valuable to it; and on the other side, Christ and his apostles preferring charity before it.

If man, as our divines maintain against Hobbes, is a social creature, who naturally loves his own species, and is full of pity, tenderness, and benevolence; and if reason. which is the proper nature of man, can never lead men to any thing but universal love and kindness, and there be no part of natural religion, or any faith it requires, but highly tends to improve this kind and benign temper; how comes it to pass that what is taught for religion in so many places of Christendom has transformed this mild and gentle creature into fierce and cruel, and made him act with rage and fury against those who never did, or intended, him the least harm? Is not this chiefly owing to such a "faith" as "works" not "by love," (Gal. 5:6) and such a zeal as, not being according to knowledge, has destroyed all good works, and is utterly inconsistent with the end of all religion?

VI

That the religion of nature is an absolutely perfect religion; and that external revelation can neither add to nor take from its perfection; and that true religion, whether internally or externally revealed, must be the same.

A. Let me ask you why you believe the Gospel a law of absolute perfection, incapable of any addition, diminution, or alteration?

B. Because 'tis the last law of God's giving.

A. Were there any thing in this argument, it makes wholly for the law of nature, since that is not only the first but the last law of God's giving, if that can be said to be last which is eternal—a law by which God governs his own actions, and by which he expects all the rational world should govern theirs. And therefore, notwithstanding the promulgation of the Gospel, he continues daily to implant it in the minds of all men, Christians as well as others; and consequently, 'tis as necessary for them as for others, as necessary since as before the coming of Christ. And I may add, too, not only necessary to be observed in this world, and ten thousand more, were there so many, but in heaven itself, and that too for ever.

B. Should I grant that my argument, from the Gospel's being the last law of God's giving, does not fully prove its absolute perfection, yet it will undeniably follow from the great agreement there is between that and the law of nature, it neither forbidding what that requires, nor requiring what that forbids; and in a word, containing nothing in it unworthy, but every thing worthy, of an absolutely perfect law-giver.

A. In saying this, you own the law of nature to be the standard of perfection, and that by it we must judge antecedently to any traditional religion what is, or is not, a law absolutely perfect, and worthy of such a being for its legislator. I desire no more than to be allowed that there's a religion of nature and reason written in the hearts of every one of us from the first creation, by which all mankind must judge of the truth of any instituted religion whatever; and if it varies from the religion of nature and reason in any one particular, nay, in the minutest circumstance, that alone is an argument which makes all things else that can be said for its support totally ineffectual. If so, must not natural religion and external revelation, like two tallies, exactly answer one another, without any other difference between them but as to the manner of their being delivered? And how can it be otherwise? Can laws be imperfect, where a legislator is absolutely perfect?

To plead that the Gospel is incapable of any additions, because the will of God is immutable and his law too perfect to need them, is an argument, was Christianity a new religion, which destroys itself; since from the time it commenced you must own God is mutable, and that such additions have been made to the all-perfect laws of infinite wisdom as constitute a new religion. The reason why the law of nature is immutable is because it is founded on the unalterable reason of things. And in truth all laws, whether the law of nations, or those of particular countries, are only the law of nature adjusted and accommodated to circumstances.

In a word, if the highest internal excellence, the greatest plainness and simplicity, unanimity, universality, antiquity, nay, eternity, can recommend a law, all these do in an eminent degree belong to the law of nature. A law which does not depend on the uncertain meaning of words and phrases in dead languages, much less on types, metaphors, allegories, parables, or on the skill or honesty of weak and designing transcribers (not to mention translators) for many ages together, but on the immutable relation of things always visible to the whole world.

VII

*That natural and revealed religion having the
same end, their precepts must be the same.*

B. Allowing that the natural knowledge we have
of God, ourselves, and our fellow creatures, is the
foundation of all religion, may not external revelation, building on this foundation, effect a larger and
nobler edifice, by extending it to such things as the
light of nature could not reach, without contradicting
any thing it teaches?

A. I thought I had obviated this objection by proving that the religion of nature was so perfect that
nothing could be added to it; and that the truth of
all revelation was to be judged of by its agreement
with it. However, since this objection is the most
plausible of any you have yet made, I reply that if
our natural notions of the divine perfections demonstrate that God will require nothing of his creatures
but what tends to their good, whatsoever is of this
kind is a superstructure that belongs to the law of
nature.

By the law of nature as well as the Gospel, the
honor of God and the good of man being the two
grand or general commandments, all particular precepts must be comprehended under these two, and
belong alike to the law of nature as well as the Gospel; and what does not, can belong to neither. And
yet these would be to little purpose, could not reason
tell men how to apply them in all conditions and
circumstances of life.

B. Supposing no particular precepts can oblige if

they chance to clash with either of those commandments, yet what is to be done if these two interfere
with one another? Must the good of man or the honor
of God take place?

A. These two grand laws are in effect the same,
since what promotes the honor of God necessarily
promotes the good of man. The more we love and
honor God, the more we shall imitate him in our extensive love to our fellow-creatures, who are equally
the children of God. The greater our veneration is
for our maker, the more it will excite us to copy
those perfections of goodness and benevolence we
adore in him. So that the duty of a truly religious
person and of a good subject and citizen are the same
with relation to God and man. For the more he
honors God, the more zealous will he be to act the
patriot; and the more he does that, the more he
honors God, because the happier men are, the more
reason they have to honor that God who made
them so.

Though we have received our all from God, we
can give him nothing; and therefore the only way
we have to show our real gratitude to our great
creator and benefactor is to be as useful as we can
to his creatures, whom we ought to love as ourselves.
If there can now be a sin against the Holy Ghost, I
should not scruple to say it is making religion the
means of destroying the end of all religion, and ren-
dering the creature miserable on pretense of doing
honor to the creator, who, as he has impressed on
bodies, in order to preserve the natural world, a tendency to each other, so he has implanted in minds,
the better to support the moral world, a tendency to
be kind and beneficent to one another.

B. This, I own, is a beautiful description of human

nature, and a strong evidence of the goodness of its author; but do men act as if they had such an innate love for virtue, or such a benevolent disposition?

A. An execrable superstition has in many Christian countries, in a manner, extinguished these kind sentiments, and even all humanity and pity, insomuch that the tender sex can rejoice to hear the shrieks and see the agonies of men expiring under the most cruel tortures. Therefore I shall not scruple to affirm that he who steadfastly adheres to what the light of nature teaches him concerning the divine goodness, as he will avoid the comfortless prospect of the atheist, the perpetual anxiety of the superstitious, the wild perturbation of the enthusiast, and the pernicious fury of the bigot, so he can't fail of the true religion, happily seated in the middle between these extremes. And as such a person can't but love God as he ought, so in imitation of the divine goodness, which influences all his actions, he will contribute his utmost to the good of others, and his love and kindness will be as extensive as human nature; and going on rational and evident principles he will act a steady uniform part. What can be wanting to a man who has this heavenly, this god-like disposition, which renders him happy in himself, and, as far as it is in his power, makes the whole world so too?

VIII

That the not adhering to those notions reason dictates concerning the nature of God has been the occasion of all superstition, and all those innumerable mischiefs that mankind, on the account of religion, have done either to themselves or one another.

A. Had the heathen believed God to have been a purely spiritual, invisible being, they could never have supposed him visible to mortals, or have thought that an unlimited being could appear under the limited form of a man or other animal; or that an omnipresent being could any more be present in one place or creature than another; or that such a being could be confined to a small spot of earth, while another equally omnipresent was in heaven, and a third descending from thence, etc. Or that one God could be sent on the errand of another God, after the manner that God Mercury was by God Jupiter; though there was nothing too absurd for the heathen to believe, after they had destroyed the unity of God, except it was that Jupiter and Mercury, the sender and the sent, were the same God.

The primitive fathers bitterly inveighed against these heathenish notions. Justin Martyr, for instance, says: "None who have the least sense will dare to affirm that the maker and father of the universe did appear in a small spot of earth; the God of the universe can neither ascend nor descend or come into any place." Tertullian says: "He would not believe the sovereign God descended into the womb of a woman, even though the Scriptures itself should say it." Thus the fathers exposed the pagan polytheism.

A good deal more might be said on this head, but now I shall briefly consider what pernicious effects the having wrong and unnatural conceptions of the deity has occasioned among men with relation to themselves and one another.

Had not numbers in all ages thought that God delighted in the pain and misery of his creatures, they could never have imagined that the best way to render themselves acceptable to him was by tor-

menting themselves with immoderate watchings, fast-
ings, penances, and mortifications of all sorts, and the
greater the more pleasing. Even at present there are
among Christians, Mahometans, and pagans numbers
of men who devote themselves to exercises full of
pain and corporal sufferings, and either wound or
mangle their own persons. Indeed, the superstitious
everywhere think the less mercy they show to their
bodies, the more mercy God will show to their souls.
'Twas owing to these superstitious notions that such
numbers of monasteries and nunneries were founded
to the great oppression and depopulation of the Christian world.

Had such notions been adhered to concerning the
divine goodness as the light of nature dictates, the
Egyptians and some other pagan nations could never
have thought that cutting off the foreskin could have
been esteemed a religious duty acceptable to a good
and gracious God, who makes nothing in vain, much
less what requires the cutting off, even with extreme
danger as well as anguish. Had nature required such
an operation, nature, being always the same, would
still have required it.

The heathen world must have very gross conceptions, not only of their inferior Gods, but of the
father of Gods and men, when they imagined him of
so cruel a nature as to be delighted with the butcher-
ing of innocent animals, and that the stench of burnt
flesh should be such a "sweet-smelling savour in his
nostrils" as to atone for the wickedness of men. 'Tis
probable that the heathen priests who shared with
their Gods, and reserved the best bits for themselves,
had the chief hand in this as well as in all other
gainful superstitions; while the deluded people, who
many times suffered by the scarcity of provisions,

caused by the great number of sacrifices, were at vast expense in maintaining these holy butchers, whose very trade inspired them with cruelty.

The pagans' sacrificing of beasts was not so bad in itself as what it soon occasioned, human sacrifices, which, men being of greater value than beasts, were believed to be more acceptable.

B. I pity those deluded people, and wonder how men can persuade themselves that the mercy of heaven can be purchased by such barbarities as human nature left to itself would start at.

A. Had the author of the Epistle to the Hebrews thought the Jews abhorred all human sacrifices, he would not, at least without some apology for the lawfulness of human sacrifices, have declared one such sacrifice, where the same person was both sacrificer and sacrifice, to have been of infinite value, in saying that "Christ offered up himself"; and that "He put away sin by the sacrifice of himself," and endeavored to show the Hebrews that the blood of the beasts that were sacrificed was of no value in comparison of "the blood of Christ who, through the eternal Spirit, offered up himself without spot to God." (Heb. 7:27; 9:26; 9:13f.)

B. Yet the Christian religion, sure, forbids all human sacrifices.

A. If putting innocent and conscientious men to death on account of religion may be called sacrificing them, there have been many more human sacrifices than ever were before in the world.

B. I must own, this bigotry which has had such terrible effects among Christians was little felt or known in the pagan world.

A. The fiery zeal of such wretches is capable of any mischief. Most other men, though ever so wicked, have some remains of pity and humanity, some checks of conscience, and though ever so much provoked, time will assuage their anger. But the bigot feels not the least remorse, nor can time abate his fury. And he is so far from having any pity that he glories in the cruelest actions, and thinks the more hellish facts he commits, the more he merits heaven, and very often gets the reputation of a saint for acting the part of a devil. So that his notions of God and religion serve only to make him infinitely a worse man than if he had been without any belief.

B. You represent bigotry more odious than it is, in making it worse than atheism itself.

A. As bigotry is the worst sort of superstition, so you know the philosophers in general suppose superstition to be worse than atheism itself. I grant that next to a real bigot, an atheist in masquerade may do most mischief; but then it is by hiding the atheist and personating the bigot, and under color of promoting religion advancing priestcraft.

But to return, if what the light of nature teaches us concerning the divine perfections is not only sufficient to hinder us from falling into superstition of any kind whatever, but demonstrates what God, from his infinite wisdom and goodness can or cannot command, how is it possible that the law of nature and grace can differ? How can it be conceived that God's laws, whether internally or externally revealed, are not at all times the same, when the author of them is and has been immutably the same for ever?

IX

Human happiness being the ultimate design and end of all traditional, as well as original revela-

tion, they must both prescribe the same means,
since those means which at one time promote
human happiness equally promote it at all times.

B. Should I grant you that natural and revealed religion, as they have the same author must have the same end, and that the ultimate end of all God's laws is human happiness, yet there are several things to be considered as subordinate ends. Here, may not original and traditional religion differ, since 'tis allowed by all that the means to promote these ends are various and mutable?

A. Your allowing these means to be various and mutable supposes no such means so prescribed in the Gospel but that, agreeably to the law of nature, they are to be varied as best suits the end for which they were ordained. The more necessary any end is, there's the more reason for people to be left at liberty to consider in the vast variety of circumstances, and those too perpetually changing, what means may be most proper for obtaining that end. Mankind are not to expect that the divine legislator will, from time to time, make any change in his laws, and communicate them to all nations in the languages they understand; nor can there be any judges with a power to oblige people by their determinations, because such a power, being without any appeal, is the same as a power to make divine laws. Consequently, the only tribunal God has erected here on earth (distinct from that he has mediately appointed by men for their mutual defense) is every man's own conscience, which, as it can't but tell him that God is the author of all things, so it must inform him that whatever he finds himself obliged to do by the circumstances he is in, he is obliged by God himself, who has disposed things in that order and placed him in those circumstances.

B. You know that divines, though they can't deny what you say to be true in general, yet they think there's an exception as to church-matters, and that here men are not permitted to use such means as they themselves think best, but such only as those who set up to be their spiritual governors shall appoint.

A. While every church, or congregation of Christians, as in the apostolical days, chose and maintained their own ministers, and ordered among themselves whatever required a special determination, no inconveniences happened. But as soon as this simple and natural method was broke, and the clergy were formed into a closely-united body, with that subordination and dependence they had on one another, the Christian world was enslaved, and religion forced to give way to destructive superstition.

In a word, if we consider the infinite variety of circumstances, the different manners and customs that prevail in different places, the prejudices of the weak, ignorant, and superstitious, and the designs of ambitious men, there's nothing of a mutable nature, if once esteemed immutably fixed by God, but must sometimes become prejudicial to the end 'twas intended to promote. There are but two ways of avoiding this inconvenience: either to suppose that the founder of this religion will, from time to time, himself ordain such alterations in things of a mutable nature as those circumstances which are different in different places do require; or else, that he has left the parties concerned to act in all places according to discretion in such mutable matters.

B. The reasons you have given do not fully satisfy me but that some things may be required by God as governor of the universe which are merely positive; nay, that rites and ceremonies, signs, or symbols might be arbitrarily enjoined, and so intermixed with matters of morality as to bind the consciences of all men at all times.

A. This alone is the point that must decide this question, whether natural and revealed religion do really differ. Though 'tis difficult to prove a negative, yet I think I can fully show you, by adding other reasons to those already mentioned, that God can't give mankind any such precepts.

X

> *God does not act arbitrarily, or interpose unnecessarily, but leaves those things that can only be considered as means (and as such are in their own nature mutable) to human discretion, to determine as it thinks most conducing to those things which are in their own nature obligatory.*

A. As to matters relating to the worship of God, it is the voice of nature that God should be publicly worshipped, and that men should do this in the most convenient way, by appointing amongst themselves time, place, persons, and all other things which require special determination. Certainly there's as much reason that things of this nature should be left to human discretion as any other whatever, considering the different conditions and circumstances which Christians may be under, and the handle designing

men might otherwise take to impose upon weak persons what they please, on pretense of divine right.

There's nothing in itself so indifferent, either as to
matter or manner, but if it be engrafted into religion,
and monopolized by the priests, may endanger the
substance of it. This has been plainly shown by those
divines who, at the Reformation and since, have
argued against all impositions; they have proved that
most of the corruptions of popery began at some
rites which seemed at first very innocent, but were
afterwards abused to superstition and idolatry, and
swelled up to that bulk as to oppress and stifle true
religion with their number and weight. Indeed,
there's no sect but complains how superstitiously rites
and ceremonies are used by all, except themselves.

Whatsoever is in itself indifferent, whether as to
matter or manner, must be so to an all-wise being,
who judges of things as they are; and for the same
reason that he commands things which are good,
and forbids those which are evil, he leaves men at
liberty in all things indifferent.

'Tis men's not being governed by the reason of
things which makes them divided about trifles, and
lay the utmost stress on such things as wise men
would be ashamed of. 'Tis on the account of these
that the different sects set the highest value on themselves and think they are the peculiar favorites of
heaven, while they condemn all others for opinions
and practices not more senseless than those themselves look on as essentials. What reason has a papist,
for instance, to laugh at an Indian, who thinks it
contributes to his future happiness to die with a
cow's tail in his hands, while he lays as great a stress
on rubbing a dying man with oil.

While priests of what denomination soever pretend

authority to absolve sinners, and the people are so void of sense as to rely on their absolution, natural religion, which puts the whole stress on internal penitence and all true virtue in the soul, will be despised as allowing no commuting or compounding with heaven. Indeed, all such commuting or compounding powers, wherever they are supposed to be lodged, serve as a bank of credit for the transgressors, and are a mighty incitement to all manner of villainy. This doctrine, that one man may not only merit for himself by doing more than God requires of him, but that the merit of such actions may be transferred to another who has done less than God requires of him, has been a great incitement to wickedness; and those who have acted a most immoral part during their whole lives have believed they might comfortably rely on it, nothing being thought too hard for merit and mediation.

The law of nature leaves men at liberty to act as they please in all indifferent matters; and if any traditionary law abridges this liberty, so far 'tis contrary to that of nature, and invades those rights which nature and its author has given mankind. And herein the whole of human liberty consists, the contrary being a state of mere vassalage; and men are more or less miserable, according as they are more or less deprived of this liberty, especially in matters of mere religion, wherein they ought to be most free.

XI

The supposing things merely positive to be made the ingredients of religion is inconsistent with the good of mankind as well as the honor of God.

A. It is a general observation in history that where anything has had the appearance only of piety, and might be observed without any virtue in the soul, it easily found entertainment among superstitious nations. A strict observance of such things as require no virtue in the practice, and may with great ease be punctually observed, makes the superstitious liable to be everywhere cheated by your Tartuffes, while men who put the whole stress on morality are represented not only as enemies to religion, but even as encouragers of immorality and mere libertines, because they are for liberty in thinking, though this can't fail to make men see the folly of licentiousness in acting.

Upon the whole, nothing can be of worse consequence than thus to depreciate morality by mixing things of an indifferent nature with it, because, as experience shows, men are more or less virtuous according to the value they put on virtue; and can a man who acts contrary to reason not be an enemy to a religion founded on reason? The precepts of natural religion and the rules of right reason can't but make strong impressions on rational creatures; what is fixed on the minds of men, and wrought in, as it were, with their very constitution, can't easily be broke through; human nature is apt to start and recoil at any such attempt. And yet some have found a most effectual way to break through it, by teaching men that the most moral actions, without a right notion forsooth in certain things of another nature, are to be looked on as *splendida peccata* [1] and partaking of the nature of sin.

---

[1] An allusion to the Augustinian notion that virtues, apart from love of God, are deficient, and become "splendid vices."

It is the chief business of preachers to show the reasonableness of the doctrines they teach, as the most effectual way of operating on rational creatures. All the laws of natural religion being built on their own reasonableness, they who attend to the dictates of their reason can scarce fail to pay a ready and cheerful obedience to all its laws. But when men take things merely on authority, and would have taken the contrary on the same authority, reason is discarded, and rational motives cease to operate; nor can men any longer perform moral duties with a free and cheerful mind, but slavishly obey, out of fear, the supposed arbitrary commands of a being too mighty to be contended with.

As long as men believe the good of the society is the supreme law, they will think it their duty to be governed by that law; and believing God requires nothing of them but what is for the good of mankind, will place the whole of their religion in benevolent actions, and to the utmost of their abilities copy after the divine original.

All religion inclines men to imitate what they worship; they who believe God will damn men for things not moral must believe that in order to prevent damnable opinions from spreading, and to show themselves holy as their heavenly father is holy, they can't show too much enmity to those against whom God declares an eternal enmity, or plague them enough in this life, upon whom in the life to come God will pour down the plagues of eternal vengeance. Hence it is that animosity, enmity, and hatred has over-run the Christian world; and men, for the sake of these notions, have exercised the utmost cruelties on one another.

Though we cry up the great advantage we have

above all other animals in being capable of religion, yet those animals we despise for want of it herd most socially together, except such carnivorous creatures which necessity separates. The ants, notwithstanding they have stings, are crowded in vast numbers in the same hillock and, having all things in common, seem to have no other contention among them but who shall be most active in carrying on the common interest of their small republic. And much the same may be said of bees and other animals. Yet men, though they can't subsist but in society, and have hands, speech, and reason to qualify them for the blessing of it above all other animals; nay, what is more, have religion, designed to unite them in the firm bonds of love and friendship, and to engage them to vie with one another in all good offices; and the good natured laity too have, at a vast expense, hired persons to inculcate these generous notions; yet alas! in spite of all these helps and motives, religion has been made by these very persons a pretense to render men unsociable, fierce and cruel, and to act everything destructive to their common welfare.

B. Granting that a deluge of every thing that's ill has overflowed Christendom, and does so still in most places, and that religion has been made a handle for such barbarities as human nature, left to itself, would startle at, yet how is this to be remedied?

A. Education is justly esteemed a second nature, and its force so strong that few can wholly shake off its prejudices, even in things unreasonable and unnatural. Must it not have the greatest efficacy in things agreeable to reason and suitable to human nature? Let those, therefore, who have the education of youth recommend morality as the end of all religion; and let everything not tending to promote the honor of God and the good of man be accounted superstition; let the youth be taught to join the ideas of virtue with the ideas of beauty, pleasure, and happiness, and the ideas of vice with those of deformity, grief, and misery; there would then be little room for so odious a thing as vice to take possession of people's minds, and jostle out virtue so firmly rooted.

B. But if everything, as you contend, ought to be looked on as superstitious which is not of a moral nature, superstition has spread itself over the face of the earth, and prevailed more or less in all times and places.

A. 'Tis the observation of naturalists that there is no species of creatures but what have some innate weakness, which makes them an easy prey to other animals that know how to take the advantage of it. Now the peculiar foible of mankind is superstition, which at all times had made them liable to be practiced on, not by creatures of different species but by those of their own who, by a confident pretense of knowing more than their neighbors, have first circumvented the many, the credulous and unwary, and afterwards forced the free-thinking few into an outward compliance. The more superstition the people have, the easier they may be imposed on by designing ecclesiastics. And the less religion the clergy have, the more unanimous they will be in carrying on their common interest. And when the clergy are without religion, and the people abound in superstition, the church, you may be sure, is in a flourishing condition, but in great danger when men place their religion in morality.

There are two ways which never fail to make superstition prevail: mysteries to amuse the enthusiasts, especially the pretenders to deep learning, and all that admire what they do not understand; and gaudy shows and pompous ceremonies, to bewitch the vulgar.

B. Sensible things make a deeper impression on the minds of the common people than words; and, therefore, the using symbolical representations being for the advantage of religion, why may they not be ordained of God?

A. If you must have recourse to words to explain the signification of such symbols, are they not arbitrary marks whose meaning cannot be known but from words, and, not being capable of expressing things more fully than words, wholly needless as to that purpose? Nay, words themselves being but arbitrary signs, to multiply such signs needlessly would be very absurd.

As to sensible things making a deeper impression on the common people, that, I presume, is a just reason against their use in religion. Because the vulgar, who generally look no further than externals, do not use them barely, as they do words, to express their meaning, but conceive in them I know not what internal holiness, and think such symbolical representations as necessary as the things represented by them; nay, by degrees forgetting the reason of their institution, come to idolize them, as the Israelites did the brazen serpent. And this the people have always done in all religions whatever where these symbolical representations have been used.

And now don't you think we may justly conclude that whatsoever God requires of us to believe, or practice, is purely for our good; and consequently that no belief, or practice, which does not contribute to that good can come from God; and therefore as

long as we adhere to what reason reveals to us concerning the goodness of God, by admitting everything into religion which makes for the good of man,
and nothing that does not, we can't mistake our duty
either to God or man?

XII

*That they who, to magnify revelation, weaken
the force of the religion of reason and nature,
strike at all religion; and that there can't be two
independent rules for the government of human
actions.*

B. In my opinion, you lay too great stress on
fallible reason, and too little on infallible revelation.

A. Whatever is true by reason can never be false
by revelation. If God can't be deceived himself, or be
willing to deceive men, the light he hath given to
distinguish between religious truth and falsehood cannot, if duly attended to, deceive them in things of so
great moment.

They who do not allow reason to judge in matters
of opinion or speculation are guilty of as great absurdity as the papists, who will not allow the senses
to be judges in the case of transubstantiation, though
a matter directly under their cognizance. Nay, the
absurdity, I think, is greater in the first case, because
reason is to judge whether our senses are deceived.
If no texts ought to be admitted as a proof in a matter contrary to sense, they ought, certainly, as little
to be admitted in any point contrary to reason.

In a word, to suppose any thing in revelation inconsistent with reason, and at the same time pretend it to be the will of God, is not only to destroy that proof on which we conclude it to be the will of God, but even the proof of the being of a God. If our reasoning faculties duly attended to can deceive us, we can't be sure of the truth of any one proposition, but every thing would be alike uncertain, and we should for ever fluctuate in a state of universal skepticism. Which shows how absurdly they act who, on pretense of magnifying tradition, endeavor to weaken the force of reason, and thereby foolishly sap the foundation to support the superstructure.

B. I don't think we ought to have the same regard for reason as men had formerly, when that was the sole rule God had given them for the government of their actions; since now we Christians have two supreme, independent rules, reason and revelation, and both require an absolute obedience.

A. I can't see how that is possible; for if you are to be governed by the latter, that supposes you must take every thing on trust, or merely because it's said by those for whose dictates you are to have an implicit faith. For to examine into the truth of what they say is renouncing their authority; as, on the contrary, if men are to be goverend by their reason, they are not to admit anything further than as they see it reasonable. To suppose both consistent is to suppose it consistent to take, and not to take, things on trust.

To receive religion on the account of authority supposes that if the same authority promulgated a different religion we should be obliged to receive it; and indeed, it's an odd jumble to prove the truth of a book by the truth of the doctrines it contains, and at the same time conclude those doctrines to be true because contained in that book; and yet this is a jumble everyone makes who contends for men's being absolutely governed both by reason and authority.

B. Though reason may be the judge, yet the Scripture, we say, is the rule by which reason must judge of the truth of things.

A. If it be such a rule, must it not have all the qualifications necessary to make it so? But if reason must tell us what those qualifications are, and whether they are to be found in Scripture; and if one of those qualifications is that the Scripture must be agreeable to the nature of things; does not that suppose the nature of things to be the standing rule by which we must judge of the truth of all those doctrines contained in the Scriptures? So that the Scripture can only be a secondary rule, as far as it is found agreeable to the nature of things, or to those self-evident notions which are the foundation of all knowledge and certainty.

If you allow that men by their reasoning faculties are made like unto God, and framed after his image, and that reason is the most excellent gift God can bestow, do they not destroy this likeness, deface this image, and give up the dignity of human nature, when they give up their reason to any person whatever?

Can we lay too great a stress on reason when we consider 'tis only by virtue of it God can hold communication with man? Nor can otherwise, if I may so speak, witness for himself, or assert the wisdom and goodness of his conduct, than by submitting his ways to men's cool deliberation and strict examination? Since 'tis from the marks we discern in the laws of

the universe and its government that we can demonstrate it to be governed by a God of infinite wisdom
and goodness.

They only answer the end for which their reason
was given them who judge of the will of God by
the reasonableness and goodness of doctrines, and
think his laws, like his works, carry in them the
marks of divinity. They likewise do the greatest
honor to the Scripture who suppose it deals with men
as with rational creatures, and therefore admit not
of any of its doctrines without a strict examination.
Those who take a contrary method would, if they
lived in Turkey, embrace Mahometanism, and believe in the Alcoran.

Indeed, a blind submission is so far from doing
credit to true religion that it puts all religions on the
same foot; for without judging of a religion by its
internal marks, there's nothing but miracles to plead;
and miracles true or false, if they are believed (and
where are they not?) will have the same effect. Nay,
if miracles can be performed by evil as well as by
good beings, the worst religion may have the most
miracles, as needing them most.

Would not Christians themselves think it a sufficient proof of a religion's not coming from God if
it wanted any of those internal marks by which the
truth of all religion is to be tried, without inquiring
into its miracles or any other external proofs? Consequently, wherever these internal marks are found,
are not external marks needless?

B. Do not our divines say mankind were for many
ages in a deplorable state for want of an external
revelation?

A. Is it not incumbent on those who make any
external revelation so necessary to the happiness of

mankind to show how it is consistent with the notion of God's being universally benevolent not to have revealed it to all his children, when all had equal need of it? Was it not as easy for him to have communicated it to all nations as to any one nation or person? Or in all languages, as in any one? Nay, was it not as easy for him to have made all men, for the sake of this noble end, speak in one and the same language, as it was at first, to multiply languages to prevent their building a tower up to heaven? When God acts as governor of the universe, his laws are alike designed for all under his government, that is, all mankind. Consequently, what equally concerns all must be equally knowable by all. If the universality of a law be the only certain mark of its coming from the governor of mankind, how can we be certain that which wants this mark comes from him?

B. Though reason, on which you lay such stress, may demonstrate that there are not more Gods than one; yet reason can never tell us that there's more than one that is God. Though reason tells us that there are not three Gods, yet reason could never tell us that, though in the idea of a divine person the idea of God be included, each person being by himself God, yet that multiplying of divine persons was not the multiplying of Gods. And though reason declares there's a difference between three and one; yet reason will never discover that there's no more in three persons than in one, all three together being the same numerical God as each is by himself. There's nothing reason can tell us more plainly than that God and a man are two distinct, intelligent persons; but can reason tell us they may become one intelligent person, even while their personal natures and properties remain infinitely distinct and different? Thus you see how reason must submit to faith.

A. I, for my part, not understanding these orthodox paradoxes, can only at present say I do not disbelieve them; but must add that, as I am a rational creature, and God requires of me a "reasonable service," (Rom. 12:1) I ought not, nay, I cannot have any faith which will not bear the test of reason. Therefore, notwithstanding your maxim of reason's submitting to faith, I will venture to affirm if a book assert (supposing the words of it are taken in their plain, literal sense) immoral or impious doctrines, and there are not in that book certain marks to tell us where they are to be taken literally, and where figuratively, or what is the figurative sense, that men in these points are as much to be determined by their reason as if there was no such book.

B. Do not you, by laying such a stress on reason, in effect set aside revelation?

A. No, if revelation be a reasonable revelation, the greater stress we lay upon reason the more we establish revelation.

B. But not on the foot of its own authority, but only as you judge it agreeable to reason; and therefore I question whether any of our eminent divines talk thus in commendation of reason to the disparagement of authority.

A. If reason is all we rational creatures have to trust to, being that alone which distinguishes us from brutes incapable of religion, divines, even those of the most narrow principles, however they may shuffle a while, must make reason their *dernier* resort. Does it not follow that 'tis our duty before we embrace any instituted religion to examine, by that light which God has given us, into every part of it, and after a scrupulous trial pass sentence on it? If the interest of truth and the honor of man's nature require them to perform this grand duty, must not their reason, antecedently to all external revelation, afford certain tests to distinguish between truth and falsehood in all religious matters?

And if it be evident that we can't discern whether any instituted religion contains everything worthy, and nothing unworthy, of a divine original except we can antecedently by our reason discern what is or is not worthy of having God for its author, it necessarily follows that natural and revealed religion can't differ. Because whatever reason shows to be worthy of having God for its author must belong to natural religion; and whatever reason tells us is unworthy of having God for its author can never belong to the true revealed religion. 'Tis upon this very plan that I have endeavored to show you wherein true and genuine Christianity consists.

B. By such reasoning, religion is the plainest thing in the world. We, it seems, have nothing to do but to examine what notions are worthy of God in order to know his will. I should readily approve what the authors you quote have said to show the reasonableness of the divine law in every instance, were there not in religion propositions to be believed which are above reason.

A. Although designing men very well know that it's impossible to believe when we know not what it is we are to believe; or to believe an absurd or contradictory proposition; yet they, because without examination people may be brought to fancy they believe such things, and it being their interest to confound men's understandings, and prevent all inquiry, craftily invented the notion of believing things above reason. Here the ravings of an enthusiast are on a level with the dictates of infinite wisdom, and nonsense rendered most sacred; here a contradiction is of great use to maintain a doctrine that, when fairly stated, is not defensible; because by talking backward and forward, by using obscure terms, and taking words in different senses, they may easily amuse and puzzle the people.

If the end of God's giving a revelation was to direct men's thoughts and actions, it must be delivered in such a way as is plain and easy to be understood, even by mean capacities. Consequently, to suppose it dark and mysterious in any part is to represent it as unworthy of having God for its author. Therefore, upon the whole, I must needs say, happy is the man who is so far, at least, directed by the law of reason and the religion of nature as to suffer no mysteries, or unintelligible propositions, no allegories, no hyperboles, no metaphors, types, parables, or phrases of an uncertain signification to confound his understanding.

B. You suppose, then, that the bulk of mankind are taught by God himself to know what religion comes from him, even though they want letters to make them capable of understanding those external proofs on which all traditional religions do and must depend.

XIII

The bulk of mankind by their reason must be able to distinguish between religion and superstition; otherwise they can never extricate themselves from that superstition they chance to be educated in.

A. Religion either does not concern the majority, as being incapable of forming a judgment about it; or it must carry such internal marks of its truth as men of mean capacity are able to discover; or else, notwithstanding the infinite variety of religions, all who do not understand the original languages their traditional religions are written in, which is all mankind, a very few excepted, are alike bound in all places to pin their faith on their priests and believe in men who have an interest to deceive them, and who have seldom failed to do so when occasion serves.

I see no middle but that we must either own that there are such internal marks fixed to every part of the true religion as will enable the bulk of mankind to distinguish it from all false religions, or else that all traditionary religions are upon a level. Since those who in every country are hired to maintain them will not fail to assert they all have external marks, such as: uninterrupted traditions, uncontested miracles, confession of adversaries, number of proselytes, agreement among themselves, and all those other external arguments that the papists and Mahometans set so high a value on. Had the people of Rome, in the primitive times of Christianity, been governed by external marks, none of them had quitted their old religion, which had exery external mark proper to recommend it, and under which they were so blessed as to become masters of the best part of the known world.

If what has been already said may not be sufficient to show that it can't be imputed to want of wisdom or goodness in God, or to any defect in reason, which he has at all times given mankind for the discovery of his will, that the nature of religion is so little understood, and so many things which do not show themselves to be the will of God are mixed with it, let me ask you whether God has a greater kindness for the brute than the rational creation?

B. That, certainly, must be a needless question.

A. If God, then, in the very frame and make of those animals we term irrational, has implanted the sense of everything necessary to answer the end of their creation, can we imagine he has not as great a care of his creatures endowed with reason and made after his own image, and for ends infinitely more noble than the brute creation? When we see with what skill and contrivance birds, without being taught by any but the God of nature, build their nests; and how artfully the spiders frame their webs, the bees their little cells, and the beasts avoid all noxious herbs; and, not to multiply instances, how all animals are endowed with sufficient sagacity for preserving themselves and species; must we not own that what we call instinct is a certain and infallible guide for inferior animals? And can we doubt whether man, the lord of the creation, has not from his superior reason sufficient notices of whatever makes for his greatest, his eternal happiness?

If we can't charge God with acting thus partially, must we not be obliged to own that reason is as certain a guide for rational creatures as instinct is for irrational? And, consequently, that those men are below brutes who, wanting instinct, will not govern themselves nor suffer others to be governed by reason?

B. If what you say be true, the principles on which all religion is founded must be so obvious that men, even of the meanest capacity, may from thence discern their duty both to God and man.

A. You shall confess there are such principles by my asking you a question or two. Is not the foundation of all religion the believing there's only one self-existent being, to whom all others owe their being and their continuance in being? And is it not as certain that he did not create mankind to supply any wants of his own, or give them rules for their conduct but to oblige them to act for their common good? If then an action is for their good, is not that alone an infallible test of its being approved by God? And if it tends to their hurt, is not that as certain a mark of its being disapproved by him?

B. Though all rational creatures who, to their utmost, imitate their great creator and benefactor in communicating happiness to each other, do all that God requires of them, yet 'tis on supposition that they do not judge wrong in relation to their common good.

A. If men, according to the best of their understanding, act for their common good, they then govern themselves by the same rule God governs them; their will is the same with his, and they concur in the same design with him. And should they, in some nice and difficult cases, mistake in applying the rule, yet in being entirely governed by it they have done all that God requires, who, having made men fallible, will not impute to them want of infallibility. And the best way not to mistake in applying this rule is to consider duly all circumstances, and follow what upon the whole seems best. As this is the rule both of God and man, so is it in common to the unlearned as well as learned, for have not all alike faculties given them by God to distinguish between good and evil, right and wrong, and to know that, as they would not suffer wrong themselves, so they ought not to do wrong?

B. The common people may have sufficient abilities to know their duty to man; but can they as well know what they owe to God?

A. In what point is it that men of the meanest abilities may not know their duty, whether it relates to God or man? As to the first, can't they tell what sentiments inspire them with love and reverence for the deity? And need they much reflection to know that the more any sentiments do this the more they ought to be cherished? And that every notion which tends not to raise in them the highest conceptions of the divine being is derogatory to his perfection, and that the highest honor and worship they can render him is solemnly to own him to be what he is?

As to their duty to one another, can't they perceive that 'tis fit in the nature of things, and agreeable to the mind of their creator, (who has endowed them with reason for this end) to introduce into his creation as much happiness as they can, by being ready to assist one another in all good offices? And, indeed, the reciprocal duties are so very evident that even children are sensible of doing as they would be done unto; and the mind with the same ease sees the agreeableness or disagreeableness in outward objects.

And the meaner people are, and the lower their station, the fewer are the things their duty consists in, and those so very plain that they cannot well mistake, with relation either to God or man, were they not imposed on by artful men. They, peace and quiet being their interest, are naturally good subjects and good neighbors, and upon all accounts most useful members of the community, except when their priests (on pretense of the good of the church) work them up to tumults, mutiny, sedition, and rebellion, because their governors presume to give equal protection to all their subjects, notwithstanding their different opinions.

B. You all along argue that the rule of action being everywhere the same (as founded on the nature of God and man and the relation we stand in to him and one another), true religion, in all places and times, must ever be the same, eternal, universal, and unalterable, and such as every intelligent creature must have sufficient understanding to discover and abilities to comply with. Hence you conclude that external revelation can only be a republication of this unchangeable rule of life.

A. I have said nothing of the plainness, simplicity, and even universality of religion but what is agreeable to the description which St. Paul, from the prophet Jeremiah, gives of the Gospel dispensation, the express terms of which run thus: "I will put my laws into their mind, and write them in their hearts; and I will be unto them a God, and they shall be to me a people. And they shall not teach every man his neighbor, and every man his brother, saying, know the Lord, for all shall know me, from the least to the greatest." (Heb. 8:10f.; Jer. 31:33f).

B. You place religion in the practice of morality in obedience to the will of God, and suppose there can be no other distinction between morality and religion than that the former is acting according to the reason of things considered in themselves, the other acting according to the same reason of things considered as the will of God. Can you hope to escape being pelted by some for such a crime as this?

A. I am sensible the showing religion to be no arbitrary institution, but founded on the nature of things and their relations, obvious to the capacity of all that dare use their reason, must provoke all ecclesiastics of what denomination soever who expect a blind submission from the laity.

B. I should find it difficult not to yield, had I not so able a combatant as Dr. S. Clarke for my second, who, in his excellent *Discourse of the Unalterable Obligation of Natural Religion, and the Truth and Certainty of the Christian Revelation,* not only shows that they are distinct religions, but the infinite advantage the latter has above the former.

XIV

Dr. Clarke's Discourse considered; and from thence is shown, how inconsistent soever with the design of that discourse, that nothing can be a part of religion but what is founded on the nature and reason of things.

A. I own the Doctor got immortal honor by that discourse. Since 'tis your pleasure, I will fully consider this discourse, and begin with the character he gives the law of nature, and see whether he does not represent it so absolutely perfect as to take in everything that God requires of mankind; and then examine what he says in behalf of revelation, in contradistinction to the religion of nature.

The Doctor's hypothesis is that upon God's framing mankind after the manner he has done, there are certain things resulting from thence which naturally and necessarily conduce to their good or hurt; and that the way to know the will of God is to know what those things are, in order to do the one and to avoid the other. For which reason God gave mankind understanding, which must be allowed to be sufficient to answer the end for which it was given. And that a being infinitely wise and good can require nothing of men but what they, for the sake of their own interest, were obliged to do; and consequently that whoever acts for his own good, in subserviency to that of the public, answers the end of his creation. As this scheme of things, to do the Doctor justice, gives us the highest idea of the goodness, wisdom, and perfection, of the divine being, so to complete his moral character, the Doctor represents the laws of God by which mankind are to govern all their actions most plain and obvious, and even impressed on human nature.

As it would be endless to mention all the Doctor says of the irresistible evidence, as well as the absolute perfection, of the eternal and immutable law of nature, I shall recite but one passage: "This is the law of nature to which the reason of all men, everywhere, as naturally and necessarily assents as all animals conspire in the pulse and motion of their heart and arteries; or as all men agree in their judgment concerning the whiteness of snow, or the brightness of the sun."

B. This indeed is so full that no ancient or modern deist could have said more in praise of the unlimited wisdom and universal goodness of God, than in supposing the common parent of mankind has given all his children, even those of the lowest capacities, and at all times, sufficient means of discovering whatever makes for their present and future happiness; and that no man can plead ignorance of a law as evident as that the sun is bright, or snow white;

and as inseparable from rational nature as the pulse or the heart and arteries are from animals.

A. If this be talking like a deist, all who write on this subject talk thus. The latter part of the Doctor's discourse is chiefly levelled against those he calls the "true deists." The deists, no doubt, will own that the Doctor has done them justice, since all their principles as he represents them have a direct tendency to make them good men, and contain nothing to divert them from entirely attending to all the duties of morality, in which the whole of their religion consists. I do not perceive the Doctor himself finds any defect in their principles, but only objects to their manner of taking them as they are discoverable by the light of nature and the reason of things.

B. Is not that a very just objection?

A. Not from one who supposes that "the eternal reason of things ought to be the rule by which all men should govern all their actions," and who affirms that "the original obligation of all is the eternal reason of things."

B. Why do you think this favors deism?

A. Because, if the eternal reason of things is the supreme obligation, must not that, if there's any difference between it and external revelation, take place? And must not that rule which can annul any other be not only the supreme but the sole rule? In short, 'tis the view with which an action is done that makes it moral; he who pays his debts out of a principle of honesty does a moral action, while he who does the same for fear of the law can't be said to act morally. And can he who does a thing to avoid being punished, or in hopes of being rewarded hereafter, and for the same reason is ready to do the contrary, merit equally with him who is in love with his duty, and is governed by the original obligation of the moral fitness of things, in conformity to the nature, and in imitation of the perfect will, of God? This the Doctor will not deny to be true deism, and that they who do not act thus deserve not the title of "true deist."

If Christianity, as well as deism, consists in being governed by the original obligation of the moral fitness of things, in conformity to the nature, and in imitation of the perfect will, of God, then they both must be the same. But if Christianity consists in being governed by any other rule, or requires any other things, has not the Doctor himself given the advantage to deism?

These "true Christian deists," as I think the Doctor ought to call them, say that though the Doctor's discourse is chiefly levelled against them, yet he can't differ with them without differing from himself, and condemning in one part of his elaborate treatise what he has approved in the other.

For if Christianity has not, say they, destroyed men's moral agency, or forbid them to act as moral agents, they must now as well as formerly judge of the will of God by that reason given them by an all-gracious God to distinguish between good and evil. The difference between those who would engross the name of Christians to themselves and these Christian deists is that the former dare not examine into the truth of Scripture doctrines, lest they should seem to question the verity of the Scriptures, whereas the latter, who believe not the doctrines because contained in Scripture, but the Scripture on account of the doctrines, are under no such apprehension.

B. I thought the Doctor had built his arguments in favor of revelation upon the obscurity of the law of nature, and would not have declared that "the reason of all men as naturally assents to it, as all animals conspire in the pulse and motion of their heart and arteries, or as all men agree in their judgment concerning the whiteness of snow, or the brightness of the sun."

A. Have patience, and you shall see that snow is no longer white, or the sun bright! The Doctor's new scheme consists in supposing that, though "in the original uncorrupted state of human nature, right reason may justly be supposed to have been a sufficient guide, yet upon the fall, mankind were in a very bad state, as wanting greater help and assistance than the light of nature could afford them, and that there was plainly wanting some extraordinary and supernatural assistance that was above the reach of bare reason and philosophy to procure. There was plainly wanting a divine revelation to recover mankind out of their universally degenerate state into a state suitable to the original dignity of their nature."

This is supposing God had left all mankind for 4000 years together, and even the greatest part to this day, destitute of sufficient means to do their duty and to preserve themselves from sinking into a corrupted and degenerate state, and that it was impossible for them when thus sunk to recover themselves, and yet that God (their duty being the same after as before the fall) expected impossibilities from them. But what he calls a state of universal degeneracy and corruption must be the state God designed they should be in. And it would seem not only to be in vain, but a crime in them, to endeavor to change that state in which God of his infinite wisdom and goodness thought fit to place them.

But if all men alike, at all times, owe their existence to God, they at all times must be created in a state of innocence, capable of knowing and doing all God requires of them. The Doctor's scheme out-does that of the most rigid predestinarians, for that at all times saves the elect; but here are no elect, but all, for many ages, are inextricably involved in a most depraved, corrupted, and impious state. The Doctor justly says, "Let none on pretense of main-taining natural religion revile and blaspheme the Christian, lest they be found liars unto God." And for the same reason, may not I say, let none blas-pheme natural religion. Though, if natural and re-vealed religion can differ, it must be a greater crime to revile a religion that is eternal, universal, and un-changeable, than a religion that is not so.

Though I pay a due deference to the Doctor's deep penetration in matters of religion, I dare not say there's the least difference between the law of nature and the Gospel, for that would suppose some defect in one of them, and reflect on the author of both. Nor dare I be so rash as to charge the light of nature with "undeniable defects," as the Doctor presumes to do; since if that light was sufficient to answer the end designed by God, there could be no deficiency. If not, then there must have been an undeniable de-fault in the giver of it, in appointing means not suf-ficient to answer their designed ends.

It can't be imputed to any defect in the light of nature that the pagan world ran into idolatry, but to their being entirely governed by priests, who pre-tended communication with their gods, and to have thence their revelations, which they imposed on the credulous as divine oracles. Whereas the business of the Christian dispensation was to destroy all those traditional revelations, and restore, free from all idolatry, the true primitive and natural religion implanted in mankind from the creation. The Doctor, however, seems afraid, lest he had allowed too much to the light of nature.

The apostle Paul, though quoted by the Doctor, is so far from favoring his hypothesis of any invincible ignorance even in the wisest and best of the philosophers that he, by saying "the Gentiles that have not the law, do by nature the things contained in the law," (Rom. 2:14) makes the law of nature and grace to be the same; and supposes the reason why they were to be punished was their sinning against light and knowledge: "That which may be known of God was manifest in them, and when they knew God, they glorified him not as God." (Rom. 1:19, 21) I think it no compliment to external revelation, though the Doctor designed it as the highest, to say it prevailed when the light of nature was, as he supposes, in a manner extinct, since then an irrational religion might as easily obtain as a rational one.

How can the Doctor know there are defects in the light of nature but from that light itself? Which supposes this light is all we have to trust to; consequently, all the Doctor has been doing, on pretense of promoting the honor of revelation, is introducing universal skepticism.

B. I can't apprehend how these philosophers who made it their business to study and practice natural religion could be entirely ignorant of any doctrines absolutely necessary for the reformation of mankind. Therefore, I should like to know what are these absolutely necessary doctrines they were thus entirely ignorant of?

A. It must be owned, they were not in the least

acquainted with the Doctor's glorious scheme of all mankind's being for 4000 years together, and the greatest part too at present, placed by God in a most depraved, degenerate state, without possibility of recovering from it.

"There philosophers," he says, "were ignorant of the original dignity of human nature." Because he frequently insists on it, I shall fully consider this matter, and will confess 'tis probable they thought that human nature, men at all times having the same common faculties, was always the same. Had they known the sacred story of Adam and Eve, that would have confirmed them in their sentiments. The most they could perceive by it would be that the first pair came into the world in every sense naked, destitute of all that knowledge, experience, gave their posterity. How weak was their reason, how strong their appetites, when they could not abstain from the fruit of but one tree! Upon the whole, I grant, these philosophers would be far from finding out this original dignity in the first pair! They would see that the Christians are now ashamed of the literal interpretation of this story.

Those philosophers would not think the matter a jot mended by substituting (did the story afford room for it) a devil instead of a serpent, since they could not see how an infinitely good God could permit a most malicious cunning spirit to work on the weakness of a woman just placed in a new world, and yet that after the fact was committed God should thus revenge it on all their innocent posterity forever.

But to return to the Doctor, where is the difference, in relation to the goodness of God and the happiness of mankind, between God's creating them in a state of universal degeneracy and corruption or causing them, by the folly of Adam (which infinite wisdom could not but foresee) to fall unavoidably into this bad state? What dignity, what perfection could Adam's nature have that the nature of his posterity has not? How can we suppose his understanding was in the least impaired by this crime, since God himself says, "Behold the man is become like one of us, to know good and evil"? (Gen. 3:22) Would it not be very strange that his posterity, while his understanding received no hurt, should suffer so greatly in theirs as the Doctor would have it thought? I may venture to say that the Doctor's description of human nature in all but one pair (and that, too, perhaps but for a day) is a libel on the dignity of human nature, and a high reflection on the wisdom and goodness of its author.

But let us see whether the Doctor has better success with his other arguments by which he endeavors to curtail the universal goodness of God. "That which of all things the best and wisest of the philosophers were entirely and unavoidably ignorant of, and yet was of the greatest importance for sinful men to know, viz., the method by which such as have erred from the right way, and have offended God, may yet restore themselves to his favor." He concludes "that there arises from nature no sufficient comfort to sinners, but an anxious and endless solicitude about the means of appeasing the deity."

Had the Doctor only said that we can't know from the light of nature that "there's more joy in heaven over one sinner that repents than over ninety-nine just persons who need no repentance," (Lk. 15:7) that, if strictly taken, might perhaps be better disputed. But nothing, sure, can be more shocking than to suppose the unchangeable God, whose nature and property is ever to forgive, was not, at all times, equally willing to pardon repenting sinners, and equally willing they should have the satisfaction of knowing it. If God always acts for the good of his creatures, what reason can be assigned why he should not from the beginning have discovered such things as make for their good, but defer the doing it till the time of Tiberius?

If revelation was absolutely necessary to recover mankind out of their universally degenerate and corrupted state, and replace them in a state suitable to the original dignity and excellency of their nature, must not revelation have had its intended effect, and made Christians much more perfect and excellent than men could possibly be when under times of unavoidable corruption? And yet the Doctor, having taken a large passage from Cicero, where the orator very rhetorically describes the great corruptions of his time, make this remark: "That a livelier description of the present corrupt state of human nature is not easily to be met with." Which, I think, is sufficiently owning that human nature at present is far from being exalted to so high a state of perfection, or in the least mended.

What impartial man who has compared the former and present condition of mankind can think the world much mended since the times of Tiberius; or, though ever so well versed in church history, can, from the conduct of Christians, find that they are arrived to any higher state of perfection than the rest of mankind, who are supposed to continue in their degeneracy and corruption? Monsieur Liebnitz, a great statesman as well as philosopher, in comparing the Christians at present with the infidels of

China, does not scruple to give the preference to the latter in relation to all moral virtues.

We have no great reason to hope it will ever be so well with mankind but that there will always be too much room for such arguments as the Doctor urges, from the corruption of mankind, for new revelations. Have not impostors always made use of this plea? Was it not on the carnality of the primitive orthodox Christians that the spiritual Montanus founded his new gospel? And it was the ill lives of the professors of Christianity, as 'tis owned by Christian as well as Arabic writers, which prepared the way for that success which Mahomet met with.

The Doctor further says: "That as no man ever denied but that the benefit of Christ's death extended backward to those who lived before his appearance in the world, so no one can prove but the same benefit may extend itself forward to those who never heard of his appearance though they lived after it." Even on this supposition, the Doctor must have owned that all men living up to that light God has given them are upon a level in relation to their future happiness. Indeed, if sinners since the coming of Christ are not to be saved without repentance and amendment, and sinners at all times were to be saved on these terms, must not repentance and amendment (which suppose a knowledge of what was to be repented of and amended) put all mankind at all times upon a level? Can anything be more evident than that, if doing evil is the only foundation of God's displeasure, ceasing to do evil and doing the contrary must take away that displeasure? I wish the Doctor had been more explicit, and told us what benefit those who never heard of Christ's appearance could gain by his death.

B. The Doctor says that "Christ died to show God's irreconcilable hatred to sin, and to vindicate the honor of his laws."

A. These reasons, sure, could never influence those who never heard of Christ; or, if they had, perhaps would have been so perverse as not to imagine that pardoning the guilty and punishing the innocent could either show irreconcilable enmity to guilt or love for innocence. Perhaps, governed by prejudices, they might think very oddly of a king who, though he freely pardoned his repenting rebels, yet should cause his most loyal and only son to be put to death, to show his hatred to rebellion; and to vindicate the honor of those laws which forbid putting an innocent person to death. Could these philosophers, who did not imagine any virtue in sacrificing of beasts, easily conceive a human sacrifice, which they believed human nature abhorred, to be an expiation for sins? Or that sins freely pardoned could want any expiation?

Though I have omitted several things which well deserve to be criticized, I think I have said enough to show the inconsistency of the Doctor's scheme, and the weakness of those arguments by which he attempts to destroy the all-sufficiency, absolute perfection, plainness, and perspicuity of the law of nature which he had before so fully demonstrated. Who could expect, after we had been told that, as God governs all his own actions by the eternal rule of reason, so all his rational creatures are obliged to govern themselves in all theirs by the same eternal rule, who, I say, could imagine that all this should be unsaid, and the utmost art employed to show the imperfection, insufficiency, obscurity, and uncertainty of the light of nature?

B. I must own you have produced several weighty arguments to prove that religion was and always must be invariably the same.

A. If, after all, I am still criminal, it must be in not owning that God created the greatest part of mankind to be damned, or, which is the same, made such things necessary to their salvation as they were incapable of knowing. And in my asserting that "God is a rewarder of those who diligently seek him," (Heb. 11:6) though they do not seek him under the direction of this or that set of men. In believing, with St. Peter, that "God is no respecter of persons, but in every nation he that feareth him, and worketh righteousness, is accepted with him." (Acts 10:34f.) And in believing with our savior that "the whole need not a physician." (Matt. 9:12) And in believing the description that God himself gives of the new covenant, "I will put my laws into their minds, and write them in their hearts." (Heb. 8:10)

WILLIAM LAW

Law (1686–1761) was a Fellow of Emmanuel College, Cambridge. He early gained a reputation as a controversialist in the so-called Bangorian affair (Bishop Hoadly), and because of his attacks on Mandeville and Tindal. Today he is better known for his devotional and mystical writings, especially the *Serious Call to a Devout and Holy Life*. Both through his writings and through personal relations, Law had an impact on the early development of John and Charles Wesley, though they later rejected his more advanced mysticism.

The Case of Reason

I

> *Inquiring whether there be anything in the nature and condition of man to oblige him to think that he is not to admit of any doctrines or institutions as revealed from God but such as his own reason can prove to be necessary from the nature of things.*

I begin with inquiring what there is to oblige a man to hold this opinion, because if there is not some strong and plain proof arising from the nature and condition of man to oblige him thus to abide by the sole light of his own reason, it may be so far from being a duty which he owes to God, that it may be reckoned amongst his most criminal presumptions. And the pleading for this authority of his own reason may have the guilt of pleading for his greatest vanity. The claiming this authority to our own reason must either be a very great duty, or amongst the greatest of sins.

All the light we can have in this matter must arise from a thorough consideration of the state and condition of man in this world. If without revelation he is free from mysteries as a moral and religious agent, then he has some plea from his state and condition to reject revealed mysteries. But if in a state of natural religion, and mere morality, he cannot acknowledge a divine providence, or worship and adore God, without as much implicit faith and humble submission of his reason as any revealed mysteries require, then his state and condition in the world condemns his refusal of any revelation sufficiently attested to come from God.

The writers against revelation appeal to the reason and nature of things as infallibly discovering everything that a revelation from God can teach us. But this whole argument proves directly the contrary to that which this author intended to prove by it. I here therefore join with this author: I readily grant that the nature, reason and relations of things and persons, and the fitness of actions resulting from thence, is the sole rule of God's actions. And I appeal to this one common and confessed principle as a sufficient proof that a man cannot thus abide by the sole light of his own reason without contradicting the nature and reason of things, and denying this to be the sole rule of God's actions.

For if the fitness of actions is founded in the nature of things and persons, and this fitness be the

sole rule of God's actions, it is certain that the rule
by which he acts must in many instances be entirely
inconceivable by us, so as not to be known at
all, and in no instances fully known or perfectly
comprehended.

For if God is to act according to a fitness founded
in the nature of things, and nothing can be fit for
him to do but what has its fitness founded in his
own divinely perfect and incomprehensible nature,
must he not necessarily act by a rule above all
human comprehension? This argument supposes that
he cannot do what is fit for him to do unless what he
does has its fitness founded in his own nature; but
if he must govern his actions by his own nature, he
must act by a rule that is just as incomprehensible
to us as his own nature.

For instance, look at the reason of things, and
the fitness of actions, and tell me how they moved
God to create mankind in the state and condition
they are in. Nothing is more above the reason of men
than to explain the reasonableness and infinite wisdom of God's providence in creating man of such
a form and condition, to go through such a state of
things as human life has shown itself to be. No revealed mysteries can more exceed the comprehension
of man than the state of human life itself.

Now if the imperfect state of human nature, the
miseries and calamities of this life, the diseases and
mortality of human bodies, the methods of God's
continual providence in governing human affairs, are
things that as much concern us and as nearly relate
to us as any methods of revealed religion; and if
these are things that we cannot examine or explain,
according to any fitness or unfitness founded in the
nature of things, but must believe a great deal more

of the infinite wisdom of God than we can so explain; have we any reason to think that God cannot, or ought not, to raise us out of this unhappy state of things, help us to a higher order of life, and exalt us to a nearer enjoyment of himself by any means but such as our own poor reason can grope out of the nature and fitness of things?

Now what is the reason that all is thus mysterious and unmeasurable by human reason in these matters so nearly concerning human nature? 'Tis because God is not an arbitrary being, but does that which the incomprehensible perfections of his own nature make it fit and reasonable for him to do.

Again, what is the nature of a human soul, upon what terms and in what manner it is united to the body, how far it is different from it, how far it is subject to it, what powers and faculties it derives from it, are things wherein the wisdom and goodness of God and the happiness of man are deeply concerned. Is it not necessary that these things should have their foundation in the reason and fitness of things, and yet what natural reason, uninspired from above, can show that this state of soul and body is founded in the reason and fitness of things?

Again, the origin of sin and evil, or how it entered into the world consistently with the infinite wisdom of God, is a mystery of natural religion which reason cannot unfold. Here the man of natural religion must drop his method of reasoning from the nature and fitness of things, and that in an article of the highest concern to the moral world, and be as mere a believer as he that believes the most incomprehensible mystery of revealed religion.

Now as there have been in the several ages of the world some impatient, restless and presuming spirits who, because they could not in these points explain the justice of God's providence, have taken refuge in horrid atheism, so they made just the same sober use of their reason as our modern unbelievers, who because they cannot comprehend the fitness and necessity of certain Christian doctrines resign themselves up to a hardened infidelity. For it is just as wise and reasonable to allow of no mysteries in revelation as to allow of no mysteries or secrets in creation and providence.

And whenever this writer, or any other, shall think it a proper time to attack natural religion with as much freedom as he has now fallen upon revealed, he need not enter upon any new hypothesis or different way of reasoning. For the same turn of thought, the same manner of cavilling, may soon find materials in the natural state of man for as large a bill of complaints against natural religion and the mysteries of providence as is here brought against revealed doctrines.

To proceed: if the fitness of actions is founded in the nature and relations of beings, then nothing can be fit for God to do but so far as it is fit for the governor of all created beings. Now what is fit for the governor of all created nature to do in this or that particular part of his creation is as much above our reason to tell as it is above our power to govern all beings. How mankind ought to be governed, with relation to the whole creation, is a matter equally above our knowledge, because we know not how they are a part of the whole, or what relation they bear to any other part, or how their state affects the whole or any other part, than we know what beings the whole consists of.

Again, if the fitness of actions is founded in the

relations of beings to one another, then the fitness
of the actions of God's providence over mankind
must be in many instances altogether mysterious and
incomprehensible to us. For the relation which God
bears to mankind, as their all-perfect creator and
continual preserver, is a relation that our reason
conceives as imperfectly as it does any of the divine
attributes. When it compares it to that of a father
and his chidren, a prince and his subjects, a pro-
prietor and his property, it has explained it in the
best manner it can, but still has left it as much a
secret as we do the divine nature when we only say
it is infinitely superior to everything that is finite.

By the natural light of our reason we may know
with certainty several effects of this relation, as that
it puts us under the care and protection of a wise
and just and merciful providence, and demands from
us the highest instances of humility, duty, adoration
and thanksgiving. But what it is in its own nature,
what kind of state or degree of dependency it signifies, what it is to exist in and by God, what it is to
see by a light that is his, to act by a power from
him, to live by a life in him, are things as incomprehensible to reason, left to itself, as what it is to be in
the third heavens, or to hear words that cannot be
uttered.

But if this relation consists in these inconceivable
things, in a communication of life, light, and power,
if these are enjoyed in God and in ourselves, our own
and yet his, in a manner not to be explained by anything that we ever heard or saw, then we must
necessarily be poor judges of what is fit for God to
require of us because of this relation. It teaches us
nothing but the superficialness of our own knowl-

edge, and the unfathomable depths of the divine perfections.

For what the relation betwixt God and sinners makes it fit and reasonable for God to require or accept of them cannot be determined by human reason. This is a new state, and the foundation of a new relation, and nothing can be fit for God to do in it but what has its fitness resulting from it. We have nothing to help our conceptions of the fore-mentioned relative characters of God, as our governor and preserver, but what we derive from our idea of human fathers and governors. Which idea only helps us to comprehend these relations, just as our idea of human power helps us to comprehend the omnipotence of God. For a father or governor no more represents the state of God as our governor and preserver than our living in our father's family represents the true manner of our living in God.

These relations are both very plain and very mysterious; they are very plain and certain as to the reality of their existence, and highly mysterious and inconceivable as to the manner of their existence. That which is plain and certain plainly shows our obligations to every instance of duty, homage, adoration, love and gratitude. And that which is mysterious and inconceivable is a just and solid foundation of that profound humility, awful reverence, internal piety, and tremendous sense of the divine majesty with which devout and pious persons think of God, and assist at the offices and institutions of religion.

To return, as there is no state in human life that can give us a true idea of any of the forementioned relative characters of God, so this relative state of

God toward sinners is still more remote, and less capable of being truly comprehended by anything observable. To ask whether God in punishing sinners acts as a physician toward patients, or as a creditor toward debtors, or as a prince toward rebels, or a judge over criminals, is the same weakness as to ask whether God as our continual preserver acts as our parents, from whom we have our maintenance, or as a prince that only protects us. For as the maintenance and protection that we receive from our parents and prince are not proper and true representations of the nature and manner of our preservation in God, but only the properest words that human language affords us to speak of things not human but divine and inconceivable in their own proper natures, so a physician and his patients, a creditor and his debtors, a prince and his rebels, or a judge over criminals, neither separately nor jointly considered, are proper and strict representations of the reasons and manner of God's proceedings with sinners, but only help us to a more proper language to speak about them than any other states of human life.

Since the relation which God bears to sinners can only be so known as to make it highly reasonable to prostrate ourselves before him in every instance of humility, but not so fully known as to teach us how, or in what manner, God must deal with us; it plainly follows that if God is not an arbitrary being, but acts according to a fitness resulting from this relation, he must, in this respect, act by a rule or reason known only to himself, and such as we cannot possibly state from the reason and nature of things.

For reason, by consulting the nature and fitness of things, can no more tell us what the guilt of sin is,

what hurt it does us, how far it enters into and alters
our very nature, what contrariety to and separation
from God it necessarily brings upon us, or what supernatural means are or are not necessary to abolish
it; our reason can no more tell this than our senses
can tell us what is the inward and what is the outward light of angels.

And he who rejects the atonement for sins made
by the Son of God, as needless because he cannot
prove it to be necessary, is as extravagant as he that
should deny that God created him by his only Son,
because he did not remember it. For our memory
is as proper a faculty to tell us whether God at first
created us and all things by his only Son, as our reason is to tell us whether we ought to be restored to
God with or without the mediation of Jesus Christ.

This writer says, "Can anything be more evident
than that if doing evil be the only cause of God's
displeasure, that the ceasing to do evil must take
away that displeasure?" Just as if he had said, if con-
versing with a leper has been the only cause of a
man's getting leprosy, must not departing from him
be the removal of the leprosy? It is as impossible for
him to know the guilt and effects of sin as to know
the shape of an angel. It is as impossible to know by
the mere light of reason what God's displeasure at
sin is, what contrariety to or separation from sinners
it implies, or how it obliges God to deal with them,
as to know what the internal essence of God is. For
though it is very evident that in the case of sin reason
can prescribe nothing but repentance, yet it is equally
evident that reason cannot say nothing more is required to destroy the effects of sin, and to put the
sinner in the same state as if it had never been
committed.

It is objected that the atonement made by Jesus Christ represents God as punishing the innocent and acquitting the guilty, or as punishing the innocent instead of the guilty. But this proceeds upon mistake, for the atonement made by Jesus Christ, though it procures pardon for the guilty, yet it does not acquit them, or excuse them from any punishment or suffering from sin which reason could impose upon them. Natural religion calls men to repentance for their sins; the atonement made by Jesus Christ does not acquit them from it, or pardon them without it, but calls them to a severer repentance, a higher self-punishment and penance, than natural religion alone prescribes.

God therefore does not by this proceeding show his dislike of the innocent and his approbation of the wicked. How can God be thought to punish our blessed savior out of dislike, if his sufferings are represented of such infinite merit with him? Or how can he show thereby his approbation of the guilty, whose repentance is not acceptable to him, till recommended by the infinite merits of Jesus Christ?

Again, supposing some supernatural means to be necessary for destroying the guilt and power of sin, or that that mediation, sufferings, and intercession of the Son of God incarnate is that true supernatural means, it necessarily follows that a revelation of such, or any other supernatural means, cannot possibly be made obvious to our reason and senses, as the things of human life or the transactions among men are; but can only be so revealed as to become just occasions of our faith, humility, adoration, and pious resignation, to the divine wisdom and goodness.

For to say that such a thing is supernatural is only saying that it is something which, by the necessary

state of our own nature we are as incapable of knowing as we are incapable of seeing spirits. If therefore
supernatural and divine things are by the letter of
Scripture ever revealed to us, they cannot be revealed
to us as they are in their own nature; for if they
could, such things would not be supernatural, but
such as were suited to our capacities. Such supernatural matter can only be revealed to us by being
represented to us by its likeness to something that
we already naturally know.

All objections therefore raised from any difficulties
about the nature of atonements, propitiations, and
satisfactions, as these words are used to signify in
human life and common language, are vain and entirely groundless. For all these objections proceed
upon this supposition, that atonement, or satisfaction,
when attributed to Jesus Christ, signify neither more
nor less, nor operate in any other manner, than when
they are used as terms in human laws, or in civil life.
Take away this supposition, and all objections are
entirely removed with it.

And as in our account of the existence of things
we are obliged to have recourse to a being whose
existence must not be ascribed to any cause, because
everything cannot have a cause, no more than everything can be created, so in our account of wisdom
and goodness there is the same necessity of having
recourse to an infinite wisdom and goodness, that
never began to be, and that is as different as to its
reason and manner of existence from all other wisdom
and goodness that have a beginning, as the existence
of God is different from the existence of the creatures.

But if it be necessary to hold that there is an infinite wisdom and goodness that never began to be,
then it is as necessary to affirm that such wisdom and

goodness can no more be founded upon the relations of things, than the unbeginning existence of God can be founded upon the existence of things. And to seek for any reasons of a wisdom and goodness that could not begin to be, is like seeking the cause of that which can have no cause, or asking what it is that contains infinity.

Nothing is more certain than that the relations of things is only the particular state of their nature or manner of existence; there can therefore no eternal and unalterable relations exist, but of things that eternally and unalterably exist. As all causes and effects are what they are, and owe their nature to the omnipotence of God, so the relations of things are what they are, and owe their nature to the wisdom and will of God.

Our author says, "Dare anyone say that God's laws are not founded on the eternal reason of things?" I dare say it with the same assurance as that his existence is not founded on the eternal existence of things. And that it is the same extravagance to say that God's laws are founded on the eternal reasons of things as to say that his power is founded on the eternal capacities of things. But as the omnipotence of God cannot be said to be founded upon the nature of causes and effects, so the infinite wisdom of God, though in giving laws to the world it acts suitably to the natures and relations of rational beings, yet cannot be said to be founded upon such relations because such relations are the effects of the divine wisdom and owe their existence to it.

This writer affirms that God's wisdom and goodness must be founded on the nature and reason of things, otherwise it could not be proved that God was not an arbitrary being. Now to seek for reasons to prove that God is not an arbitrary being, that is a being of the highest freedom and independency, that does everything according to his own will and pleasure, is as vain as to seek for reasons to prove that all things and all natures are not the effect of his will. For if everything besides God received its existence from him; if everything that exists is the effect of his will, and he can do nothing but because he wills the doing it, must he not be free and arbitrary in as high a manner as he is powerful?

For if God is omnipotent, he must act according to his own will. And though will and power, when considered as blind or imperfect faculties in men, may pass for humor and caprice, yet as attributes of God, they have the perfection of God. And if the will of God, as such, is in the highest state of perfection, then we have the highest reason to love and adore God because he is arbitrary, and acts according to his own all-perfect will.

And as God's will has thus all the perfection of the divine nature, and has no rule or reason or motive to any goodness that comes from it but its own nature and state in God; so this great will is the only law of all creatures, and they are all to obey and conform to it for this reason, because it is the will of God. Nothing has a sufficient moral reason or fitness to be done but because it is the will of God that it should be done.

It may be asked, is there then no reason or nature of things? Yes, as certainly as there are things. But the nature and reason of things, considered independently of the divine will, or without it, have no more obligation in them than a divine worship considered independently of, and without any regard to the existence of, God. For the will of God is as absolutely necessary to found all moral obligation upon as the existence of God is necessary to be the foundation of religious worship.

It may be asked, can God make that fit in itself which is in itself absolutely unfit to be done? This question consists of improper terms. No things, nor any actions, have any absolute fitness of and in themselves. A gift, a blow, the making of a wound, or shedding of blood, considered in themselves, have no absolute fitness, but are fit or unfit according to any variety of accidental circumstances. When therefore God by his will makes anything fit to be done, he does not make the thing fit in itself, but it becomes fit for the person to do it because he can only be happy, or do that which is fit for him to do, by so doing the will of God.

Supposing therefore God to require a person to do something which according to his present circumstances, without that command, he ought not to do; God does not make that which is absolutely unfit in itself fit to be done, but only adds new circumstances to an action that is neither fit, nor unfit, moral, nor immoral, in itself, but because of its circumstances.

To instance in the case of Abraham, required to sacrifice his son. The killing of a man is neither good nor bad, considered absolutely in itself. It was unlawful for Abraham to kill his son because of the circumstances he was in with regard to his son. But when the divine command was given, Abraham was in a new state, the action had new circumstances, and then it was as lawful for Abraham to kill his son as it was lawful for God to require any man's life, either by sickness or any other means he should please to appoint. And it had been as unlawful for Abraham to have disobeyed God in this extraordinary command, as to have cursed God at any ordinary calamity of providence.

This writer makes further advances in errors. "Hence," says he, "we may contemplate the great dignity of our rational nature, since our reason for kind, though not for degree, is of the same nature with that of God's." But what greater absurdity can a man fall into than to suppose that a being whose existence had a beginning but a few years ago differs only in degree from that which could not possibly have a beginning; or that a dependent and independent being should not be different in kind but only in degree.

The truth of the matter is this. Reason is in God and man, as power is in God and man. And as the divine power has some degree of likeness to human power, yet with an infinite difference from it, so that perfection which we call reason in God has some degree of likeness to reason as it is in man, yet is infinitely and beyond all conception different from it.

II

Showing from the state and relation between God and man that human reason cannot possibly be a competent judge of the fitness and reasonableness of God's proceedings with mankind, either as to the time, or matter, or manner of any external revelation.

If God does things, not because they are easy, but because they are infinitely good and fit to be done, and founded in the relation of a fore-knowing creator to his free creatures, then the reason why God has afforded different revelations to different ages and persons is this: that his manner of revealing everything might be worthy of his own fore-knowledge of the effects of it, and that everything that is particular in the time or manner of any revelation might have its fitness resulting from the relation between a good God and his creatures, whose changing state, different conduct, tempers, and actions are all eternally foreknown by him.

God ordains a revelation in this or that manner, time, and place, not because it is a justice that he cannot refuse, not because it is a matter of favor or free goodness, and therefore may be given in any manner at pleasure, but because he has the whole duration of human things, the whole race of mankind, the whole order of human changes and events, the whole combination of all causes and effects of human tempers, all the actions of free agents, and all the consequences of every revelation, plainly in his sight. And according to this eternal fore-knowledge, every revelation receives everything that is particular in it, either as to time, matter, manner, or place.

He shows his goodness in a revelation to this part of the world, not because it is a part that alone wants it, not because he can bestow his favors as he pleases, but because by acting so with such a part he best shows his goodness and regard to the whole. He reveals himself at such a time, not because he at that time begins to have a partial or particular kindness, but because by so timing his goodness he best shows his care and goodness throughout the whole duration of human things, from the beginning to the end of the world. And it is because he had the same good will toward mankind in every age that he does what he does in any particular age.

III

Showing how far human reason is enabled to judge of the reasonableness, truth and certainty of divine revelation.

We are not without some natural capacity of judging right of God, of finding out his perfections, and proving what is or is not worthy to be ascribed to him. But what the divine perfections are in themselves, what they imply and contain in their own nature and manner of existence, is altogether mysterious and inconceivable by us at present.

Though we are insufficient for comprehending the reasons on which the particular matter or manner of any divine revelation is founded, yet we may be so far sufficient judges of the reasons for receiving or not receiving a revelation as divine as to make our conduct therein justly accountable to God.

For if God can show a revelation to proceed from him by the same undeniable evidence as he shows the creation to be his work; if he can make himself as visible in a particular extraordinary manner as he is by his general and ordinary providence; then, though we are as unqualified to judge of the mysteries of a revelation as we are to judge of the mysteries in creation and providence, yet we may be as fully obliged to receive a revelation as to acknowledge the creation to be the work of God, and as highly criminal for disbelieving it as for denying a general providence.

Adam, Noah, Abraham, and Moses were very incompetent judges of the reasons on which the par-

ticular revelations made to them were founded. But
this did not hinder their sufficient assurance that
such revelations came from God, because they were
proved to come from God in the same manner and
for the same reasons as the creation is proved to be
the work of God.

And if their posterity will let no messages from
heaven, no prophecies and miracles persuade them
that God can call them to any duties but such they
must enjoin themselves; or to the belief of any doctrines but such as their own minds can suggest; nor
to any methods of changing their present state of
weakness and disorder for a happy immortality but
such as suit their own taste, temper, and way of
reasoning; it is because they are grown senseless of
the mysteries of creation and providence with which
they are surrounded, and forget the awful prerogative
of infinite wisdom over the weakest, lowest rank of
intelligent beings.

For the excellence of a revelation is to be acknowledged by us for the same reason that we are to
acknowledge the excellence of creation and providence; not because they are wholly according to human conception and have no mysteries, but because
they are proved to be of God.

And a revelation is to be received as coming from
God not because of its internal excellence, or because
we judge it to be worthy of God, but because God
has declared it to be his, in as plain and undeniable
a manner as he has declared creation and providence to be his. For though no revelation can come
from God but what is truly worthy of him, and full
of every internal excellence, yet what is truly worthy
of God to be revealed cannot possibly be known by
us but by a revelation from himself. As we can only

know what is worthy of God in creation by knowing what he has created, so we can no other way possibly know what is worthy of God to be revealed but by a revelation.

This writer's argument, if it were allowed, leads directly to atheism. For if a revelation cannot be divine if it contains anything mysterious whose fitness and necessity cannot be explained by human reason, then neither creation nor providence can be proved to be divine, for they are both of them more mysterious than the Christian revelation. And revelation itself is therefore mysterious because creation and providence cannot be delivered from mystery.

For if everything is arbitrary whose fitness and expedience human reason cannot prove and explain then surely an invisible over-ruling providence, that orders all things in a manner and for reasons known only to itself; that subjects human life and human affairs to what changes it pleases; that confounds the best laid designs, and makes great effects arise from folly and imprudence; that gives the race not to the swift, nor the battle to the strong; that brings good men into affliction, and makes the wicked prosperous; surely such a providence must be highly arbitrary.

And therefore if this argument is to be admitted, it leads directly to atheism, and brings us under a greater necessity of rejecting this notion of divine providence, on the account of its mysteries, than of rejecting a revelation that is mysterious in any of its doctrines. There is nothing half so mysterious in the Christian revelation, considered in itself, as there is in that invisible providence which all must hold that believe a God. And though there is enough plain in providence to excite the adoration of humble and pious minds, yet it has often been a rock of atheism to those who make their own reason the measure of wisdom.

The true grounds and reasons on which we are to believe a revelation to be divine are such external marks and signs of God's action and operation as are a sufficient proof of it. And if God has no ways of acting that are peculiar and particular to himself, and such as sufficiently prove his action and operation, then revelation can have no sufficient proof that it comes from God.

I appeal therefore to the miracles and prophecies on which Christianity is founded, as a sufficient proof that it is a divine revelation. Every reason for ascribing the creation to God is the same reason for ascribing such miracles and prophecies to God; and every argument against the certainty of those miracles and prophecies coming from God is the same argument against the certainty of the creation's being the work of God.

As the existence of things is the highest and utmost evidence of God's having created them, and not to be tried by our judgments about the reasonableness and ends of their creation; so a course of plain undeniable miracles, attesting the truth of a revelation, is the highest and utmost evidence of its coming from God, and not to be tried by our judgments about the reasonableness or necessity of its doctrines.

And as miracles thus considered in themselves are the highest and most undeniable evidence of the truth and divinity of any external revelation, so Christianity stands fully distinguished from all other religions by the highest and most undeniable evidence, since it has all the proof that the highest state of miracles can give, and every other religion is without any support from them.

And though this writer, with a boldness worthy of himself, often puts all "traditional religions" upon a level, yet he might have shown himself as much a friend to truth and sobriety by asserting that all arguments are equally conclusive, all tempers equally virtuous, all designs equally honest, and all histories and fables equally supported by evidence of fact.

IV

Of the state and nature of reason, as it is in man; and how its perfection in matters of religion is to be known.

This writer and others who take to themselves the names of free-thinkers make their court to the world by pretending to vindicate the right that all men have to judge and act according to their own reason. Though, I think, the world has no more to thank them for on this account than if they had pretended to assert the right that every man has to see only with his own eyes, or to hear only with his own ears.

For their own reason always did, does, and ever will govern rational creatures, in everything they determine, either in speculation or practice. It is not a matter of duty for men to use their own reason, but of necessity, and it is as impossible to do otherwise as for a being that cannot act but from choice to act without choice. A being whose principle of action is reason and choice can no more act without it, or contrary to it, than an extended being can be without extension.

The dispute therefore betwixt Christians and unbe-

lievers concerning reason is not whether men are to
use their own reason, but whether every man's reason
must needs guide him by its own light, or must
cease to guide him as soon as it guides him by a
light borrowed from revelation. This is the true state
of the question, not whether reason is to be followed,
but when it is best followed. Not whether it is to be
our guide, but how it may be made our safest guide.

Christians oppose unbelievers not because they reason, but because they reason ill. They receive revelation, not to suppress the natural power, but to give
new and heavenly light to their reason; not to take
away their right of judging for themselves, but to
secure them from false judgments. Christians therefore do not differ from unbelievers in the constant use
of their reason, but in the manner of using it, as
virtuous men differ from rakes, not in their desire of
happiness, but in their manner of seeking it.

Now although every man is to judge according to
the light of his own reason, yet his reason has very
little light that can be called its own. For as we derive
our nature from our parents, so that which we generally call natural knowledge, or the light of nature,
is a knowledge and light that is made natural to us
by the same authority which makes a certain language, certain customs, and modes of behavior, natural to us.

Nothing seems to be our own but a bare capacity
to be instructed, a nature fitted for any impressions;
as capable of vice as virtue, as ready to be made a
vicious animal as a religious rational creature; as
liable to be made a Hottentot by being born among
Hottentots, as to be a Christian by being born among
Christians.

It is not my intention by this to signify that there

is not a good and evil, right and wrong, founded in the nature of things; or that morality has any de-pendence upon the opinions or customs of men; but only to show that we find out this right and wrong, come to a sense of this good and evil, not by any inward strength or light that our natural reason of itself affords, but by such external means as people are taught articulate language, civility, politeness, or any other rules of civil life.

Now if this is the state of reason as it is in man; if this is all the light that we have from our own nature, a bare capacity of receiving good or bad im-pressions, right or wrong opinions and sentiment, according to the state of the world that we fall into; then we are but poorly furnished to assert and main-tain the absolute perfections of our own reason.

If we are nothing without the assistance of men; if we are a kind of foolish, helpless animals till educa-tion and experience have revealed to us the wisdom and knowledge of our fellow-creatures; shall we think ourselves too wise and full of our own light to be further enlightened with a knowledge and wisdom revealed to us by God himself?

This gentleman, speaking of education, saith, "Edu-cation is justly esteemed a second nature, and its force is too strong, that few can wholly shake off its prejudices." And our author can no more tell what man would be without human education, or what nature would do for those who had no foreign in-struction, than he can tell what sort of beings dwell in the moon. And yet he that does not know this, how can he know what the light of nature is in itself?

For if most of our judgments, opinions, tempers, and ways of thinking are owing to education, and the authority of that part of the world where we dwell; if these impressions have the power of a "second nature" upon us, then the light of "nature" can no more be distinguished from the light of education than the strength which we have from nature can be distinguished from the strength which we have from our food.

So that to declare the light of nature so absolutely perfect as to be incapable of all improvement even by divine revelation is no less an extravagance than to declare the education of mankind to be absolutely perfect in the same degree. When therefore it is just and fitting for all people to abide by the absolute perfection of their education, the infallible light of their second nature, as the unerring standard, measure, and rule of all that is to be esteemed moral, religious, and divine; then it may be just to appeal to the natural light of all men, of all ages, and all places, as a sufficient teacher of all that ought or ought not to be a matter of religion.

For till it can be shown that men are not liable to a second nature from education, or that there is or can be any nature without it, the state of nature must differ all over the world, and in every age of the world, just as the light and advantages of education have differed in the several parts and ages of the world. In a word, the religious and moral light of our first nature is just as great as the first strength of infants; and the religious and moral light of our second nature is just as perfect as our education, and as much of our own growth as the first language that we are taught to speak.

Their objection against revelation is founded upon the pretended sufficiency and absolute perfection of the light and strength of human reason to teach all men all that is wise, and holy, and divine in religion.

But how do they prove this perfection of human reason? Do they appeal to mankind as proofs of this perfection? Do they produce any body of men, in this or any other age of the world, that without any assistance from revelation have attained to this perfection of religious knowledge? This is not so much as pretended to; the history of such men is entirely wanting. And yet the want of such a fact as this has even the force of demonstration against this pretended sufficiency of natural reason. To talk of a light and strength of reason, natural to man, which fact and experience have never yet proved, is as egregious nonsense as to talk of natural senses, or faculties of his body, which fact and experience have never yet discovered.

He that asserts the sufficiency of the light and strength of reason to guide men in matters of religion is not only without any positive proof from fact or experience on his side, but has the history of all ages, for near six thousand years past, fully demonstrating the quite contrary. This is exactly the case of these gentlemen, their opinion has neither more nor less absurdity in it: they only affirm such a sufficiency of light and reason to be natural to all men, as cannot be supported by a single instance of any one man that ever lived, and is fully contradicted by the experience and history of every age since the creation of the world.

V

Showing that all the mutability of our tempers, the disorders of our passions, the corruption of our hearts, all the reveries of the imagination,

> *all the contradictions and absurdities that are*
> *to be found in human life, and human opinions,*
> *are strictly and precisely the mutability, dis-*
> *orders, corruption, and absurdities of human*
> *reason.*

Although common language ascribes a variety of faculties and principles to the soul, yet in strictness of truth everything that is done by us is the action and operation of our reason, and is to be ascribed to it as the sole faculty or principle from whence it proceeded, and by which it is governed and effected.

As our passions not only make us different from other men, but frequently and almost daily different from ourselves, loving and hating under great inconstancy, so our reason is not only different from the reason of other men, but is often different from itself, by a strange inconstancy setting up first one opinion and then another.

So that when we talk of human reason, or a reason common to mankind, we talk of as various, uncertain, and unmeasurable a thing as when we talk of a love, a liking, an aversion, a good nature, or ill nature, common to mankind; for these qualities admit of no variation, uncertainty, or mutability but such as they directly receive from the reason of mankind. For it is as much the reason of man that acts in all these tempers, and makes them to be just what they are, as it is the reason of man that demonstrates a mathematical proposition.

A laudable good nature, or a laudable aversion, is only reason acting in a certain manner; a criminal good nature, or a criminal aversion, is nothing else but an ill-judging reason. But it is still reason or our understanding that is the only agent in our bad passions as well as good passions, and as much the sole agent in all our passions and tempers as in things of mere speculation.

So that the state of reason in human life is nothing else but the state of human tempers and passions. And right reason in morality is nothing else but right love and right aversion.

Brutes are incapable of imprudence and immorality because none of their actions are the actions of reason. Everything therefore that is imprudence, immorality, baseness, or villainy in us must be the act of our reason; otherwise it could no more be imprudent or immoral than the action of brutes. As therefore all that is faithful, just, and wise, can only be attributed to that which is done by our reason, so by plain consequence all that is vain, false, or shameful, can only be imputed to any acts as they are the acts of reason.

All the good, therefore, that there is in any of the desires or aversions of the mere natural man is the good of our reason; and all the evil or blindness that there is in any of our passions is solely the evil and blindness of our reason. So that all that which we call different faculties of the soul, tempers and passions of the heart, strictly speaking means nothing else but the various acts and operations of one and the same rational principle, which has different names according to the objects that it acts upon and the manner of its acting.

To all this it may, perhaps, be objected that our passions and tempers arise from bodily motions, and depend very much upon the state of our blood and animal spirits, and that therefore what we do under their commotions cannot be attributed to our reason.

It is readily granted that the body has this share in our passions and tempers; but then the same thing must be granted of the body in all the acts and operations of the mind. For the most abstract thought and calm speculation of the mind has as truly the concurrence and conjunct operation of bodily spirits as our strongest desires or aversions. And it is as much owing to the state of the body that such speculations are what they are, as it is owing to the state of the body that such passions are what they are.

To draw now some plain consequences from the foregoing account. First, if reason be, as above represented, the universal agent in the natural man; if all the difference among such men, either in speculation or practice, is only such a difference as reason makes, then nothing can be more extravagant than to affirm anything concerning the degree of perfection or imperfection of reason as common to man.

Secondly, granting that all matters of religion must be agreeable to right, unprejudiced reason, yet this could be no ground for receiving nothing in religion but what human reason could prove to be necessary, for human reason is no more right unprejudiced reason than a sinner is sinless, or a man an angel.

Granting, again, that a man may go a great way toward rectifying his reason and laying aside its prejudices, yet no particular man can be a better judge of the rectitude of his own reason than he is of the rectitude of his own self-love, the sagacity of his own understanding, the brightness of his own parts, the justness of his own eloquence, and the depth of his own judgment. For there is nothing to deceive him in self-love, in the opinion of his own merit, wit, judgment, and eloquence, but what has the same power to deceive him in the opinion of his own reason.

Thirdly, a man that has his religion to choose, and with this previous privilege, that he need not allow anything to be matter of religion but what his own right reason can prove to be so, is in as fair a way to be governed by his passions as he that has his condition of life to choose, with the liberty of taking that which his own right reason directs him to.

Does anyone suppose now that nothing but right reason would direct him in the choice of his condition? Or that he would make the better choice because he proceeded upon this maxim, that nothing could be right but that which was agreeable to his reason? Or that his tempers, his prejudices, his self-love, his passions, his partiality, would have no influence upon his choice because he had resigned himself to his own right reason?

For as our choice of a condition of life is not a matter of speculation, but of good and evil, so however it is recommended to our reason, it chiefly excites our passions. And our choice will be just as reasonable as our tempers and passions are. And he that is made the most positive of the sufficiency of his own right reason will be the most likely to be governed by the blindness of his own passions.

Now it is just the same in the choice of a religion as in the choice of a condition of life. As it is not a matter of speculation but of good and evil, so if it is left to be stated and determined by our own reason, it rather appeals to our tempers than employs our reason; and to resign ourselves up to our own reason to tell us what ought or ought not to be a matter of religion is only resigning ourselves up to our tempers, to take what we like and refuse what we dislike in religion.

For it is only natural and easy for him, who believes that nothing can be a part of religion but what his reason can prove necessarily to be so, to take that to be fully proved which is only mightily liked; and all that to be entirely contrary to reason which is only vastly contrary to his tempers.

Lastly, if this be the state of reason, as has been fully proved, then to pretend that our reason is too perfect to be governed by anything but its own light is the same extravagance as to pretend that our love is too pure to be governed by anything but its own inclinations, our hatred too just to be governed by anything but its own motions. For if all that is base and criminal in love, all that is unjust and wicked in hatred, is strictly and solely to be imputed to our reason, then no perfection can be ascribed to our reason but such as is to be ascribed to our love and hatred.

HENRY DODWELL

Dodwell (c. 1700–1784) studied at Oxford, and then read law. His late entrance into the deist discussion, in the work here presented, provoked significant controversy, since it is most unclear whether the piece represents a subtly ironic attack on orthodoxy by reducing the argument for it to absurdity, or whether it is to be taken seriously.

Christianity Not Founded
on Argument

I recur to the subject of our last meeting: the subject of the world where it is most material to think right, where it is indeed of the most tremendous consequence to be mistaken. What are all your ingenious discoveries of speculative truths, which at best serve but to entertain and amuse the imagination, if, in the main point, in the one essential truth, you are still to seek? There only it is that ignorance and error are fatal, and knowledge truly of importance. Had you erred in any branch of human science, your penetrating reason would, in all probability, have recovered and set you right again; but here, be assured, it will have no such effect, as proudly as you insist upon its admired all-sufficiency.

If once you allow yourself in doubting, I will take upon me to answer for the consequence that you never will well believe; if once you come fairly to your proposed situation for "proving all things," be

assured that you will never "hold fast" (I Thess.
5:21) anything. To offer to sit down to examine
seems to me to be absolutely giving up the cause of
religion, and desiring me to dispute, to be begging
the question. For is it not most absurd to require a
belief if previous examination be requisite? If skepticism be this necessary qualification for the obtaining of a true faith, how can we ever be secure that
it shall not improve into direct unbelief? If doubting
be at all admitted, conviction can never with any
propriety be insisted on. Conviction is a dubious and
uncertain consequence wherever there is ground for
debate, and therefore not to be promised for, any
more than any other contingency. If I am once left
free to examine, I can by no means be tied up in the
issue. It is in its own nature a necessary and independent event, under no influence of mine, where
I have no power to interpose to direct its course or
operations, or any further interest or concern than
merely as a looker-on.

There is no medium betwixt believing and not believing. If, as I apprehend you, you do indeed intend
to waive all religion till your reason is satisfied about
it, know that from the very moment of that resolution
so long you actually apostatize from Christianity and
renounce your baptismal vow. A strange method this!
To turn one's back upon religion in order to meet it,
to discard it as a means to commence acquaintance.

Never believe but I am convinced as well as you
that opinions founded on prejudice and ignorance
are not that truth which the Gospel requires at our
hands. It is yet further evident to me that where
reason is to determine the cause, she must be left to
herself to determine fairly; that it is the greatest
injustice and mockery to invite her to give sentence

where there have been practices beforehand, and are practices still continued, to obstruct or limit her influence. Thus far it seems then I readily agree with you in all your preliminaries in behalf of reason and her rights, but you will defer building too much upon the concession till you hear the ground I profess for this agreement, which is my looking upon the subject before us to be absolutely out of her jurisdiction. I am fully persuaded that the judging at all of religious matters is not the proper province of reason, or indeed an affair where she has any concern.

I shall attempt to show you, *first*, that reason could not possibly, both from its own nature and that of religion, be the principle intended by God to lead us into a true faith; *secondly*, that neither is it so in fact from the plain account given us of it in Holy Scripture; and, *thirdly*, by tracing plainly from the same indisputable authority what it positively is, and by ascertaining the proper and prescribed means to come at the knowledge of divine truths.

In the first place, then, can it be by the exercise of their reason that men can be required to think all alike? You understand too well what the principle of reason is to expect any such consequence from it; nay, not to be certain of its producing a direct contrary effect. A thinker of a much lower degree of proficiency would disdain, very justly, to bestow a second thought upon so preposterous a scheme as that of unity in opinion proposed to be effected by reasoning. He sees readily at first view that the different light things appear in to different men must necessarily create a different sense of things; that an infinity of sects is but the natural and unavoidable consequence of every man's thinking for himself; that from the very notion of speculative inquiry, and the immense variety of human understandings, private judgments must of course run into the greatest latitude.

In the next place, with what regard, with what patience rather, can one of this class be supposed to attend to questions propounded to him under the restraints of threats and authority, to be talked to of danger in his decisions, and have the rod held out with the lesson, to have propositions tendered to his reason with penalties annexed? His reason, ever necessitated to determine just as she does of herself, and by her nature incapable either of paying compliments or giving offense. He is conscious all the while that he has no such free vote to dispose of, and therefore disdains with all justice an attempt, equally weak and unjust, of frightening him into a compliance out of his power.

I ask further; can a man be baptized into a rational religion? Where is reason concerned when babes accept the terms of salvation by deputy, and are entitled to all the privileges of the most extensive faith by another's act? A fresh instance from the manner of its culture that reason was to have originally no share in making the graft: we are to pray for increase of our faith. Had we been expected to have contributed to its establishment by any endeavors or pains of our own, we might have had cause to suspect yet further that the ground-work too was to be something wherein we were to be ourselves accessories. But if prayer be the effectual means proposed for the attaining the perfection of our faith, there is a strong presumption too that our labors of every other kind were to be spared throughout the whole progress, and that it was to be introduced after a like manner by methods purely divine and without any of our assistance.

If religion admits at all of examination, it must necessarily admit likewise of (at least a temporary) disbelief. The rational Christian, whoever he be, must of course have originally set out a skeptic, and hesitated for a time even whether the Gospel were true or false. Tell me, I beseech you that contend for a rational belief, since the first moments of doubt are but necessary preparatives in your scheme, and therefore not in themselves criminal, by what authority (if the evidence happens never to take the effect) can a man be obliged ever to be resolved? If a man may, nay must, disbelieve a while for information's sake, why may he not e'en disbelieve forever for want of due information? If doubting be indeed one moment allowable, who shall ascertain the precise time for summing up the evidence and pronouncing sentence? Who shall take upon him to settle the last lawful point of hesitation, making the proper indulgence to the tardy apprehension, and exacting a more ready decision from the more capable? For all this reasonable allotment of time in proportion to their several abilities, men must innocently take who are to "work out their salvation" (Phil. 2:12) by the use of their reason; they must be permitted to acquaint themselves fully and perfectly with the merits of the cause before they can be expected to form maturely and give in their important determinations upon it; and the more fair and severe the scrutiny, the more time it must necessarily cost them. The very integrity of the examiner will be the natural impediment to his dispatch.

Now if this be the case, that a man must go thus

long without his religious determinations, it will, I think, be something very difficult to prove them necessary at all; since 'tis probable they may now come too late to answer the end for which they were designed. For let us ask ourselves, what is the proposed use and purpose of this faith required? Is it not to influence our actions, and direct our conduct through life? And when have we more occasion for such a monitor than at the crisis when our passions are most prevalent, in those early years when reason is least able to form her judgments in our assistance? The use of faith is to enable us "to overcome the world." (I John 5:4) But what shall become of this promised victory if the contest must be so long depending, and if we must be so long taken up with "fitting on our armor"? (Eph. 6:11ff.)

Meantime the powers of darkness, and our own corrupt dispositions, will be fatally gaining ground upon us every day, long before this boasted ally can have raised her forces to come in to our protection, or be qualified in any degree to deal with them. Our passions will be beforehand with our reason, in spite of all her pretensions. The habits of vice will be taking deep root the while, let her preparations be never so expeditious, or her motions never so watchful to oppose them; they must needs have got the start in their advances before she can, by her nature, have made any considerable progress in those salutary discoveries which are to regulate or subdue them. Now for want of this timely notice, and the secret of distinguishing, we may more than probably have embarked in wrong measures at setting out, and be lost in the power of habit beyond recovery, before we know where we are. Unprovided of all restraining considerations, and at a loss for a better guide, we shall, of course, give up ourselves wholly to our natural bias and the law of inclination; and when we have lived the best part of our lives thus at adventure, and strayed so far without the lessons of this sage counsellor, they will go near, when they arrive, to find us actually engaged already, and beyond the power of precept to retrieve. Whilst I am myself in search after just notions of right and wrong, and attempting to learn by speculative discoveries what they are, 'tis not much to be expected that anyone else shall find them in my conduct. And the misfortune is that in our present situation there is no standing still to look about us, even so much as to find out the way. We must be running on ourselves in life, let our systems proceed never so heavily.

But were it possible still that our doubting disciple should not be in the meantime at this supposed loss for his duty on any occasion, let his natural obligations, as he may pretend, be never so obvious and self-evident, and his practice never so strictly conformable; what if without this previous acquisition and devout temper I contend for, the best of lives is no circumstance to recommend or qualify us for any regard from the throne of grace? "Good works done before faith," and without the special influence of this sanctifying principle, are so far from being accepted themselves as the terms of a complete obedience that they do not so much as put men into a nearer state for favor, or a capacity of being the sooner enlightened; they do not, as our church expresses it, make men "meet to receive grace." [1] The exactest observer of moral laws is a vile and wretched

---

[1] From Art. XIII of the Articles of Religion of the Church of England.

sinner in God's account, as long as he proceeds by
human lights and motives, and upon the strength of
mere ethics only.

If beyond these uses assigned, the discovery of our
rule of action or the purifying and stamping a value
upon the fruits of common morality, there be still
further something abstractedly of a necessary qualification in a true faith, something of a meritorious
nature in the thing itself, considered merely as a
proper test of our obedience, we must yet, if reason
be the allotted guide, be obliged to wait at least till
that reason can bring us her report. Meantime in this
infidel interim should death surprise us, what shall
now become of our hopes without this necessary
preparative for our introduction? You will examine,
you say; "thou fool! this night shall thy soul be required of thee." (Lk. 12:20) And is it now any un-
warrantable conclusion, from all these considerations,
to infer that religion therefore can never be a thing
to be taught, that it must needs be something that
does not require time to attain, like other common
lessons and sciences, which are indifferent in their
consequences? Since the very same reasons that make
it necessary at all, make it equally so for every moment of our lives. The souls of the multitude are
lodged in their hands, and that for the wisest purposes. They are formed entirely with a view to active
life. What an injurious representation, what an arbitrary image is this then of our wise and good
creator! Requiring a just judgment of things, and not
giving abilities to judge at all; making salvation a
matter of blind chance and guess-work, and setting
out precious souls upon the hazard of a random conjecture; and all this, too, where the determining either

right or wrong must in itself be equally meritorious. For the nature of the evidence of religion in your rational way, being founded entirely on the credit and authenticness of history, a very critical point to pronounce upon, it is impossible, without a good natural turn for reasoning, and even some very considerable acquisitions of learning superadded, to give any rational decision at all in the case.

Whereas, in my humble sense the truth of the history itself is by no means the matter in question, but my obligation to assent to it. It is one thing whether a proposition be indeed true in itself, and another whether a man be bound to apprehend and believe it. A distinction, not sufficiently attended to on this subject. For that absolute and certain truth of the Gospel, which shines out indeed so conspicuously upon a proper discussion and acquaintance, does yet not at all hinder but that it may very possibly appear otherwise to the rude and short-sighted understandings of many that cannot enter sufficiently into the argument to become apprised of its merits. It is still a speculative truth, whose explanation and whole force depends upon a just apprehension of moral proofs, and it is to be learnt only by reasoning; and therefore must from its nature be liable to be often misconceived, and have its opponents so far necessitated, and therefore innocent, in their opposition, without some further cause and principle of offense to justify their being damned for mistaking. Demonstrative, doubtless it is; but what is that to me, who have not the talents requisite for entering into demonstrations? It is by no means sufficient that your argument be indeed conclusive in itself, unless you can adapt it effectually to my understanding too, and make it conclusive to me. It must be upon such a connection only that all my duty in the case can possibly be grounded.

For the same reason, all the ingenious applications of mysterious prophecies, and their references, are in my opinion never to be mentioned as arguments and means of conviction in behalf of a truth destined to be universally received. The excellent *Analogy of Reason and Revelation*[1] lately communicated might induce me yet more powerfully to acknowledge at least a very great and specious appearance of truth in its traced connections and inferences, if the subject were indifferent in its consequences, and I were left to myself to pronounce freely what occurred naturally to my mind from the consideration of it. But when I consider all these enlightening lucubrations as proofs actually insisted on, and whose force I am bound to admit, as calculated for the general and ready use of all those to whom the precept of believing is addressed; or, in short, as that which any part of the evidence is to stand upon, or depend for its support; however I may honor the sagacious authors of these new lights for their particular discoveries, I cannot but draw to myself very different consequences from those they seem to expect from their proposal of them. Instead of availing to convince my reason of the truth of any particular religious system, they have a contrary effect, and suggest strongly to me that such a position can never be that necessary truth, which stands in need of any such far-fetched apologies and labored accounts to reconcile and explain it.

---

[1] Bishop Joseph Butler's *The Analogy of Religion, Natural and Revealed.*

Whenever I reflect with myself upon the general importance and end of religion, I cannot found its evidence by any means on any complication of circumstances to be traced out by industry or address, for the illustration of its authority. I cannot but form to myself some more simple characteristic of full sufficiency always accompanying it. I cannot but conclude in my mind that the whole force of its evidence must have been contemporary with the original institution itself, and have been entirely complete for the purpose ever since its first publication; that necessary truths were not revealed by halves, and left to be perfected afterwards at leisure by the efforts of human wit; that the evidence of the Gospel must have this one property of its great author, to be the "same yesterday, today, and forever" (Heb. 13:8); and consequently must have been equally plain and affecting to such as never lived to be in the way of these supplemental revelations, and who never heard a syllable in their lives of *Analogies.*

We are to remember always that the terms of salvation are equally calculated for the benefit of such as cannot so much as read, as they were chiefly published to the world by men actually under that incapacity themselves. Now it is to be remembered all along, and carried carefully with us through all these considerations, that the great command to believe is peremptory and absolute; no conditions in the case that we shall believe if we have time, if we have abilities, or if preceding prejudices have not first taken too fast hold to prevent us.

Let us however suppose that our rational inquirer has happily labored through all impediments to his wish; that he is crowned with all imaginable success in his undertaking, and confirmed at last beyond all

remains of doubt and scruple in his religious persuasions. Let us consider him for the present as having
attained to the highest degree of satisfaction in the
point that reason can possibly help him to. Will a
faith thus built upon syllogisms ever furnish out any
of those miraculous effects which are described to
attend a just and finished belief? Can this be the
faith whose promised influence was to supersede the
powers of second causes, and triumph over the whole
course of nature in its operations? Can this be the
faith whose efficacy was to "remove mountains," and
make men "walk upon the water"? (Matt. 17:20;
14:22ff.) Or will it even serve to produce any of those
more known and ordinary characteristics that are
given us to distinguish the true believer? The calm
votary of reason's dictates will not so readily be
brought to express all that sanguine concern for his
opinions which is required of a disciple of Christ.
He will be apt to be very much wanting in that
laudable warmth with which religious truths are to
be asserted and promoted, since the best warrant of
human reason can never give such assurance of the
truth but that we may possibly be mistaken; and if
we may, it is madness of partiality to attack another's
principles with vehemence, as if we were the only
persons not liable to error. It is, he is sensible, but
a very unpromising dependence for disciples where
the guide himself is liable to alter his mind, which
must ever be the necessary situation of every teacher
who derives his authority from no higher a principle
or stronger light than that of his own reason. If he
deal ingenuously in his researches, and prosecute
truth with that honesty and vigor which he ought,
he must be unavoidably liable to recantation every
moment of his life without remedy. For the decrees

of a human understanding can, in their nature, have no pretension to be irreversible.

And this is another very singular and essential defect of a rational faith, that it must always be so very precarious. For what reason first established, it is evident the same reason must ever have the power to repeal. Hence a rational faith will ever be subject to change, and the most fixed resolves and mature determinations that reason can make must be always ready to be "turned about with every wind of doctrine," (Eph. 4:14) as the evidence shall shift to another point. Whereas it is the religious man's resolution, as it is his duty, to persist in the faith he has once espoused to his life's end. Convinced of the truth of his adopted Gospel, he disclaims henceforth all further trial, and triumphs forthwith in such a supposed certainty that he piously implores the protection of heaven to preserve him firm in his present situation against the dangerous power of any innovation whatsoever, and all new principles that might possibly alter and corrupt him.

But the reverential part of our adherence, which takes its rise from a supposed sacred authority, being once removed, it is impossible we should ever after be brought back again to pay the same profound and religious deference to our own uncertain reasonings, and discoveries of our own making. The just horror of venturing at all upon such a question, where the truth of religion is concerned, and where a possibility of its falsehood is actually supposed, is the best and only security of our proper veneration for the subject. When once these important out-works are demolished, when once we are come so far as to make no scruple of examining freely for ourselves, the main hold upon our religious engagements is then broke through, and farewell forever all the true spirit of discipleship. The very presuming that we have a right to call these matters to a rehearing, and abilities to decide in them for ourselves, is an effectual step taken toward the throwing off for the future all that obsequious awe and dependence which is the life of this cause. When once we have made a practice of traversing with so much freedom the avenues and approaches of the sanctuary, whence once we have presumptuously inured ourselves to the stamping thus boldly and familiarly over holy ground, we shall with difficulty be recovered to a tender sense of the reverence and devotion due to the place, to the pious posture of humble supplicants, and prostration.

In the last place, no conviction drawn from reasoning can ever have force enough to make us virtuous against our inclinations; the highest degree of moral assurance will never be a sufficient balance for present temptations. The mortifying all our most beloved affections, and restraining all the strongest propensities of our nature, (in which our obedience to religious rules consists) is too substantial a sacrifice to be made to the most specious suggestions of our own fallacious reasonings. Venerable tradition and historical records, though never so plausible and well attested, can yet never be a sufficient basis for a belief which is to produce a new course of life and an absolute mastery of our passions, in opposition to all the importunate solicitations of sense and the violent appetites of depraved nature. It is still all but human testimony this, in its nature ever liable to error as depending only on fallible authors. And however forcibly such an evidence may operate for the present upon our judgment whilst actually under consultation, we shall see all its true amount and weight in a juster light at those seasons when we expect to make use of it and feel its influence, and shall be apt to remember involuntarily when we come to action, and some darling passion crossed by it puts the question in good earnest home to us, that it is nothing more than the precarious conjecture of a fallible judge, upon the traditional testimony of a fallible witness. Can a scheme thus vouched and ascertained be ever expected to gain that prevailing ascendancy over our minds as to change thus wonderfully all our obvious and palpable interests, and take off all our regard from objects present and familiar to our desires, to bring us to depend confidently on distant expectations and promises for our compensation? We shall hardly be induced to quit what we actually feel, for any less consideration than something which we actually know; nothing less than a thorough conviction can effectually secure a thorough reformation.

And if this rational faith will not serve us even defensively, and on common emergencies, so much as to make a good living Christian, much less will it produce a faithful martyr upon occasion, if ever so severe an exercise of it be demanded at our hands. Here is yet a more conspicuous instance of that absolute certainty which there ought to be in our faith for such a purpose, since the strongest operations of our reason can never point out truth to us in a light glaring and forcible enough to furnish such an experiment. The philosopher thus pressed would be apt, with a very natural casuistry, to distinguish between opinions and principles, and to remit much of his tenaciousness under such circumstances. Rational conviction will readily be distrusted when

matters come to such a crisis. The rationalist may
indeed, in his retirement, be wonderfully affected
with the abstracted contemplation of his discoveries,
and his formed resolutions of constantly persisting in
them; but when once he is called upon to exert its
promised influence, and put to a test like this, he
will soon be convinced that he must call in much
greater aid than that of plausible hypotheses to confirm him steadfast amidst the rage and cruelty of
malicious murderers, and enable him to be faithful
to the last to a persecuted religion, and that nothing
but a fixed and well-grounded confidence of being
happy forever in another world can effectually prevail
on him to renounce all his hopes and interests in
this. "The exceeding weight of glory" (II Cor. 4:17)
will have but little weight with us, till it be first
fully revealed; we must have this heaven actually
"opened to our view," and "behold the Son of Man
standing plainly before our eyes," (Acts 7:55f.) (not
through the dim and obscure perspectives of history
and tradition) to support and reward us.

II

My next proof proposed was that reflection and
common sense were seconded and confirmed in this
point by the divine word itself, and that it was plain
from Scripture that no such appeal to the understanding was actually ever made or intended.

Now this part of my assertion would, I think, demand of me only a small degree of my industry for
its justification. I should, I apprehend, have little
more than merely to collect and range for the purpose all those expressions, both literal and figura-

tive, that treat of the nature of faith, or have any relation to the subject. Such as: lest they should "understand with their hearts" (Matt. 13:15); their foolish "heart" was darkened (Rom. 1:21); purified their "hearts" by faith (Acts 15:9). Expressions applicable with no propriety to the intellectual faculty, but evidently descriptive of the will only.

But as quotations in behalf of doctrinal points are many times liable to have their application disputed, and it is perhaps often difficult enough to ascertain critically their just sense and meaning against all the specious exceptions of prejudiced wit, I shall choose rather, for the present, to enlarge upon a particular which appears to me entirely uncontrovertible, and that is the plain narrative part of that history, as far as it relates to the business of planting the Gospel and the manner by which it was attempted.

Did our savior himself, then, lay the arguments and proofs of his mission frankly before his disciples, and then give them time to consider calmly of their force, and liberty to determine thereon, as their reason should direct them? Or did they, when thoroughly persuaded, ever take any such course themselves amongst their intended proselytes? No such matter. For his part, "he taught them, as one having authority." (Mark 1:22) He considered himself as the person he was, as one who derived from heaven the instructions he was communicating, and therefore taught them very justly, as a master who had a right to dictate and prescribe to his pupils without reply. With what strong circumstances of approbation and applause is a ready acquiescence always recorded for our imitation? What matter of greater merit do we meet with than this of an extempore subscription? Whereas reason is naturally a slow, distrustful scholar, ever backward to give any great confidence as long as she can find the least room to start new difficulties. "We will hear thee again of this matter" (Acts 17:32) is the true adjourn-ing spirit and style of the academic; whereas the language of the Gospel is at once "believe you that I am able to do this?" (Matt. 9:28) The conviction, you see, was to precede the evidence, as the terms of the favor to be consequently conferred. The Pharisees, it is said, "tempting him, asked a sign," that is, some testimonial of the truth of his declared mission. And what did this request produce? Why, he sighed deeply at their perverseness, who were so hard to be convinced, and styled them a "foolish and adulterous generation" (Matt. 16:1-4) for their presumption.

The successors in the ministry we find continuing the same method of practice exactly in their turn, and treading punctually in their master's steps in the ex-ecution of their office, insisting constantly on the ready acknowledgement of their doctrines without any concessions of time for doubt or deliberation. Nor could it possibly be otherwise, if we consider the situation of the preacher in the infancy of revela-tion, and what an extensive province he had to run through with his intelligence. He must of course be always in haste to get on, and could have no time to spare, if he were so disposed. His commission re-quired him to keep stirring. "The harvest was plenteous" (Matt. 9:37) upon his hands, and that alone must oblige his hearers to come in at short warning, to snatch the critical opportunity, or fairly expect to stand to the loss.

Nor were indeed these instructors in themselves qualified to go through with any such regular way

of attack, if the nature of their commission had admitted it. They wanted as much the skill and address
to manage a controversy as the leisure to attend it.
They were no proficients in any science but, on the
contrary, the most artless and illiterate persons living. A shrewd intimation that such were purposely
chosen out to be the instruments to convey this
knowledge to us, that there might not be the least
seeming room for any mistaken notion of the kind;
that we might not possibly be tempted to attribute
to reason's force, or impute to any personal art or
acquisition of their own, an effect which was to be
the sole and immediate act of the divinity, and
wherein the power of God was in a particular manner to be glorified. For the same reason the single
person amongst them who was possessed of the supposed advantages of human learning resolves, we
see, immediately from the first moment of his com-
mencing apostle, to leave it all behind him, and absolutely to disclaim all further acquaintance with it.
He was determined to "know nothing else" amongst
his disciples "but Christ crucified," nor to make any
use of "the wisdom of words," lest "the cross of Christ
should be made of none effect." (I Cor. 2.2ff.)

But here again I have, I am very sensible, been
holding you for some time past in the highest impatience of zeal to interpose and remind me that if
these founders of Christianity did not indeed make
their appeals to men's reasoning faculty, it was because they were endowed with a readier and more
decisive means of conviction in its stead, one more
suitable both to the capacities of their audience and
their own necessary course of dispatch; and this, by
an immediate appeal to their senses, by performing

works before their faces, in attestation of those doctrines, which it was confessedly not within the reach of any human power to produce.

To all which one might not unplausibly suggest in return, what has been so often urged upon the occasion, that miracles have, time out of mind, been undoubtedly performed as well in favor of false doctrines, and therefore can never be singly, and of themselves alone, any certain marks of a true. This the Scripture itself confesses, when it warns us of "lying wonders, and false Christs" (Matt. 24:24); to take the most exact care and caution what we give credit to of the kind; and recommends to us the further and more secure trial of them by what it calls "their fruits." (Matt. 7:15ff.) It allows plainly, by sending us thus to trace analogies, and consult more known relations for the experiment, that we have no proper ground to ascertain any truth from these appearances, distinctly considered, without having this recourse to a surer standard, and calling in the foreign aid of moral considerations to confirm their authority. One might allege yet further that all this wonderful and miraculous evidence was indeed, in strictness, but the natural effect of their doctrine, instead of any supernatural proof of its veracity, which may be best learned by considering the nature of these extraordinary actions, and the occasions on which they were generally produced.

The healing of the sick seems to want no labored account to explain it, but to speak itself sufficiently in its own beneficial tendency. It was a suitable instance of that universal benevolence they were recommending, and which it would be very hard to consider apart from its merits and influence. It must seem strange too, if our Lord had any such meaning as to convince by these works, that he should be always so remarkably upon the reserve in that respect whenever he happened amongst unbelieving company; that he should be so particularly sparing of these supposed arguments amongst the very persons who seemed most to want them.

We find our master ever disclaiming, with the severest resentment, all followers of that complexion; and no temper checked and discouraged with so constant an aversion as this of "seeking a sign." (Cf. Mark 8:11-13, etc.) There cannot be a stronger and more express reproof to all such notions and constructions of his good offices, than that he makes use of, in jealousy of heart, upon being applied to for an instance of this extraordinary assistance in favor of the nobleman's child: "Unless you see signs and wonders, you will not believe." (John 4:48) Indeed, so far from any view of the kind, or with any tendency toward the reclaiming men's minds to a proper sense and reverence for the actor, do all these extraordinary essays seem directed; so far from having any the least connection with the thought of procuring disciples from the influence of the spectacle, that a certain degree, and that no ordinary one, of previous confidence and persuasion appears to have been constantly stipulated for beforehand, to entitle them to have their applications at all listened to or regarded; and to be the sole measure and rule of dispensing these occasional favors. Wherever we find them conferred, it was still first perceiving that the patient "had faith to be healed." (Acts 14:9)

Thus much I have ventured to intimate of my own sentiment upon this stronghold, as it is by some esteemed, of miraculous evidence; and such it is, as I cannot but imagine, must needs appear sufficiently

conclusive and satisfactory for the purpose for which
it is produced. But what if now, in deference to some
contrary opinions, I am still disposed to give up all
this part of the argument? What if I am yet content,
after all, to grant you readily to the extent of your
demand that these miracles were indeed displayed
merely for that end you suppose, and carry with them
all that invincible demonstration you contend for?
How will this yet serve the purpose? To whom were
they such demonstration? To those only who saw
them. Certainly to none else. They were conviction
enought at that instant of time, and upon that spot,
when and where they were exhibited. But wherever
either of these circumstances fail all that resistless
force of the evidence must fail with it. What they
saw will serve well to convict that one generation to
which these wonders were immediately addressed.
These mighty works could be no demonstration to
any that were not actually and personally present
when they were done; and, for the same evident reason, can be none to us now. All that we can possibly
know of the matter at this distance will amount, in
the strictest calculation, to no more than moral appearances of truth, and probable attestations of the
fact.

And are we to imagine now that God would ever
leave a matter of such consequence upon such a
foundation? That he who vouchsafed at first to create,
and then to redeem, at so great an expense, the souls
of all mankind, would have sat down after all, lightly
contented to have scattered thus partially and accidentally his necessary light amongst a very few,
and leave all the rest of us to the courtesy only of
a few reporters, to such a testimony as, if it were
never so false, it were absolutely impossible we

could, in our situation and circumstances, ever discover to be so?

If miracles were necessary in the infancy of the Gospel, they are so still, and will be to the end of the world; whenever they cease, the authority of the evidence which depended on them ceases with them. That divine demonstration to by-standers, the voice of God himself, "This is my beloved Son," (Lk. 3:22) has been, by one intervening age, dwindled long long since to human tradition; God no longer bears witness to his Son, but men only bear witness to God. The date will quite change the property of the evidence, and really make all this difference. We hear no more that awful sound but by repetition and echo, and all that commanding force of the great original attestation and acknowledgement is sunk with us into the uncertain assertions of fallible men relating it after one another. The light of conviction which is thus received can extend no further than to the eyewitness himself, lost and extinguished the first moment it is offered to be imparted. Here then it commences human authority, and, as such, becomes the proper subject of our free inquiry and debate. It recurs in that shape to the province of reasoning, and can now claim no longer to be treated with any other deference than it shall appear from its own proper merits to be entitled to. Now whatever degree of credit it may, by this means, in time acquire in my mind from strict trial and probation, this can surely never be of itself that kind of flagrant and incontestable evidence which God expects should work such an instant effect on our minds, and be accepted by us at first mention with so much readiness and acquiescence. The hesitating upon the genuineness of a particular tradition can never be that offense which

God has professed himself to take so heinously at
our hands as an affront to his personal veracity (with
which it has no connection). "He that believeth not
God hath made him a liar, because he believeth not
the record that God gave of his son." (I John 5:10)

And yet that there must be somewhere still, we
may be certain, (from the consideration of his reasonable nature who enjoined the duty) some general
uniting principle in being which, if well attended to,
will be a proper foundation in all for this general
assent. That it cannot be human reason, we have
seen clearly on many accounts, both from the natural effects of reason itself, and the known methods
by which faith was first introduced. Perhaps then we
have amongst us some visible fountain of truth, some
universal dictator assigned us upon the spot, to whom
we may all have recourse in our doubts to be resolved alike, and determined alike. Alas! the evidence of such a qualification is but still fresh matter
for dispute; the authority of this assumed character,
and claim of infallible must be grounded still on some
positive warrant; and the truth of such a pretension
is again itself a new question, which can apply only
to reason for decision, and must of consequence be
still liable to all the objections to our former scheme,
and to the same variety of persuasions about it.
Hitherto then, it seems, we are absolutely at a loss
for this general standard and principle, so much
wanted, of universal conviction. Have we no prospect left for making the discovery?

III

Strange is it to my apprehension that any man who
has ever looked into the sacred writings to be re-

solved, the authentic oracles from which alone all our intelligence of that kind can be drawn, could possibly overlook it, and mistake the rule there so plainly delineated to our hands. There we find laid down, in the first place, in the strongest terms, the negative preliminary I have been advancing, and reason ever entirely excluded the question. We are there expressly assured that no man ever attained to the belief of revealed truths by the strength or assistance of his natural faculties, as we have at once from the same authority the further positive instruction communicated and the true principle assigned us.

The third article I proposed mentioning, and which we have in one plain word thus fully set forth to us: "No man can say that Jesus is the Lord, but by the Holy Ghost." (I Cor. 12:3) Here is pointed out to us at once that great dictator and infallible guide we have been seeking for, and indeed the only character we can possibly think of any way equal to such a province. It could be nothing less than omniscience and omnipresence itself, nothing but this inexhaustible fountain of all truth that could be sufficient to such a demand. And he it is, the promised oracle, who is to attend the charge of believers to the end of the world, to keep alive his divine light constantly in their hearts; not to teach them rudiments of logic, but to irradiate their souls at once with a thorough conviction, and perform more by one secret whisper than a thousand clamorous harangues from the schools. From the satisfaction consequent to the mind from his performance of this great office it is that he is so eminently styled "the Comforter," (John 14:26) as his operations are in another place very strongly and significantly termed "the power of God unto salvation." (Rom. 1:16) "He that believeth on the Son

of God hath the witness in himself." (I John 5:10)
In this sense it is that we are properly styled "the
temples of the Holy Ghost," (I Cor. 6:19) the consecrated scenes of his constant residence, there ever
personally present, and dispensing his certain intel-
ligences to the soul, which the apostle calls the
"witnessing of the Spirit with our spirit." (Rom. 8:16)

The plainest declaration and direction what kind
of evidence Christians were always to trust to and
rely on for the information and assurance of their
minds we may find summed up in brief in their master's last instructions at parting. "The Spirit of truth,
which proceedeth from the Father, he shall testify
of me." (John 15:26) As we have both the same person and commission elsewhere again specified: "The
Spirit, whom I shall send, shall lead you into all
truth." (John 16:13) But, not to stand forever tran-
scribing particulars, I refer you once more to the
great original which will, I think, really save us both
all further trouble in quotations and comments, and
abundantly evince, in opposition to all the evasive
constructions which may be imposed on particular
passages, that he was in general to inspire conviction
as well as holiness, and to illuminate as well as
sanctify our hearts.

Now this supposition once suggested, let us for a
further trial and confirmation take a short view of
religion in the light I have been representing it, of
inspiration and infused evidence, and we shall
readily find that this principle alone fully answers
all the ends proposed, that it concurs in every particular with what we must naturally expect from
such an assistant, and has indeed all those requisite
qualities which reason so manifestly wanted for the
office. It is, in the first place, universal: "That grace

which bringeth salvation hath appeared unto all men." (Titus 2:11) "This is the light which lighteth every man that cometh into the world." (John 1:9) The uniting principle speaks the same thing to all. Thus instructed all alike, men may be brought to think all alike, which could never have possibly been effected by any other means. This again is of authority and force sufficient to countermand effectually against the most violent assaults of temptation, as it is itself of equal certainty with any gratifications they can possibly propose. Here is feeling opposed to feeling, knowledge to set against appetite, and a strong and palpable internal sense to balance all the motions of the external. Above all, it is of immediate influence, and operates without delay. Such was the happy metamorphosis of an officious persecutor into as zealous an apostle: a conversion effected not by the force of dilatory inferences and conclusions, but an "irresistible light from heaven" (Acts 23:6) that flashed conviction in a moment. This is that "still small voice" (I Kings 19:13) that bespeaks the immediate presence of the divinity, and makes its dictates, as it were, self-evident to the mind where it is lodged. In this the sum and substance of all argumentation is briefly comprised, the very spirit and extract of all convicting power, of a nature, perhaps, but little differing from that of intuition itself. We stand no longer now in need of any of the credit of ancient miracles, or of the genuineness of distant records, a very slender and insufficient ground to answer all the great purposes and insure all the rigid demands of religion. We can vouch, in its stead, a present and a standing miracle of our own, an evidence that supports all the same original authenticness which it carried with it in ages so far remote, this living witness and uncorrupt commentator in our own breasts, surviving all changes and successions, and equally contemporary with each one of us. It is our security that "he has writ his law in our hearts." (Rom. 2:15; Heb. 8:10; 10:16.) The indelible characters stamped upon those living tablets are such as are out of the power of the unfaithfulness or ignorance of transcribers to falsify or pervert. And our faithful monitor and guardian has promised to continue this office and abide with us himself (as long as our faith is expected to last) "to the end of the world," (Matt. 28:20) that we might not be left liable one moment to a possibility of error and imposition. Now, what a very different prospect this, and ground of security, from the empty notion of mere manuscript authorities and paper-revelations?

So far from resting the terms of our salvation upon a writing that must run the common hazards of all other memorials of the kind, I will venture to assert that even though a constant miracle were to interpose upon the occasion to exempt this important charge in particular from all these changes and chances incident to all other compositions; though the same almighty power that first indited were to continue hovering perpetually with a guardian hand over the sacred depositum, and the constant inspection of an immediate providence concerned to revise and keep it up in all its original purity; with all these special privileges supposed, it were still absolutely defective and insufficient for any such revealing purpose. The plainest terms, in the plainest characters that could possibly be devised, were at the best but the putting a dead letter into our hands, without the additional grace of this active interpreter to attend it.

To return to my argument, pursuant to this my explanation of the nature of faith and the means of attaining it, we may be now able to give some account of how the want of it comes to be such a crime, and so severe a penalty to be denounced against unbelief, which upon no other supposition we could possibly do. The universal tender of this conviction, however potent in its influence, must yet depend greatly upon the proper disposition of our minds to give it reception for its efficacy, and so far will give place, and afford ample matter for trial and probation, and become indeed a test of our obedience. Whereas the arbitrary determinations of reason are well known to be events entirely out of our power, and consequently to leave no such room for either our merit or offense. Hence, I say, can arise the only possible connection in nature between conscience and believing, in every other light the most ridiculous jargon in the world. The commanding men to believe rationally, commanding them to have their reason satisfied, and this with threatened imputation of guilt and infliction of punishment, is such a scheme at first view as no pretense of authority, human or divine, can command any regard or attention to, or indeed any notice but that of the contempt due to paradoxes, the most eminently impudent and ridiculous. On the other hand, a rebellious opposition of all the gracious instances of the divine spirit to enlighten our hearts, the willful repugnance to all his earnest solicitations to accept of his saving truths, may they not as deservedly expect all that so great an injury calls for, or the resentment of so great a personage can inflict? Here disbelieving and guilt have meaning again when put together, since the compliance required is no longer that of the understanding but of the will, in its nature free and there-

fore accountable; and though we are not by any
means chargeable for the effects of our apprehension,
yet there is no reason but that we may be with all
justice called to the strictest account for our obstinacy, impiety and perverseness.

There cannot indeed be on earth two things more
widely differing than this same religion humanly considered, and falling under the proper cognizance of
this supernatural inspired sense, when it is attempted
to be weighed in the unequal scales of human reason,
and when it has its just poise of being proved in "the
balance of the sanctuary." "With men this is impossible, but with God all things are possible," (Matt.
19:26) is a distinction nowhere more strongly ex-
emplified than in this subject. By his almight influence, the faith of grace shall give us demonstration
of things in a thousand instances, to which the faith
of reason could never have in any degree reconciled
us. They clash in their very first principles, their very
first lessons are the most direct contradictions to each
other. The foundation of philosophy is all doubt and
suspicion, as the foundation of religion is all acquiescence and belief. But how extremely distinct and
opposite they are in their natures and interests, we
may judge yet more certainly from their constant ex-
perienced effects, by observing that there never was
in fact any right understanding or correspondence
betwixt their several professors; that from the very
earliest accounts they have run naturally into separate parties, have manifested on all occasions a hostile
disposition and mutual antipathy, and stood ever in
the most distant remove from all possibility of amicable terms and reconcilement. The philosopher inso-
lently scoffing the believer, and he, in his turn, as
zealously proscribing the philosopher. "The wisdom

of man" has ever been reputed "foolishness with God" and his servants, and but too often the censure has been (however vainly) retorted. "The world by wisdom knows not God." (I Cor. 1:18ff.)

I am sure there is no one lesson that the holy writings have taken more care to inculcate in the strongest terms than this of denying our reason to give our faith scope. Are we not strictly enjoined to "captivate our reason to the obedience of faith"? (II Cor. 10:5) To captivate—to lay it under the most absolute restraint and prohibition, not to permit it the least opportunity or freedom to exert itself, or interpose on any occasion whatever. Is not "carnal wisdom," (II Cor. 1:12) viz., the result of human reason, everywhere industriously decried in the affair of believing? Is not philosophy at every turn degraded and branded with the name of folly, to make room for the more glorious principle of faith? And is it possible now that we can desire anything more positive and express for the purpose to convince us that this pure and divine institution (mysteries that "angels can be curious to look into"—I Pet. 1:12) was never meant to be made a subject for the challenges of logicians, and for schoolmen to play prizes upon?

It is much easier to excite a spirit to inquiry than to satisfy it. Now, if infidelity be indeed justifiable any one moment of our lives, who shall tell me what moment it ceases to be so? Who shall take upon him to determine the critical point when longer want of conviction becomes criminal, or settle the competent time we ought to be satisfied in? "O," says the rationalist in return, "as long as we are thus actually employed in the search, we may make ourselves perfectly easy in that point; God will, on his part, never certainly expect more of us than he enables us to perform. A sincere desire to know and do his will must supply, till his good time, the deficiency of the actual knowledge." So that, if we can disbelieve (as they term it) with a safe conscience, we shall do as well without it as with it. Excellent account of the necessity of a doctrine which God himself both did and suffered so much to introduce to us, and without whose actual acknowledgement he has so often assured us our offenses against him can have no remission. If the allowance of our own conscience be a sufficient security, it must be equally so under every profession; and then farewell to the notion of one only true and saving faith, and all the consequent care to discover it.

Strange paradox! that no one should believe to please God, without having first asked himself the question whether his son be not an impostor. Rather, who knows if grace may ever on any terms be vouchsafed after the having listened to such a suggestion, or once harbored so blasphemous a thought?

Amidst all the rationalist's extravagant and chimerical notions of I know not what strict justice in the case, and an equal indulgence due to the advocates of both sides, it is not, surely, to be seriously expected, even by his romantic self, that the well-grounded zeal of an enlightened preacher of the Gospel should really permit him to countenance thus equitably in his own defiance all the vain pretensions of these industrious ministers of darkness in their turn, and not rather laudably oppose to the utmost all establishment of blasphemous lectures against the truth of religion, and the erecting of common pulpits and privileges for Antichrist, avowedly to communicate his poison. All which, if religion were indeed a rational institution were, it must be confessed, no more than reasonable concessions, and the only method for cultivating a proper knowledge of her pretensions and veracity.

Questioning in religion is denying; and all suspending one's judgment (though even in order to be better informed) is, in this case, a professed and criminal opposition. Whereas, were religion indeed a rational institution, a man might surely well dispute it without a crime; the disputant could by no fair conclusion be reputed an adversary, and prosecuted with such sanguine and inveterate marks of hostility. A free and amicable correspondence might well be admitted, and the wildest opponent received upon an equal foot with his most orthodox and approved antagonist. All other methods of proceeding bespeak plainly the question already determined beyond all possibility of controversy. And so indeed it is, by that unerring principle which I have been pointing out. Thus instructed, we can consider it no longer as matter of speculation and argument, or bear with patience under any specious pretenses to have that savior which *we feel* denied in effect by being called in question. This prompts and authorizes all our just zeal and aversion on these occasions, and stamps that a laudable crusade and holy war against infidels which would else be no other than a wild and foolish sally of blind bigotry, the furious and mad spirit of superstitious frenzy and persecution.

JOHN WESLEY

Wesley (1703–1791) was a fellow of Lincoln College, Oxford, and a teacher and a scholar before he became the leading Evangelical of his day, and the father of Methodism. The following treatise exhibits both the kind of antithesis to the deist view of religion which the early Wesleyan writing took, and his specific comments on Dodwell's work.

An Earnest Appeal to Men of Reason and Religion

We are ready to give any that are willing to hear a plain account both of our principles and actions. We see (and who does not?) the numberless follies and miseries of our fellow creatures. We see on every side either men of no religion at all, or men of a lifeless, formal religion. We are grieved at the sight, and should greatly rejoice if by any means we might convince some that there is a better religion to be attained—a religion worthy of God that gave it. And this we conceive to be no other than love, the love of God and of all mankind—the loving God with all our heart, and soul, and strength, as having first loved us, as the fountain of all the good we have received, and of all we ever hope to enjoy; and the loving every soul which God hath made, every man on earth, as our own soul.

This love we believe to be the medicine of life, the never-failing remedy for all the evils of a dis-

ordered world. This religion we long to see established in the world, a religion of love, and joy, and
peace, having its seat in the inmost soul, but ever
showing itself by its fruits. We desire that others may
go the straight way to the religion of love, even by
faith.

Now faith (supposing the Scripture to be of God)
is "the demonstrative evidence of things unseen,"
(Heb. 11:1) the supernatural evidence of things invisible, not perceivable by eyes of flesh, or by any
of our natural senses or faculties. Faith is that divine
evidence whereby the spiritual man discerneth God
and the things of God. It is with regard to the spiritual world what sense is with regard to the natural.
It is the spiritual sensation of every soul that is born
of God.

Faith, according to the scriptural account, is the
eye of the new-born soul. Hereby every true believer in God "seeth him who is invisible." (Heb.
11:27) It is the ear of the soul, whereby a sinner
"hears the voice of the Son of God, and lives."
(John 5:25) It is the palate of the soul, for hereby a
believer "tastes the good word, and the powers of the
world to come." (Heb. 6:5) It is the feeling of the
soul, whereby a believer perceives both the existence
and the presence of Him in whom "he lives, moves,
and has his being," (Acts 17:28) and indeed the
whole invisible world, the entire system of things
eternal. And hereby, in particular, he feels "the love
of God shed abroad in his heart." (Rom. 5:5)

By this faith we are saved from all uneasiness of
mind, from the anguish of a wounded spirit, from
discontent, from fear and sorrow of heart, and from
that inexpressible listlessness and weariness, both of
the world and of ourselves, which we had so help-

lessly labored under for many years. In this we find
that love of God, and of all mankind, which we had
elsewhere sought in vain.

If you ask, "Why then have not all men this faith?
Why do they not believe immediately?" We answer,
"It is the gift of God." (Eph. 2:8) No man is able to
work it in himself. It is a work of omnipotence. It
requires no less power thus to quicken a dead soul
than to raise a body that lies in the grave. It is a
new creation; and none can create a soul anew but
He who at first created the heavens and the earth.

It is the free gift of God, which he bestows, not
on those who are worthy of his favor, not on such
as are previously holy, but on the ungodly and un-
holy, those in whom there was no good thing, and
whose only plea was, "God be merciful to me, a sinner." (Lk. 18:13) No merit, no goodness in man
precedes the forgiving love of God. His pardoning
mercy supposes nothing in us but a sense of mere
sin and misery; and to all who see and feel and own
their wants and their utter inability to remove them,
God freely gives faith, for the sake of him in whom
he is always "well pleased." (Matt. 3:17)

This is a short, rude sketch of the doctrine we
teach. These are our fundamental principles. According to the light we have, we cannot but believe the
Scripture is of God, and while we believe this, we
dare not turn aside from it. Will you object to such
a religion as this that it is not reasonable? Is it not
reasonable then to love God? Is it not reasonable
also to love our neighbor, every man whom God
hath made? Is it not reasonable that, as we have opportunity, we should do good unto all men? Well,
this is the sum of our preaching, and of our lives.
If, therefore, you allow that it is reasonable to love

God, to love mankind, and to do good to all men, you cannot but allow that religion which we preach and live to be agreeable to the highest reason.

Perhaps all this you can bear. It is tolerable enough; and if we spoke only of being saved by love, you should have no great objection. But you do not comprehend what we say of being saved by faith. Have patience then. By those words, "we are saved by faith," we mean that the moment a man receives that faith which is above described, he is saved from doubt and fear, and sorrow of heart, by a peace that passes all understanding; from the heaviness of a wounded spirit, by joy unspeakable; and from his sins, of whatsoever kind they were, from his vicious desires, as well as words and actions, by the love of God, and of all mankind, then shed abroad in his heart.

We grant, nothing is more unreasonable than to imagine that such mighty effects as these can be wrought by that poor, empty, insignificant thing which the world calls faith. But supposing there be such a faith on the earth as that which the apostle speaks of, such an intercourse between God and the soul, what is too hard for such a faith? O that you would at length cry to God for that heavenly gift whereby alone this truly reasonable religion, this beneficent love of God and man, can be planted in your heart.

This is scriptural Christianity, and this alone. Whenever therefore, you see an unreasonable man, you see one who is no more a Christian than he is an angel. So far as he departs from true, genuine reason, so far he departs from Christianity.

We join with you then in desiring a religion founded on reason, and every way agreeable thereto.

But one question still remains to be asked, "What do you mean by reason?" I suppose you mean the eternal reason, or the nature of things; the nature of God, and the nature of man, with the relations necessarily subsisting between them. Why, this is the very religion we preach: a religion evidently founded on, and every way agreeable to, eternal reason, to the essential nature of things. It is every way suitable thereto: to the nature of God, for it begins in knowing him, and where but in the true knowledge of God can you conceive true religion to begin? It goes on in loving him and all mankind, for you cannot but imitate whom you love. It is every way suited to the nature of man: for it begins in a man's knowing himself, knowing himself to be what he really is—foolish, vicious, miserable. It goes on to point out the remedy for this; it finishes all by restoring the due relations between God and man.

But perhaps by reason you mean the faculty of reasoning, of inferring one thing from another. There are many that utterly decry the use of reason, thus understood, in religion; nay, that condemn all reasoning concerning the things of God as utterly destructive of true religion. But we can in no wise agree with this. We not only allow but earnestly exhort all who seek after true religion to use all the reason which God hath given them. But your reasoning justly presupposes true judgments already formed, whereon to ground your argumentation. Else, you know, you will stumble at every step.

You know, likewise, that before it is possible for you to form a true judgment of them, it is absolutely necessary that you have a clear apprehension of the things of God, and that your ideas thereof be all fixed, distinct, and determinate. And seeing our ideas are not innate, but must all originally come from our senses, it is certainly necessary that you have senses capable of discerning objects of this kind: not those only which are called natural senses, which in this respect profit nothing, as being altogether incapable of discerning objects of a spiritual kind; but spiritual senses, exercised to discern spiritual good and evil. It is necessary that you have the *hearing ear,* and the *seeing eye,* emphatically so called; that you have a new class of senses opened in your soul, not depending on organs of flesh and blood, to be "the evidence of things not seen" as your bodily senses are of visible things; to be the avenues to the invisible world, to discern spiritual objects, and to furnish you with ideas of what the outward "eye hath not seen, neither the ear heard." (I Cor. 2:9)

And till you have these internal senses, till the eyes of your understanding are opened, you can have no apprehension of divine things, no idea of them at all. Nor, consequently, till then can you either judge truly or reason justly concerning them, seeing your reason has no ground whereon to stand, no materials to work upon. What then will your reason do here? How will it pass from things natural to spiritual, from the things that are seen to those that are not seen, from the visible to the invisible world? What a gulf is here! By what art will reason get over the immense chasm? This cannot be, till the Almighty come in to your succor, and give you that faith you have hitherto despised. Then upborne, as it were, on eagles' wings, you shall soar away into the regions of eternity, and your enlightened reason shall explore even "the deep things of God," God himself "revealing them to you by his Spirit." (Cf. Ex. 19:4; Isa. 40:31; I Cor. 2:10)

I expected to have received much light on this head from a treatise lately published and earnestly recommended to me; I mean *Christianity Not Founded On Argument*. But on a careful perusal of that piece, notwithstanding my prejudice in its favor, I could not but perceive that the great design uniformly pursued throughout the work was to render the whole of the Christian institution both odious and contemptible. In order to this, the author gleans up, with great care and diligence, the most plausible of those many objections that have been raised against it by late writers, and proposes them with the utmost strength of which he was capable. To do this with the more effect, he personates a Christian: he makes a show of defending an avowed doctrine of Christianity, namely, the supernatural influence of the Spirit of God; and often, for several sentences together (indeed, in the beginning of almost every paragraph) speaks so like a Christian that not a few have received him according to his wish. Meanwhile, with all possible art and show of reason, and in the most labored language, he pursues his point throughout, which is to prove that "Christianity is contrary to reason," or that "no man acting according to the principles of reason can possibly be a Christian."

It is a wonderful proof of the power that smooth words may have even on serious minds that so many have mistook such a writer as this for a friend of Christianity, since almost every page of his tract is filled with gross falsehood and broad blasphemy, and these suported by such exploded fallacies, and commonplace sophistry, that a person of two or three years' standing in the university might give them a sufficient answer, and make the author appear as irrational and contemptible as he labors to make Christ and his apostles.

CONYERS MIDDLETON

Middleton (1683–1750) was a scholarly controversialist throughout the first half of the eighteenth century. His attack on the miracles of the church (despite his insistence in his preface that "whatever be the fate of my argument, or were it allowed even to be true, the credit of the Gospel miracles could not in any degree be shaken by it") was commonly received as an attack on the whole mode of apologetic in which miracles played a significant role. Middleton's work appeared the same year as David Hume's *Philosophical Essays*, in which the famous Humian attack on miracles appeared; Hume complained that the attention given Middleton's treatise was responsible for the relatively little furor about his own.

A Free Inquiry into the Miraculous Powers

PREFACE

The present question, concerning the reality of the miraculous powers of the primitive church, depends on the joint credibility of the facts pretended to have been produced by those powers, and of the witnesses who attest them. If either part be infirm, their credit must sink in proportion; and if the facts especially be incredible, must of course fall to the ground, because no force of testimony can alter the nature of things. The credibility of facts lies open to the trial of our reason and senses, but the credibility of witnesses depends on a variety of principles wholly concealed from us, and though in many cases it may reasonably be presumed, yet in none can it certainly be known.

In the original promise of these miraculous gifts, there is no intimation of any particular period to which their continuance was limited. The next question is, by what sort of evidence the precise time of their duration is to be determined? To whatever age one may restrain it, the difficulty at last will be to assign a reason why we must needs stop there. The more we descend from those earliest fathers, the more strong and explicit we find their successors in attesting the perpetual succession and daily exertion of the same miraculous powers in their several ages. If the cause must be determined by "the unanimous consent of fathers," we shall find as much reason to believe that those powers were continued even to the latest ages as to any other, how early and primitive soever, after the days of the apostles. For as far as the church historians can illustrate or throw light upon anything, there is not a single point in all history so constantly, explicitly, and unanimously affirmed by them all as the continual succession of these powers through all ages, from the earliest father who first mentions them, down to the time of the Reformation. Which same succession is still further deduced by persons of the most eminent character, for their probity, learning, and dignity, in the Romish Church to this very day. So that the only doubt which can remain with us is: whether the church historians are to be trusted or not; for if any credit be due to them in the present case, it must reach either to all or to none, because the reason of believing them in any one age will be found to be of equal force in all, as far as it depends on the characters of the persons attesting, or the nature of the things attested.

My opinion in short is this: that in those first efforts of planting the Gospel, after our Lord's ascension, the extraordinary gifts which he had promised were poured out in the fullest measure on the apostles, and those other disciples, whom he had ordained to be the primary instruments of that great work, in order to enable them more easily to over-rule the inveterate prejudices both of the Jews and Gentiles, and to bear up against the discouraging shocks of popular rage and persecution which they were taught to expect in this novitiate of their ministry. But in process of time, when they had laid a foundation sufficient to sustain the great fabric designed to be erected upon it, and by an invincible courage had conquered the first and principal difficulties, and planted churches in all the chief cities of the Roman Empire, and settled a regular ministry to succeed them in the government of the same, it may reasonably be presumed that as the benefit of miraculous powers began to be less and less wanted, in proportion to the increase of those churches, so the use and exercise of them began gradually to decline, and as soon as Christianity had gained an establishment in every quarter of the known world they were finally withdrawn, and the Gospel left to make the rest of its way by its own genuine graces, with which it was so richly stored, faith, hope, and charity. And all this may probably be thought to have happened while some of the apostles were still living.

The Introductory Discourse

It is an opinion commonly received among Christians, and above all among those of the Romish communion, that after the days of the apostles there resided still in the primitive church, through several successive ages, a divine and extraordinary power of working miracles, which was frequently and openly exerted, in confirmation of the truth of the Gospel, and for the conviction of unbelievers. This is generally alleged by the divines of all churches, in their disputes with the skeptics, as a subsidiary proof of the divinity of the Christian doctrine; and as it is managed by the church of Rome, is rendered more persuasive and affecting to the multitude than what the Gospel itself affords, by deducing the succession of those apostolical gifts down to our own times, and offering the testimony of the same miracles to the senses even of the present age.

It must be confessed that this claim of a miraculous power, which is now peculiar to the church of Rome, was universally asserted and believed in all Christian countries, and in all ages of the church, till the time of the Reformation. For ecclesiastical history makes no difference between one age and another, but carries on the succession of its miracles, as of all other common events, through all of them indifferently, to that memorable period. But the light of the Reformation dispelled the charm. For that spirit of inquiry with which Christendom was then animated detected the cheat, and exposed to public view the hidden springs and machinery of those lying wonders by which the world had been seduced and enslaved to the tyranny of Rome.

The most prevailing opinion is that they subsisted through the three first centuries, and then ceased at the beginning of the fourth, or as soon as Christianity came to be established by the civil power. Eminent divines seem unwarily to have betrayed the Protestant cause by transferring the miraculous powers of the church into the hands of enemies, yielding up this sacred depositum to the defense and support of popish Rome. For it was in these very primitive ages, and especially in the third, fourth and fifth centuries, in which the chief corruptions of popery were either actually introduced or the seeds of them so effectually sown that they could not fail of producing the fruits which we now see. By these corruptions I mean the institution of monkery, the worship of relics, invocation of saints, prayers for the dead, the superstitious use of images, of the sacraments, of the sign of the cross, and of consecrated oil, by the efficacy of all which rites, and as a proof of their divine origin, perpetual miracles are affirmed to have been wrought in these very centuries. Our dispute with them is, not how ancient but how true their doctrines and practices are. And if they are not derived from Christ or his apostles, nor founded in the holy Scriptures, it is indifferent to us Protestants from what age they drew their birth, whether it was from the four first, or the four last centuries of the church.

We see to what a state of things the miracles of the fourth and fifth centuries would reduce us: they would call us back again to the old superstition of our ancestors. But if the miracles of these later ages must needs be rejected, and if, as I have said above, ecclesiastical history makes no difference between them and those of the earlier ages, it may reasonably be asked, where then are we to stop? And to what period must we confine ourselves?

After the strictest attention to what both the ancients and the moderns also have delivered on this subject, I find great reason to be convinced that the pretended miracles of the fourth century were not only in general, and for the greatest part, but entirely and universally the effects of fraud and imposture. I take it to be a maxim on which we may safe'y depend that wherever the bishops, the clergy, and the principal champions of the Christian cause are found to be tampering with false miracles, and establishing new rites and doctrines by lies and forgeries, it would be vain for us to look for any true miracles in that age and that church. And this was actually the case of the fourth century, in which all its most illustrious fathers, now saints of the Catholic church, have severally recorded and solemnly attested a number of miracles, said to be wrought in confirmation of some favorite institutions of those days, which, in the judgment of all learned and candid Protestants, are manifestly fictitious and utterly incredible.

This discovery of the state of the fourth century will reflect fresh light on our searches, both backwards and forwards; and from its middle situation give us a clearer view as well into the earlier as the later ages. For example, if we suppose the miraculous powers of the church to have been withdrawn in the beginning of this century, the first inference which it suggests is that they were withdrawn likewise through all the succeeding centuries. Because the reasons for which they are imagined to have ceased at this particular period grow stronger still in every later age, as the church was everyday gaining strength and a firmer establishment, not only from the protection of the magistrate but from an authority and power of its own, independent of the civil government.

The forged miracles of the fourth century must necessarily taint the credit of all the later miracles, down even to the present age. For they depend as it were upon each other, as the parts of one chain, so that wherever we draw out a link, all the rest which hang upon it must of course fall to the ground. Let us consider then, in the next place, what light the same forgeries will afford us in looking backward also into the earlier ages, up to the times of the apostles.

And first, when we reflect on that surprising confidence and security with which the principal fathers of this fourth age have affirmed as true what they themselves had either forged or what they knew at least to be forged, it is natural to suspect that so bold a defiance of sacred truth could not be acquired or become general at once, but must have been carried gradually to that height, by custom and the example of former times, and a long experience of what the credulity and superstition of the multitude would bear.

Secondly, this suspicion will be strengthened by considering that this age, in which Christianity was established by the civil power, had no real occasion for any miracles. For which reason the learned among the Protestants have generally supposed it to have been the very era of their cessation; and for the same reason the fathers also themselves, when they were disposed to speak the truth, have not scrupled to confess that the miraculous gifts were then actually withdrawn, because the church stood no longer in need of them. So that it must have been a rash and dangerous experiment to begin to forge miracles at a time when there was no particular temptation to it, if the use of such fictions had not long been tried, and the benefit of them approved and recommended by their ancestors, who wanted every help toward supporting themselves under the pressures and persecutions with which the powers on earth were afflicting them.

Thirdly, if we compare the principal fathers of the fourth with those of the earlier ages, we shall observe the same characters of zeal and piety in them all, but more learning, more judgment, and less credulity in the later fathers. If these then be found either to have forged miracles themselves, or to have propagated what they knew to be forged, or to have been deluded so far by other people's forgeries as to take them for real miracles (of the one or the other of which they were all unquestionably guilty), it will naturally excite in us the same suspicion of their predecessors, who, in the same cause and with the same zeal, were less learned and more credulous, and in greater need of such arts for their defense and security.

Fourthly, as the personal characters of the earlier fathers give them no advantage over their successors, so neither does the character of the earlier ages afford any real cause of preference, as to the point of their integrity, above the latter. The first indeed are generally called the purest, but when they had once acquired that title, from the authority of a few leading men, it is not strange to find it ascribed to them implicitly by everybody else, without knowing or inquiring into the grounds of it. But whatever advantage of purity those first ages may claim in some particular respects, it is certain that they were defective in some others, above all which have since succeeded them. For there never was any period of time in all ecclesiastical history in which so many rank heresies were publicly professed, nor in which so many spurious books were forged and published by the Christians, under the names of Christ and the apostles and the apostolic writers, as in those primitive ages. Several of which forged books are frequently cited and applied to the defense of Christianity by the most eminent fathers of the same ages as true and genuine pieces, and of equal authority with the Scriptures themselves. And no man surely can doubt but that those who would either forge or make use of forged books would in the same cause, and for the same ends, make use of forged miracles.

Now from all these considerations taken together it must, I think, be allowed that the forged miracles of the fourth century give us just reason to suspect the pretensions of every other age both before and after it. My argument would be much the same if it were grounded on the allowed forgeries of any later age. The earlier miracles rest on no better foundation, nor are supported by any better evidence, than the later. But then, if these later, after all the confidence of their advocates, may certainly be discredited, and must consequently be rejected, it follows that the earlier may with as much reason be rejected too. Which brings me at last to that general conclusion which I have undertaken to illustrate: *that there is no sufficient reason to believe, from the testimony of antiquity, that any miraculous powers did ever actually subsist in any age of the church after the times of the apostles.*

But this will be the proper business of the subsequent treatise, in which I shall endeavor to evince, by particular facts and testimonies, what this general view of the question here given, and the reflections naturally arising from it, would previously dispose us to suspect: that the pretended miracles of the primitive church were all mere fictions, which the pious and zealous fathers, partly from a weak credulity and partly from reasons of policy, believing some perhaps to be true and knowing all of them to be useful, were induced to espouse and propagate for the support of a righteous cause.

As far as miracles can evince the divinity of a religion, the pretensions of Christianity are confirmed by the evidence of such as of all others on record are the least liable to exception, and carry the clearest marks of their sincerity, being wrought by Christ and his apostles for an end so great, so important, and so universally beneficial as to be highly worthy of the interposition of the deity; and wrought by the ministry of mean and simple men, in the open view of the people, as the testimonial of that divine mission to which they pretended; and delivered to us by eye-witnesses, whose honest characters exclude the suspicion of fraud, and whose knowledge of the facts which they relate scarce admits the probability of a mistake. This is the genuine ground on which Christianity rests: the history of our savior's doctrine and miracles, as it is declared and comprised within the canon of the holy Scriptures. Whenever we go beyond this, we weaken its foundation by endeavoring to enlarge it, and, by recurring to an evidence less strong and of doubtful credit, take pains only to render a good cause suspected, and expose it to the perpetual ridicule of the skeptics and free-thinkers. We admit no miracles but those of the Scriptures; the rest are either justly suspected or certainly forged. In truth, it has always been considered as a fundamental principle of the Reformation that *the Scriptures are a complete rule both of faith and manners, and as such are clear also and intelligible, in all fundamental points, to every private Christian.* In this, all Protestant churches agree, how much soever they may differ in any other article. If this be true, then whatever be the character of the ancient fathers, or whatever they may have taught and practiced in any age of the church, is a matter wholly indifferent, and makes no part in the religion of a Protestant. Consequently, no difference of judgment with regard to those fathers ought to give any cause of offense or hatred among the members of that communion. If the Scriptures are sufficient, we do not want them as guides; or if clear, as interpreters. Everyone therefore may enjoy his opinion of them with the same liberty as of any other writers whatsoever, with this caution only, that an esteem of them is apt to carry us too far, and has actually carried many into great and dangerous errors; whereas the neglect of them cannot be attended with any ill consequence, since the Scriptures teach everything that is necessary, either to be believed or practiced.

But though this doctrine of the sufficiency of the Scriptures be generally professed through all the reformed churches, yet it has happened in our own that its divines have been apt, on all occasions, to join the authority of the primitive church to that of the sacred writ, to supply doctrines from the ancient councils in which the Scriptures are either silent or thought defective, to add the holy fathers to the college of the apostles, and by ascribing the same gifts and powers to them both, to advance the primitive traditions to a parity with apostolic precepts.

The design of the present treatise is to give some check to the current of this zeal, and to fix the religion of Protestants on its proper basis, that is, on the sacred Scriptures, not on the authority of weak and fallible men, the detection of whose errors and the suspicion of whose frauds would necessarily give a wound to Christianity itself. Their very errors afford a profitable lesson to us; for the many corruptions which crept into the church in those very early ages are a standing proof and admonition to all the later ages that there is no way of preserving a purity of faith and worship in any church but by reviewing them from time to time, and reducing them to the original test and standard of the holy Scriptures.

Inquiry

I. I propose to draw out, in their proper order, all the principal testimonies which relate to the miraculous gifts of the church, as they are found in the writings of the fathers from the earliest ages after the days of the apostles. Whence we shall see, at one view, the whole evidence by which they have hitherto been supported.

Our first thoughts are carried of course to the apostolic fathers, that is, to those who had lived and conversed with the apostles, and who were ordained to succeed them in the government of the church. As there are several whose writings still remain to us, so it is natural to expect that in these valued remains the history of the miraculous gifts, which are so much celebrated by the writers of the New Testament, should be carried on still in the same manner by these their immediate successors. It is remarkable that there is not the least claim or pretension, in all their several pieces, to any of those extraordinary gifts which are the subject of this inquiry. The whole power of their ministry seems to have lain in the innocent and amiable character of their lives, and in the pious, charitable and fervent strain of their pastoral exhortations. Here then we have an interval of about half a century, the earliest and purest of all Christian antiquity after the days of the apostles, in which we find not the least reference to any standing power of working miracles for the conviction of unbelievers, but, on the contrary, the strongest reason to presume that the extraordinary gifts of the apostolic age were by this time actually withdrawn, and the Gospel left to make its way by its own strength and the authority of those credentials and original miracles with which Christ had furnished it.

But if the apostolic writers have left us in the dark with regard to our present argument, their successors, it must be owned, as far as their authority reaches, have cleared it from all obscurity by their strong, explicit, and repeated attestations of many extraordinary gifts and miraculous powers which were constantly and publicly exerted in the Christian church through each succeeding age.[1]

It has already been observed that the silence of the apostolic writers on the subject of these gifts must dispose us to conclude that in those days they were actually withdrawn. Surely the pretended revival of them after a cessation of forty or fifty years cannot fail of infusing a suspicion of some fiction in the case. If they really did cease for so long an interval, and at a time when the Christian cause seemed to want them the most, we cannot conceive any reason why they should afterwards be revived, when the church, without any such help, had been gathering more and more strength by its own natural force. But it is remarkable that as the church continued to increase in power and credit, so its miraculous gifts are said to have increased also in the same proportion. For though by an increase of power it certainly

---

[1] Middleton cites Justin Martyr, Irenaeus, Theophilus of Antioch, Tertullian, Minucius Felix, Origen, Cyprian, Arnobius, Lactantius.

stood less in need of true miracles, yet by the same power it became more able to reward, and more likely therefore to excite false pretensions to them.

Again, the difference between the miraculous gifts of apostolic days and these of the following ages will greatly confirm the suspicion just intimated. The apostles wrought their miracles on special occasions, when they felt themselves prompted to it by a divine impulse, but at other times were destitute of that power. We never find them calling out upon the magistrates and people to come and see the mighty works which they were ready to exhibit before their eyes on all occasions. Whereas this confident and ostentatious manner of proclaiming their extraordinary powers carries with it an air of quackery and imposture as it was practiced by the primitive wonder-workers who, in the affair especially of casting out devils, challenge all the world to come and see with what superiority of power they could chastise and drive those evil spirits out of the bodies of men.

II. I propose to throw together all which those fathers also have delivered concerning the condition of the persons who are said to have been endued with those gifts and to have wrought the miracles to which they appeal. None of the "venerable saints" have anywhere affirmed that either they themselves or the apostolic fathers before them were endued with any power of working miracles, but declare only in general that "such powers were actually subsisting in their days, and openly exerted in the church." But as to the persons who wrought them, they leave us strangely in the dark. Of what condition soever the actors were, it is certain that in the performance of their miracles they were always

charged with fraud and imposture by their adversaries. We may fairly conclude that the celebrated
gifts of those ages were generally engrossed and
exercised by private Christians, chiefly of the laity,
who used to travel about from city to city to assist the
ordinary pastors of the church and preachers of the
Gospel in the conversion of the pagans, by the extraordinary gifts with which they were supposed to
be endued by the spirit of God.

Here again we see a dispensation of things ascribed
to God quite different from that which we meet with
in the New Testament. In those days the power of
working miracles was committed to none but the
apostles and to a few of the most eminent of
the other disciples. Upon the pretended revival of the
same powers in the following ages we find the ad-
ministration of them committed not to those who
were instructed with the government of the church.
But if those venerable saints and martyrs were not
endued with them when living, they had amends
made to them when dead, if we can believe the
reports of their successors, by a profusion of them
on their bones and relics, which suggests a further
cause of suspecting the faith and judgment of those
early ages. How can we think it credible that God
should withhold his distinguishing favors from his
faithful servants when living, to bestow them on their
rotten bones?

These things, I say, are so strange as to give just
reason to suspect that there was some original fraud
in the case, and that those strolling wonder-workers,
by a dexterity of juggling which art, not heaven, had
taught them, imposed upon the credulity of the pious
fathers, whose strong prejudices and ardent zeal for

the interest of Christianity would dispose them to embrace, without examination, whatever seemed to promote so good a cause.

III. I propose to illustrate the particular characters and opinions of the fathers who attest those miracles, so as to enable us to determine with more exactness what degree of credit may be due to their testimony. The authority of a writer who affirms any questionable fact must depend on the character of his veracity and of his judgment. As far as we are assured of the one, so far are we assured that he does not willingly deceive us; and from our good opinion of the other, we persuade ourselves that he was not deceived himself. In many cases, the want of judgment alone has the same effect as the want of veracity toward invalidating the testimony of a witness, especially in cases of an extraordinary or miraculous nature, where the weakness of men is the most liable to be imposed upon, and the more so as it happens to be joined to the greater piety and simplicity of manners. I shall examine what proofs of a sound judgment and strict veracity are to be found in the writings of those fathers who attest the miraculous stories which we are now considering.

Justin Martyr's genius will best be illustrated by some specimens of it from his writings. Among the endowments conferred in an extraordinary manner on the primitive Christians, the gift of expounding the holy Scriptures was reckoned one; this, as Justin frequently affirms, "was granted by the special grace of God to himself." Let us inquire, then, what use he made of this divine gift. If ever he was really enlightened by it, we might surely expect to find the effects of it where he is discoursing on the mystery of the cross, which he declares to be the greatest symbol of power and dominion, and explains in the following manner: "Consider all the things in the world, whether they could be administered, or have any communication with each other, without this form of the cross. The sea could not be passed, unless that trophy called the sail were preserved in the ship; the earth could not be tilled without it, for neither diggers nor artificers could do their work but by instruments of this shape. The form of man differs in nothing else from other animals but in the erection of his body and the extension of his arms, which shows nothing else but the figure of the cross." Again, "Hear," says Justin, "how Christ, after he was crucified, fulfilled the symbol of the tree of life in paradise, and of all the other things which were to happen afterwards to the righteous. For Moses was sent with a rod to redeem his people; with this rod he divided the sea, brought water out of the rock, and with a piece of wood made the bitter water sweet. Jacob also with sticks made his uncle's sheep bring forth such lambs as were to be his own again." And so he goes on, in this way of allusion, to apply all the sticks and pieces of wood in the Old Testament to the cross of Christ. It would be endless to run through all the interpretations of the same kind which are to be found in this father, since his works are but little else than a wretched collection of them, the pure flights of an enthusiastic fancy and heated brain, which no man in his sober senses could mistake for divine revelation. Yet this pious father insists that they were all suggested to him from heaven. What credit then can be due to this father, in the report of other people's gifts and inspirations, who was so grossly deceived himself, or willing at least to deceive others, in this confident attestation

of his own? It will be said perhaps that these instances show indeed a weakness of judgment, yet do
not impeach the veracity of Justin as a witness of
fact. With regard to which, we must call to mind
that the want of judgment alone may, in some cases,
disqualify a man as effectually from being a good
witness as if he wanted veracity too.

For example, Justin expressly affirms that he had
seen the cells in which the seventy were shut up
to the task of translating the Bible.[1] Now it is certain
that there never were any such cells, nor any such
translators; and the best excuse which can be made
for him is that he was imposed upon by some Jews
or Christians of Alexandria, who might show him
some old ruins under the name of cells. Should we
allow these cases to be clear of any fraud or design
to deceive, yet they yield so bad a sample of his understanding as to render his testimony of very little
weight in any other relation whatsoever. For if he
was deceived in such plain and obvious facts, where
a common discernment and moderate knowledge of
history would have enabled him to have discovered
the truth, how much the more easily would he be
caught by a confederacy of subtle and crafty impostors, employing all their arts to amaze and dazzle
the senses of the credulous, and to put off their surprising tricks for the miraculous effects of a divine
power?

If a gross absurdity of opinions, and the belief of
things impossible, be the proof of a weak mind; if
expositions of the Scriptures void of reason and common sense betray a great want of judgment; then

---

[1] A reference to a legend about the translation of the Greek
version (Septuagint) of the Old Testament.

we may justly charge those defects upon these ancient fathers. Since the very earliest of all traditions,
and the nearest to the fountain's head, are found
to be so corrupt, it will demonstrate at least what
a treacherous foundation they must be to build any
opinion upon, and much more any article of our
faith.

These facts show likewise the weakness of that
argument for the truth of doctrines from the unanimity with which they are asserted by the ancient
writers. If the unanimity of the primitive fathers
must be allowed to have so great a force as to
evince the truth of any opinion, it would necessarily
establish all those monstrous doctrines above specified,[1] since it would be difficult to produce any other
whatsoever in which there was so great a harmony
among them, or so general a consent of the whole
church, through the three first centuries, and that
entirely grounded upon the pretense of apostolic
tradition.

IV. I propose to review all the several kinds of
miracles which are pretended to have been wrought,
and to observe from the nature of each how far the
credibility of them may reasonably be suspected.

1. As to the first, and the principal indeed of all
miracles, that of raising the dead, it is very strange
that from the time of the apostles there is not an
instance of this miracle to be found in the first three
centuries, except a single case, slightly intimated by
Eusebius from the books of Papias, which he seems
to rank among the other fabulous stories delivered by
that weak man.

---

[1] Middleton has pointed particularly to the millenarianism
in Irenaeus, and the common belief in demons and in
magic.

2. The next gift said to have resided in it is that of healing the sick, in favor of which the ancient testimonies are more full and express, though with some variation concerning the method of cure. But be that as it will, the pretense of curing diseases by a miraculous power was so successfully maintained in the heathen world by fraud and craft that, when it came to be challenged by the Christians, it was not capable of exciting any attention to it among those who themselves pretended to the same power. Every man's experience has taught him that diseases thought fatal and desperate are often surprisingly healed of themselves, by some secret and sudden effort of nature, impenetrable to the skill of man. But to ascribe this presently to a miracle, as weak and superstitious minds are apt to do, to the prayers of the living or the intercessions of the dead, is what neither sound reason nor true religion will justify. Wherefore when the narratives of these pretended cures are delivered to us by partial and interested or by weak and credulous men, they will always furnish reason to suspect that the relators were either deluded themselves, or willing to delude others. And unless we know more precisely in this case the real bounds between nature and miracle, we cannot pay any great regard to such stories, especially when we are informed at the same time by the Christians themselves that the same cures were performed also by knaves and impostors of all sects and nations.

3. The most eminent and celebrated of all the miraculous powers of the primitive church was the gift of casting out devils, or the cure of demoniacs. To this the ancient fathers make the most frequent appeals. It is not easy however to collect from their accounts what was the real cause of these demon-

iacs. The fathers themselves seem to have been fully persuaded that they were actually possessed and tormented by devils; yet many learned men of modern times have imagined them rather to have been affected by epilepsy. It is very remarkable that all the fathers who lay so great a stress on this particular gift yet allow the same power both to the Jews and the Gentiles, as well before as after our Savior's coming. But there is such uniformity in all the primitive accounts of them that they all seem to have been cast in the same mold. And from the testimony of antiquity itself it is evident that many of their demoniacs could not possibly be cured by all the power of the exorcists, and that the cures which are pretended to have been wrought on any were but temporary, and appear to have been the cessation rather of a particular fit than the real expulsion of a demon. Whence we may reasonably conclude that it was nothing else but a false mimicry of that genuine power which was exercised by our Lord and conferred afterwards on his apostles.

4. The next miraculous gift ascribed to the primitive church is that of prophetic visions and ecstatic trances. But how credible soever these visions might appear to the generality of Christians in those days, yet there were many at the same time, as Cyprian himself confesses, who condemned and made a jest of them, as mere illusions and impertinent fancies. To declare freely what I think, whatever ground there might be in those primitive ages, either to reject or to allow the authority of those visions, yet from all the accounts of them that remain to us in these days there seems to be the greatest reason to suspect that they were all contrived, or authorized at least, by the leading men of the church, for the

sake of moderating and governing with more ease
the unruly spirit of the populace in those times of
danger and difficulty. For they are generally applied
to excuse the conduct of particular persons in some
instances of it liable to censure, or to enforce some
particular doctrine or discipline warmly pressed by
some and not well relished by others, or to confirm
things not only trifling and frivolous but sometimes
even superstitious and hurtful to true religion.

5. As to the gift of expounding the Scriptures by
a divine inspiration, which is claimed likewise by
the primitive fathers, there is not the least trace of
it to be found in any age of the church from the days
of the apostles. For in the second and third centuries,
the very period in which all the other miraculous
gifts are supposed to have flourished in their greatest
vigor, it is certain that a most senseless, extravagant,
and enthusiastic method of expounding prevailed,
which has ever since been utterly slighted and rejected. Whereas in these later days, when all extraordinary gifts are confessedly ceased, a clear,
solid, and rational way of interpreting generally ob-
tains. If those fathers through a fervency of zeal,
or an enthusiastic turn of mind, could mistake such
fanciful expositions for divine inspirations, I see no
reason why they might not as easily be deluded in
every other instance of those pretended gifts, which
flattered the same zeal and spirit that so strongly
possessed them.

6. The gift of tongues is also claimed, and affirmed to have been actually possessed by the primitive Christians. But from the time of Irenaeus there
is not a single father in all the succeeding ages who
has ventured to make the least claim to it, or to speak
of it in any other manner than as a gift peculiar to

the first Christians. If we trace the history of this gift from its origin, we shall find that, in the times of the Gospel, in which alone the miracles of the church are allowed to be true by all Christians, it was the first gift which was conferred upon the apostles in a public and illustrious manner. But in the succeeding ages, when miracles began to be of a suspected and dubious character, this gift is mentioned but once by a single writer, and then vanished of a sudden.

In the case of these miracles, there is one circumstance common to all the writers who attest them, that though their assertions be strong, their instances are weak. In short, when we reflect on the corrupt and degenerate state of the church in the end of the fourth century, allowed by the most diligent inquirers into antiquity; and that this age was the pattern to all that succeeded it; we may safely conclude, without weighing the particular scruples which may arise upon each single miracle, that they were all of the same class and species, the mere effects of fraud and imposture.

V. I now propose to refute some of the most plausible objections which have hitherto been made by my antagonists, or which the prejudices and prepossessions of many pious Christians may be apt to suggest, to the general turn of my argument.

1. In the first place, it is objected that by the character which I have given of the ancient fathers, the authority of the books of the New Testament, which were transmitted to us through their hands, will be rendered precarious and uncertain. To which I answer that the objection is trifling and groundless, and that the authority of those books does not depend upon the faith of the fathers, or of any particu-

lar set of men, but on the general credit and reception
which they found, not only in all the churches, but
with all the private Christians of those ages who
were able to purchase copies of them, among whom,
though it might perhaps be the desire of a few to
corrupt, yet it was the common interest of all to
preserve and of none to destroy them.

2. It has been alleged that all suspicion of fraud
in the case of the primitive miracles seems to be
precluded by that public appeal and challenge which
the Christian apologists make to their enemies the
heathen. But this objection, to all who are acquainted
with the condition of the Christians in those days, and
the difficulty of making their apologies known to
the world, will be found to have no weight in it.
The Gospel continued to be held in such contempt
by the generality of the better sort through the three
first centuries that they scarce ever thought it worth
while to make any inquiry about it, or to examine
the merit of its pretensions. Should the case happen
in our days, that any Methodist, Moravian, or French
prophet,[1] should publish an apology for his brethren,
addressed to the King and the Parliament, is it not
wholly improbable that the government would pay
any regard to it, or take it at all into their consideration? How can it then be supposed that the Emperor
and Senate of Rome, who had a worse opinion of
the ancient Christians than we of our modern fana-
tics, would give themselves the trouble to read or
to consider the merit of their writings?

3. It is urged against me that no suspicion of craft
can reasonably be entertained against persons of so

---

[1] Cf. Ronald A. Knox, *Enthusiasm* (Oxford, 1950), chs.
15–16.

exalted piety, who exposed themselves to persecution and even to martyrdom in confirmation of the truth of what they taught. But all who are conversant with history know that nothing gives so invincible a prejudice and so strong a bias to the mind of man as religious zeal in favor of everything that is thought useful to the object which excites it. Glory or reputation was a great spur to martyrdom, for by the principles of those ages nothing was esteemed more glorious than the "crown of martyrdom," as it was called. The principal incentive to martyrdom was the assurance, not only of an immortality of glory and happiness in another world, but of extraordinary and distinguished rewards, and a degree of happiness proportionable to the degree of their sufferings. And the opinion likewise, which commonly prevailed in those days, that this world was near to its end, made them the more eager still to snatch that crown which would entitle them to such high privileges, give them a power with God so as to procure benefits for others, and make them assessors and judges with Christ himself at the last day. Lastly we must add the scandal of flying from persecution, and the infamy which attended the lapsed Christians. These principles and motives, I say, had such force as sometimes to animate even bad men to endure a martyrdom. For heretics also had their martyrs. It is not my design to detract in any manner from the real merit and just praise of those primitive martyrs who, with an invincible constancy, sustained the cause of Christ at the expense of their lives. Yet they were subject still to the same passions, prejudices, and errors which were common to all the other pious Christians of the same age. The circumstance of their martyrdom, while it gives the

strongest proof of the sincerity of their faith and
trust in the promises of the Gospel, adds nothing to
the character of their knowledge or their sagacity,
nor consequently any weight to their testimony, in
preference to that of any other just and devout
Christian whatsoever.

4. It has been frequently objected that to reject
the unanimous testimony of the fathers, in their reports of the primitive miracles, will destroy the faith
and credit of all history. This was the constant cant
of all the zealots, even of the heathen world, whenever any of their established superstitions were attacked by men of sense. That same outcry was made
by them also against the Christians, when the Gospel
first began to spread itself among them. The Christians constantly derided this plea; yet when it came
at last to their own turn to find authority on their
side, they took up the same plea which they had
before rejected, and urge it at this day as the principal objection to Protestantism: "that it is a mere
novelty, which had no existence in the world before
Luther, contradictory to the practice of all the primitive saints and martyrs of the Catholic church, and
to the unanimous consent of fifteen centuries."

If this objection therefore had ever been found to
have any force in it, the ancient Christians could
never have overruled the impostures of paganism,
nor our Reformers the superstitions of popery. But
in truth, it will appear to have no sense at all in it.
Our commerce with the times past, as they are represented to us in history, is of much the same kind with
our manner of dealing with the present. We find
many men in the world whose fidelity we have
just ground to suspect; yet a number of others whom

we can readily trust, sufficient to support that credit
and mutual confidence by which the business of life
is carried on. Just so in ancient history; we find many
things of which we have cause to doubt, many which
we are obliged to reject, yet its use still subsists. The
history of miracles is of a kind totally different from
that of common events, the one to be suspected always of course, without the strongest evidence to
confirm it, the other to be admitted of course, without as strong reason to suspect it. Ordinary facts, related by a credible person, furnish no cause of doubting from the nature of the thing; but if they be
strange and extraordinary, doubts naturally arise,
and in proportion as they approach toward the mar-
vellous, those doubts still increase and grow stronger.
For mere honesty will not warrant them; we require
other qualities in the historian—a degree of knowledge, experience and discernment sufficient to judge
of the whole nature and circumstances of the case.

The case of witchcraft affords the most effectual
proof of the truth of what I am advancing. There is
not in all history any one miraculous fact so authen-
tically attested as the existence of witches. All Christian nations whatsoever have consented in the belief
of them, and provided capital laws against them. In
our own country, great numbers have been condemned to die, at different times, after a public trial
by the most eminent judges of the kingdom. Now
to deny the reality of facts so solemnly attested, and
so universally believed, seems to give the lie to the
sense and experience of all Christendom; yet the
incredibility of the thing prevailed, and was found at
last too strong for all this force of human testimony.
So that the belief of witches is now utterly extinct,

and quietly buried without involving history in its ruin, or leaving even the least disgrace or censure upon it.

These instances are sufficient to evince the reasonableness and prudence of suspending our assent to reports of a miraculous kind, though attested by an authority which might safely be trusted in the report of ordinary events. Human nature has always been the same, agitated by the same appetites and passions, and liable to the same excuses and abuses of them, so that our experience of what passes in the present age will be the best comment on what is delivered to us concerning the past. To submit our belief implicitly and indifferently to the mere force of authority, in all cases, whether miraculous or natural, without any rule of discerning the credible from the incredible, might support indeed the faith, but would certainly destroy the use, of all history. But to distinguish between things totally different from each other, between miracle and nature, the extraordinary acts of God and the ordinary transactions of man; to suspend our belief of the one while, on the same testimony, we grant it freely to the other; and to require a different degree of evidence for each, in proportion to the different degrees of their credibility; is so far from hurting the credit of history, or of anything else which we ought to believe, that it is the only way to purge history from its dross and render it beneficial to us; and by a right use of our reason and judgment, to raise our minds above the low prejudices and childish superstitions of the credulous vulgar.

JOHN WESLEY

The bulk of Wesley's letter to Middleton consists of a detailed examination of patristic evidence; his initial charge, however, and especially his conclusion setting forth his own alternative, go beyond momentary controversy to the heart of the debate over deism.

To Dr. Conyers Middleton

Reverend Sir,

In your late *Inquiry* you endeavor to prove (1) that there were no miracles wrought in the primitive church; (2) that all the primitive fathers were fools or knaves, and most of them both one and the other; and it is easy to observe the whole tenor of your argument tends to prove (3) that no miracles were wrought by Christ or his apostles; and (4) that these too were fools or knaves, or both.

I am not agreed with you on any of these heads. My reasons I shall lay before you in as free a manner, though not in so smooth or labored language, as you have laid yours before the world.

You begin your Preface by observing that the *Inquiry* was intended to have been published some time ago; but, upon reflection, you resolved to "give out first some sketch of what you was projecting," and accordingly "published the *Introductory Discourse*" by itself, though "foreseeing it would encounter all the opposition that prejudice, bigotry, and superstition are ever prepared to give to all in-

inquiries" of this nature. But it was your "comfort that this would excite candid inquirers to weigh the merit and consequences of it."

The consequences of it are tolerably plain, even to free the good people of England from all that prejudice, bigotry, and superstition vulgarly called Christianity. But it is not so plain that "this is the sole expedient which can secure the Protestant religion against the efforts of Rome." It may be doubted whether deism is the sole expedient to secure us against popery; for some are of opinion there are persons in the world who are neither deists nor papists.

You proceed: "If the Scriptures are a complete rule (I reject the word 'sufficient,' because it is ambiguous), we do not want the fathers as guides, or, if clear, as interpreters. An esteem for them has carried many into dangerous errors: the neglect of them can have no ill consequences." I answer: (1) The Scriptures are a complete rule of faith and practice; and they are clear in all necessary points. And yet their clearness does not prove that they need not to be explained, nor their completeness that they need not to be enforced. (2) The esteeming the writings of the first three centuries not equally with but next to the Scriptures never carried any man yet into dangerous errors, nor probably ever will. But it has brought many out of dangerous errors, and particularly out of the errors of popery. (3) The neglect in your sense of the primitive fathers—that is, the thinking they were all fools and knaves—has this natural consequence (which I grant is no ill one, according to your principles), to make all who are not real Christians think Jesus of Nazareth and his apostles just as honest and wise as them.

I cannot dismiss this *Discourse* without observing that the uncommon artfulness and disingenuity which glare through the whole must needs give disgust to every honest and upright heart; nor is it any credit at all to the cause you have espoused. Nay, I am persuaded there are many in these kingdoms who, though they think as you do concerning the Christian system, yet could not endure the thought of writing against it in the manner that you have done: of combating fraud (if it were so) with fraud, and practicing the very thing which they professed to expose and abhor.

We have been long disputing about Christians, about Christianity, and the evidence whereby it is supported. But what do these terms mean? Who is a Christian indeed? What is real, genuine Christianity? And what is the surest and most accessible evidence (if I may so speak) whereby I may know that it is of God?

A Christian cannot think of the author of his being without abasing himself before him, without a deep sense of the distance between a worm of earth and him that sitteth on the circle of the heavens. He has a continual sense of his dependence on the parent of good for his being and all the blessings that attend it. To him he refers every natural and every moral endowment, with all that is commonly ascribed either to fortune or to the wisdom, courage, or merit of the possessor. And hence he acquiesces in whatsoever appears to be his will, not only with patience but with thankfulness.

And as he has the strongest affection for the fountain of all good, so he has the firmest confidence in him—a confidence which neither pleasure nor pain, neither life nor death, can shake. But yet this, far

from creating sloth or indolence, pushes him on to
the most vigorous industry. It causes him to put
forth all his strength in obeying him in whom he
confides. And as he knows the most acceptable worship of God is to imitate him he worships, so he is
continually laboring to transcribe into himself all his
imitable perfections.

Above all, remembering that God is love, he is
conformed to the same likeness. He is full of love to
his neighbor, of universal love. His love resembles
that of him whose mercy is over all his works. He
loves every soul that God has made—every child
of man, of whatever place or nation. His love is in
itself generous and disinterested, springing from
no view of advantage to himself, from no regard to
profit or praise.

The same love is productive of all right actions.
It leads him into an earnest and steady discharge
of all social offices, of whatever is due to relations
of every kind—to his friends, to his country, and to
any particular community whereof he is a member.
It prevents his willingly hurting or grieving any
man. And as he is easy to others, so is he easy in
himself. He is free from the painful swellings of
pride, from the flames of anger, from the impetuous
gusts of irregular self-will. He knows how to use all
things in their place, and yet is superior to them all.

Neither is he a slave to fame. And he who seeks
no praise cannot fear dispraise. Censure gives him
no uneasiness, being conscious to himself that he
would not willingly offend and that he has the
approbation of the Lord of all. In honor or shame,
in abundance or want, in ease or pain, in life or in
death, always, and in all things, he has learned to
be content, to be easy, thankful, happy.

This is the plain, naked portraiture of a Christian. The second point to be considered is, what is real, genuine Christianity, whether we speak of it as a principle in the soul or as a scheme or system of doctrine? Christianity, taken in the latter sense, is that system of doctrine which describes the character above recited, which promises it shall be mine (provided I will not rest till I attain), and which tells me how I may attain it.

Christianity tells me how I may attain the promise—namely, by faith. But what is faith? Not an opinion, no more than it is a form of words; not any number of opinions put together, be they ever so true. A string of opinions is no more Christian faith than a string of beads is Christian holiness. It is not an assent to any opinion or any number of opinions. A man may assent to three or three-and-twenty creeds, he may assent to all the Old and New Testament (at least, as far as he understands them), and yet have no Christian faith at all.

The faith by which the promise is attained is represented by Christianity as a power, wrought by the Almighty in an immortal spirit inhabiting a house of clay, to see through that veil into the world of spirits, into things invisible and eternal; a power to discern those things which with eyes of flesh and blood no man hath seen or can see. This is Christian faith in the general notion of it. In its more particular notion, it is a divine evidence or conviction wrought in the heart that God is reconciled to me through his Son, inseparably joined with a confidence in him as a gracious, reconciled father. To believe (in the Christian sense) is, then, to walk in the light of eternity, and to have a clear sight of and confidence in the most high reconciled to me through the Son of his love.

What Christianity (considered as a doctrine) promised is accomplished in my own soul. And Christianity, considered as an inward principle, is the completion of all those promises. It is holiness and happiness, the image of God impressed on a created spirit, a fountain of peace and love springing up into everlasting life.

And this I conceive to be the strongest evidence of the truth of Christianity. I do not undervalue traditional evidence. Let it have its place and its due honor. It is highly serviceable in its kind and in its degree. And yet I cannot set it on a level with this.

It is generally supposed that traditional evidence is weakened by length of time. But no length of time can possibly affect the strength of this internal evidence. It is equally strong, equally new, through the course of seventeen hundred years. It passes now, even as it has done from the beginning, directly from God into the believing soul.

Traditional evidence is of an extremely complicated nature, necessarily including so many and so various considerations that only men of a strong and clear understanding can be sensible of its full force. On the contrary, how plain and simple is this? Is not this the sum: "One thing I know, I was blind, but now I see"? (John 9:25)

If, then, it were posssible (which I conceive it is not) to shake the traditional evidence of Christianity, still he that has the internal evidence (and every true believer hath the witness or evidence in himself) would stand firm and unshaken.

I have sometimes been almost inclined to believe that the wisdom of God has in most later ages permitted the external evidence of Christianity to be more or less clogged and encumbered for this very end, that men (of reflection especially) might not altogether rest there, but be constrained to look into themselves also and attend to the light shining in their hearts. Nay, it seems (if it may be allowed for us to pry so far into the reasons of the divine dispensations) that, particularly in this age, God suffers all kind of objections to be raised against the traditional evidence of Christianity that men of understanding, though unwilling to give it up, yet, at the same time they defend this evidence, may not rest the whole strength of their cause thereon, but seek a deeper and firmer support for it.

Without this I cannot but doubt whether they can long maintain their cause; whether, if they do not obey the loud call of God, and lay far more stress than they have hitherto done on this internal evidence of Christianity, they will not one after another give up the external, and (in heart at least) go over to those whom they are now contending with; so that in a century or two the people of England will be fairly divided into real deists and real Christians.

And I apprehend this would be no loss at all, but rather an advantage to the Christian cause; nay, perhaps it would be the speediest, yea the only effectual, way of bringing all reasonable deists to be Christians.

Those who were blind, but now see; those who were sick many years, but now are healed; those who were miserable, but now are happy will afford you also a very strong evidence of the truth of Christianity, as strong as can be in the nature of things, till you experience it in your own soul. And this, though it be allowed they are but plain men, and in general of weak understanding; nay, though some of them should be mistaken in other points, and hold opinions which cannot be defended.

All this may be allowed concerning the primitive fathers. I mean particularly Clemens Romanus, Ignatius, Polycarp, Justin Martyr, Irenaeus, Origen, Clemens Alexandrinus, Cyprian; to whom I would add Macarius and Ephraim Syrus. I allow that some of these had not strong natural sense, that few of them had much learning, and none the assistances which our age enjoys in some respects above all that went before. Hence I doubt not but whoever will be at the pains of reading over their writings for that poor end will find many mistakes, many weak suppositions, and many ill-drawn conclusions.

And yet I exceedingly reverence them as well as their writings, and esteem them very highly in love. I reverence them, because they were Christians, such Christians as are above described. And I reverence their writings, because they describe true, genuine Christianity, and direct us to the strongest evidence of the Christian doctrine. I reverence these ancient Christians (with all their failings) the more, because I see so few Christians now; because I read so little in the writings of later times and hear so little of genuine Christianity; and because most of the modern Christians (so called), not content with being wholly ignorant of it, are deeply prejudiced against it, calling it "enthusiasm" and I know not what.

That the God of power and love may make both them, and you and me, such Christians as those fathers were, is the earnest prayer of, reverend sir,

Your real friend and servant,

John Wesley